In Our Shoes is revealing, riveting, and real. It presents a clear path for self-discovery and survival; of perspective from lessons learned and a visionary promise for all you can become. A recommended read for seekers of a better way.

— *Larry James, President, CelebrateLove.com;*
  speaker and author of How to Really Love the One You're With

In Our Shoes speaks of a courage that calls forth courage in the reader to look at his or her own life and heal. I was struck by the honesty, joy, and humor with which each woman told her story— with the willingness to be totally 'seen,' to allow the lessons of her soul to be visible. The spiritual realizations that have come through these women's experiences have anchored their ability to move forward in their lives. I think anyone would gain incredible insights through their stories.

— *Rev. Lei Lanni Burt, Director of Ministry*
  Unity of Phoenix

In Our Shoes presents the lives, hopes, and dreams of seven women. The honest, straightforward dialogue allows one to feel they are in the same room—that you are listening to the story of a wise woman's life with its trials and tribulations. Their experiences clearly have been a propelling force toward wisdom and contentment with their past, present, and future lives. The gift offered to the reader gives strength to the notion that we can choose to have our life's lessons be the power behind achieving our own serenity.

— *William H. Miller, Jr., M.D, Psychiatrist.*

All the women in my life have been mirrors of my transformation. On the pages of **In Our Shoes**, seven women mirror the journey of healing and self-discovery that every woman travels. This is a unique and dynamic portrayal of every woman's search for her authentic soul. I highly recommend **In Our Shoes** for any woman on the path of self-actualization.

— *Dr. Marilyn Powers syndicated radio show host of* Words to Empower, *KRLA, Los Angeles and KCBQ, San Diego*

In Our Shoes is an ambitious undertaking. Ms. Brown, the group's founder, refers to it as a 21st century quilting group. Instead of sharing stories over a quilting frame, they write them and then read them. The fables are interesting, but the stories are riveting. We give it four hearts.

— *Judy Schuler, Heartland Reviews*

In Our Shoes

In Our Shoes

Seven Women Reveal Their Soles

Charlotte Rogers Brown
Courtney Leigh Dyer
Jami McFerren
Ramona Sallee
Jane Norde
Karolyne Smith Rogers, Ph.D.
Rashmi Goria

Wonder Weavers.

Phoenix, Arizona

ISBN 1-932484-01-9
Library of Congress Control Number: 2003105625

Cover design ©2003 by Shanks-DMG
Cover photographs by Brandon Sullivan
Black-and-white photographs by Jorgen
Interior design by MyLinda Butterworth

Printed in the United States of America
10 9 8 7 6 5 4 3 2 1

Published by Wonder Weavers, Inc., Phoenix, Arizona

*Dedicated to the connection of hearts,
minds, and souls that brings peace
and healing to our world.*

Acknowledgements

We wish to extend our love and gratitude to everyone who has supported us in the creation of this book.

To our editor, Bob Spear, for his enthusiasm and care for this project.

To Charlie for relegating himself to the guestroom every Wednesday evening so the "shoe women" could take over the rest of the house.

To everyone whose presence in our lives has contributed to the stories told on these pages. We recognize all the people and animals we encounter—including those we find "difficult"—as valuable teachers, and we are thankful to you, one and all.

To you, dear reader, for taking the time to walk a mile in our shoes.

To the Spirit who inspires us, guides us, and loves us, each step of the way.

Contents

Introduction

The Wednesday evening ritual begins around seven o'clock when I start the coffee. Decaf, *always* decaf, though even after four months, invariably someone will check to be sure. The cups come out of the hutch, the cream pitcher and sugar bowl from the cupboard, the bottled water from the last trip to Costco. I take out a couple of baskets, line them with napkins, and fill them with offerings. Not your typical fare—no potato chips or cheese doodles—but food worthy of goddesses—crunchy Romano cheese sticks, cinnamon-coated pastry twists, and chocolate-dipped biscotti. By the time I've placed the offerings on the coffee table and lit the candles, the "shoe women" are beginning to arrive. One by one, they gather in my living room and the air becomes charged with expectation, with a knowing that magic is about to happen.

It is the same current of expectation and magic I felt surge through my body four months earlier when, in that same living room, a vision came to me during my morning meditation. The message was clear: Call together a group of women and invite each one to tell her story—to reflect upon her past, present, and future so that others, both women and men, might know what it is to walk in her shoes. I could see the book in my mind, complete with photographs of shoes, each pair decorated to reflect the journey of the past and the vision of the future, with a pair of socks illustrating the here and now. Ignited with a passion I hadn't felt in some time, I literally sprang from the couch and ran for the phone. I didn't have to think about who to invite into this project; I just knew. Intuition gave me their names. I simply dialed their numbers.

As we began the project, we were nine. We created our shoes and socks—one shoe to represent the experiences of our past, the other to represent our vision of the future, and the socks to illustrate the "here and now." We decorated them all with yarn, paint, shells, buttons, play money, dollhouse miniatures—symbols to represent the most significant events, settings, and players in our lives. A love of sports or memories of countless hours spent at a child's youth league games might show up on a shoe as a tiny baseball bat or a soccer ball. Other memories or influences might be represented less literally. A parent or sibling, for example, might be represented as a particular color or shape. It didn't matter whether the symbols we chose were decipherable to anyone else. What mattered was how closely they captured the feelings and images our life experiences evoked within ourselves.

Next, we each wrote a fable to capture the essence of what we felt about what we had just created. We began our fables by imagining how we came to be in possession of that particular pair of shoes, and then explored what happens, where the shoes take us, once we put them on. The fables were spontaneous, written under a deadline with the sole purpose of engaging our imagination and cracking open the door to the daunting prospect of examining the very nature of who we are.

With our fables fresh in our minds, we began writing our reflections on our lives—past, present, and future. Without the safety of fiction and the riddle of our symbols to hide behind, these explorations challenged us in ways none of us expected. We each had to ask ourselves: *What experiences are the most significant in shaping the person I have become? To what degree am I willing to risk exposing my life to others? What stories am I afraid to tell? Do I have the courage to tell them anyway?*

The demands and the timing of such an undertaking soon cost us two members of the group, though I firmly believe their presence richly served this project from start to finish. So now we are seven. Seven ordinary, extraordinary women who have seized the opportunity to see what they're made of. We are Charlotte, Courtney, Jami, Jane, Karolyne, Ramona, and Rashmi. We come from Jamaica, India, and the United States. We are daughters, sisters, and friends. We are wives, widows, and divorcees. We are mothers of children born, children lost, and children who are not our own. We have wounded and been wounded. We have done things we're proud of, and made mistakes we desire never to repeat. We have failed and we have succeeded. We are human and divine.

While Jami has achieved local celebrity status as a radio and television personality, all of us could walk the streets of New York or Los Angeles or San Francisco in virtual anonymity, free to present ourselves to the world in any way we choose, which in my case, used to be the safest way possible. Until quite recently, I would share enough of myself—of my thoughts, feelings, failures, even successes—to connect with other people, but not so much that I would risk turning those same people away. I nearly always considered it a risk to say what I truly thought, felt, or did. *If they knew what really lurked inside of me,* I told myself, *they wouldn't want to know me.* I looked at other people and imagined that they had lived better, more compelling lives than I had— that they had made better choices, fewer mistakes. What mistakes they had made were no doubt more forgivable than mine. Mine were egregious, shameful.

That's what I told myself.

If you have ever given yourself those messages, or any like them, the stories in this book are especially for you. The purpose of this book is to

❖ debunk the myth, the lie you tell yourself, that your mistakes or failures keep you from "measuring up" to other people;

❖ share with you the experiences of seven individuals as they explore the range, depths, and dilemmas of their humanity; and

❖ invite you into the same unique process of exploration and sharing by providing a detailed set of guidelines to follow.

This book contains the stories of seven women who have discovered—through the decorating of our shoes, and through the courageous, no-holds-barred telling of the stories those shoes represent—the paradox that we are as alike as we are diverse. Ours are the stories of beauty pageants, finishing schools, and nude modeling. They're the stories of psychiatric wards, bus stations, and the bottoms of wine bottles. They're the stories of abortions, divorces, and depression. They're the stories of childhood years spent in an orphanage and adult years in a rustic mountain cabin where rabbits give birth in the bathtub and bears get their heads stuck in the dog door. They're the stories of our physical, emotional, and spiritual journeys.

At the end of this book, you will find a detailed guide to forming your own "shoe group." One of the key elements in this process is choosing symbols that capture your memories and feelings about your life. The symbols provide a gentle means of opening the door to self-exploration; they will reveal much to you about your memories and feelings about your life without exposing too much to others before you are ready to share. The fables that follow provide a means of gently expanding your boundaries of self-discovery and of reaching out to others through a further exploration of the symbols you've chosen within a fictional framework. Together, the symbols decorating the shoes, and the fables based upon those symbols provide the invitation to the authentic telling of the stories of your life—stories with the power to connect us all as human and spiritual beings. In this way, our *soles* become the base upon which our *souls* meet.

In person and in spirit, seven of us have come together every Wednesday evening to share our individual experiences, and in so doing, to discover our common bonds.

We laugh and cry to see ourselves in each other's stories, and in the process, something amazing has happened. The power of the stories we once kept silent has been transformed from a power that held us captive with feelings of shame or separateness, to a power capable of guiding ourselves and others along our journeys. We have come to know deeply that it is not our task as women, as human beings, to strive for perfection—even perfect inner peace—but to celebrate and love the full range of our emotions and experience. It is in the co-existence of our seeming contradictions—fear and courage, selfishness and generosity, doubt and faith, sadness and joy, anger and forgiveness, success and failure, envy and the capacity to celebrate another's good fortune—that true perfection lies.

When we began, none of us had any idea what form our personal stories would take. We knew only that, given we each had forty, fifty or sixty years of history behind us, and only one chapter in which to cover them, we'd probably have to leave out a detail or two. We came to discover, among the countless moments in our lives, some would demand our attention and insist upon being included. Expecting to shape the telling of our own stories, we instead found ourselves shaped by the telling. While we may have thought we knew who we were when we began, we learned that self-knowledge is not a destination, but a ceaseless, ever-unfolding process that gives life its meaning, its passion.

As Jane writes, "When I cease to be amazed at this experience, I cease to be."

One member of our group never attended the Wednesday gatherings. Karolyne lives and works in North Idaho, more than a thousand miles from my living room in Phoenix, Arizona. Except for one occasion, near the end of this project, Karolyne never smelled the coffee brewing or tasted the snacks. She couldn't hear our voices or watch our faces as the rest of us read our stories to each other. Two of the women had never met her. Karolyne experienced our stories the same way we experienced hers—by reading them. In the process we all discovered something very important: distance does nothing to lessen the power or value of any story shared between two souls. When Karolyne did finally join the circle in my living room, just weeks before we completed our writings, it felt as though her chair had been occupied all along.

We want to stress, while all of us have addressed the paths on which our spiritual journeys have taken us, our intention is neither to promote nor condemn any religious or spiritual practice. Just as we honor every story and every life, we honor every chosen path to God, as well as every name by which God is known. In this book, as well as in our months of meeting together, our intention is to celebrate our differences, as well as our commonalities.

So, now we invite you to walk awhile in our shoes, to give us the honor of telling you our stories. It is our hope that, through the experience, you'll feel guided to call together your own group of "shoe women"—whether near or far—and you'll feel the magic of telling each other your stories.

Charlotte Rogers Brown

Charlotte's Shoes

In Our Shoes

Fable

Window Shopping

Up and down the street come familiar sounds. Doors grating against uneven doorframes. Keys jangling in the locks. The turn of engines in the back-alley parking lots where the shopkeepers all park. For them, it's closing time. But for me, it's the time I go window shopping for those things I have always wanted but can never quite seem to find.

I often begin at the women's clothing boutique, gazing in at the finely tailored and proportioned suits, trying to imagine myself—body and soul—perfectly suited for them. At the travel agency, I stare at the posters advertising safaris in Africa, or expeditions in the Himalayas and try to see me there—that is, the "me" I would be if I had more courage.

I prefer to do all my shopping this way. If I shop when the stores are open, I risk having some clerk tell me that the very thing I want is out of stock, out of style, not available in my size, beyond my means, or simply does not exist.

No matter where I start, I always end up at the bookstore, searching the window display for copies of those books I've wanted so much, for so long to get published. But the books are never there. My picture is never on the covers. My name is never on the spines. Alas, tonight is no different.

But tonight, as I finish my rounds, I come across something unexpected: an open door. It belongs to a shop I've never seen before. The neon sign in the window reads, "Curiosity Shop."

OK. I'm curious.

I step into a large room crammed with what appear to be antiques—judging from the musty, grandma's attic smell that permeates the place and the dust that moves through the air like an evening fog. Frayed wicker chairs hang from the ceiling. Every inch of the walls is covered with old family photos, dust coated oil paintings of fruit bowls and flower baskets, and faded lithographs of pastoral scenes someone once knew or perhaps simply longed for. The floor space is "arranged" in a maze of tables, dressers, trunks, and other pieces of furniture, piled one on top of the other.

As I make my way through these remnants of other people's pasts, I have a thought that they belong to my past, too, though I don't recall having seen any of them before. It also occurs to me that no one should walk through this mess without a hard hat.

The maze leads to a wall of shoeboxes at the back of the store. Intrigued—or should I say, "curious"—I select a box and open it. There is only one shoe inside, and it's an odd little Hush Puppy. Actually it's a tennis shoe, a dingy white tennis shoe covered with all sorts of gizmos. A magical-looking castle and the dove of peace are stuck to the tongue, and on the sides appear miniature sports equipment, brightly colored hands, a couple of hats, and a clock face—just to name a few. A few pale feathers sprout up from inside the heel where a small wooden egg sits nearly hidden from sight. And on the tip of the toe, a scaly, spiny, canned-pea-colored lizard looks to be leading the whole parade. The lizard looks to me like fear feels.

"Any particular size you're looking for?"

The voice startles me. I hadn't noticed the woman sitting at the desk, writing.

"There's only one shoe in here," I tell her.

"That's right," she says.

"So where's the other one?" I ask.

"You have to choose it, just as you did that one. The one you've got in your hand there is a past shoe, just like the sign says."

I look up and, sure enough, a sign above my head reads, "PAST."

"You need to choose one from the other stack if you want a pair," she says, pointing to a sign to my right that reads "FUTURE."

I look at her, wondering what on earth she's talking about. Then I can't take my eyes off of her. She looks familiar to me in a way that makes me want to embrace her and recoil from her all at once. The shape her of her powdered-blue, sequined eyeglasses makes her look like a cat with an extremely bad complexion. Her outfit is a retro nightmare of saddle shoes, plaid bellbottom pants, and a ruffled pink blouse. Under her raised arm, sweat is sneaking beyond the edges of her dress shield. She smiles at me with a mouthful of metal braces attached to a piece of headgear that encircles her head like some medieval instrument of torture.

In brief, this poor clerk exhibits every embarrassment I have ever lived. At the same time, she is the antithesis of every image of greatness I have ever aspired to attain.

"Go ahead. Pick one."

"Excuse me?" I say, unable to take my eyes off this huge pimple in the center of her forehead. I'm tempted to tell her that I once tried to cover one just like it with a headband. It was the seventies, so I thought I might get away with it.

"A shoe," she says. "Pick yourself out a future shoe."

I reach over and slide another box from the shelves lining the wall. It contains another dingy white tennis shoe, though decorated much differently from the first. This one has money sprouting from inside the heel, red-orange flames dancing around its sole, and brightly-colored feathers spreading like wings from the sides. A magical-looking castle is affixed to this shoe also, but on the back, where the rudder would be if it were a boat. With a bunch of brass sleigh bells hanging from the laces, this shoe doesn't just look like a parade, it sounds like one, too, with a lantern and great big capital letter "G" leading the way, toe first.

"Do you want to try them on?" the shopkeeper asks.

I'm thinking, *None of this is part of my plan. I'm just supposed to be window shopping here.* But seeing this woman, seeing how eager she is to please me, I find myself wanting to please her—even feeling a little ashamed of how hard I once tried not to be just like her.

"Yes," I say to her. "I want to try them on."

I try to slip them on, but my feet resist. They sweat and strain. The past shoe pinches before I can get it over my toes, and the future shoe seems to shrink three sizes before my toes ever reach it.

"You'll need these," the clerk tells me, handing me a pair of socks—white, though stained with what looks like red wine, and with one word stitched onto each:

J O Y

I look incredulously at the clerk.

"Trust me, they'll go perfectly," she says.

"Are they even clean?" I ask.

"Perfectly."

I take the socks from her and put them on. She's right. My feet now slide easily into both shoes, even the one with the wooden egg hidden down deep in the heel. I can see them in a mirror propped against the wall, the word "JOY" over each shoe, past and future. The whole effect appears almost coordinated.

"Take a walk in them, to see how they feel," the shopkeeper says.

Before I can take a step, the spiny lizard on the left shoe opens his jaw to reveal a nasty looking set of teeth, which he proceeds to sink into my big toe. I let out a scream and try to shake him off, but he just laughs and keeps on biting until I can see blood stains on the white canvas.

About that time I start to hear whispering coming from the vicinity of my new socks. The words "JOY, JOY, JOY" come floating up to my ears like feathers on a breeze. And something about the sound of those words makes me go ahead and step out with my left foot—blood, lizard, and all.

The lizard stops laughing. He looks annoyed at me for making a move, but he stops biting. He even starts to clutch at the canvas with his sharp claws, as though he's worried he might fall off and get trampled.

I take another step, this time with my right foot. When my foot comes down, it doesn't touch the floor, but comes to rest an inch or so above it, as though I were stepping on a cushion of air.

I begin to walk—left foot, right foot, left foot, right foot— and I don't know whether it's from the heaviness of the left shoe, or the lightness of the right, but I'm walking with a distinct limp. It feels uncomfortable, unnatural.

Left, right, left, right. I begin to get a rhythm going, and after awhile, I don't mind the limp so much. It reminds me of how, as a kid, I used to walk along curbs and sidewalks —one foot up and one foot down—just for the fun of it. I proceed around the shop until I manage to achieve a consistent, if somewhat awkward, gait—like a toddler with a loaded diaper.

"So how do they feel?" the clerk asks.

I don't know how to answer her in a way that makes any sense. The more I walk, the better I feel—outside and in. I came into the shop with the disappointment of all that was missing in the other shops, all closed up tight, but now I feel light, free, ignited with a sense of endless possibility.

"Can I try them outside?" I ask.

"You can take them anywhere you want," she answers.

Grabbing the shopkeeper's hand, I run through the crowded store and out the door into a perfect evening. I see that the doors to all the shops are open now, so I head straight for the book-store where a light shines brightly on a display of books in the window. *My* books.

Scarcely knowing how to express my gratitude for the mystery of fate, I hurry inside to buy the shopkeeper the very first copy.

≈⊃⊂≈

Reflections on the Past

...In brief, this poor clerk exhibits every embarrassment I have ever lived. At the same time, she is the antithesis of every image of greatness I have ever aspired to attain...

I was six years old when Hal Petrowitz prophesied my future. An unlikely prophet, Hal was a law school professor and family friend. Behind the wheel of his MG convertible, Hal wore driv-ing gloves and a spiffy cap pulled low over his forehead. He lived in a classy Los Angeles skyline apartment with a wet bar that appeared spectacularly from behind the living room wall. He knew actress Jane Wyman. He went to the ballet. He may have had the build and the hairline of Barney Fife, but from my six-year-old perspective—shaped by life with my parents and older sister in a middle-class San Francisco suburb, with a white Ford station wagon parked in our garage—Hal Petrowitz was a god.

That is why, on that day the two of us waited in line to ride the carousel at Disneyland, I took his words deep into my heart.

"You are special, Charlotte, and someday you are going to do something truly great."

Whatever prompted him to say such a thing? What did he see in me? What sort of great thing did he imagine I would do?

I didn't ask those questions back then. I simply felt giddy to be climbing onto a carousel at Disneyland with a sophisticated man of the world who actually said I was special. I couldn't recall ever having heard those words before.

But over the years Hal's words kept coming back to me, and I did ask those questions, many times, mostly to God. I grew increasingly determined, and eventually desperate, to solve the mystery of Hal's Prophecy. As child, I looked for the solution in my imagination, fantasizing about when, how, and in what form the call would come. Maybe it was those early trips to Disneyland that ignited my rich imaginary life—at least that's my husband's theory—but whatever the reason, I had no trouble seeing myself as capable of greatness. I stepped easily into the skins of my favorite heroines—Cinderella, Snow White, and Sleeping Beauty—girls who grew to be women of beauty, wealth, class, and distinction.

I could step into any character, any fantasy. At Disneyland, I didn't take a turn on the Flying Dumbo ride; I really flew on the back of a magical flying elephant. On Halloween, I didn't just dress up like a witch; I became a witch, just like Casper's friend Wendy, casting magic spells. Photos from those early years seem to indicate that fantasy wanes somewhere between the ages of six and fourteen. In one of my favorite shots, my sister Karin—who is eight years older—and I are sitting on Flying Dumbo, awaiting our flight. Another photo has us posed against the living room curtains wearing our matching witch costumes. While my sister is smiling in both photographs, it is the smile of a teenager who loves her little sister enough to endure any humiliation on her behalf. My smile, on the other hand, is one of pure ecstasy—the smile of a child who has lost an entire night's sleep in anticipation of just a few hours of being anything but an ordinary human child.

By the third grade, I was looking for the solution of Hal's Prophecy in books. I loved any good story and I fantasized about becoming a writer—a novelist like Madeleine L'Engle, or a reporter like Nellie Bly. Even in elementary school, I also knew I wanted a great romance. What little I knew about real-life romance came from episodes of *Bachelor Father*, movies such as *My Fair Lady* and *The King and I,* the sex education lecture I suffered through in the school cafeteria with my classmates and our parents, and the pamphlet my mother kept in her closet. I liked the idea of a handsome bachelor reaching his arms around my waist to teach me how to swing a golf club or dance the waltz; I figured I could pass on the rest.

In my teens I looked for the solution where most teens draw conclusions about their destinies—in the mirror. This is what I saw reflected there: a raging case of acne; glasses that got thicker with every trip to the optometrist; clothes that were somehow always on the flipside of fashionable; and teeth forced into place by a torture of braces, rubber bands, and headgear. Hardly a match for every model of greatness I had held in my imagination.

And so I enrolled myself in a John Robert Powers School. The mission of this nine-month program was to assist students of all ages in giving birth to the lovely, well-heeled woman within. As stated on my certificate of completion, "Our purpose has been to direct her efforts toward fulfilling her potentialities in beauty, charm and poise; and to install in her the desire to continue to progress even beyond the point she has reached under our tutelage."

Note that nowhere on that certificate does it say I actually achieved any of those things—only that they tried their darnedest on my behalf. As it turned out, I was one of two graduates the school chose to leave out of its annual yearbook—one of its recruiting tools. We apparently failed to live up to their standards, though I never asked why. But it is true that at the end of nine months' worth of learning how to walk, talk, pluck my eyebrows, put on make-up, and put together a decent outfit, I felt better when I looked in the mirror. Gone was the single, unruly eyebrow that had reached from temple to temple, now shaped into two gentle arches. Gone were the glasses, replaced by contact lenses. Gone were the braces. Gone were the sagging knee socks.

I might not have been chosen for the cover of *Seventeen*, but being seventeen got a little easier.

I remember the sixties, which means, I guess, I wasn't really there. And in large part, that is true. The sixties were about anti-war demonstrations, free love, and getting high with a little help from your friends—all things I never experienced, though I grew up fifty miles from Haight-Ashbury. I was too afraid of what my parents would do to me if I did. My parents even forbade me to see the movie version of *Woodstock*, though I went to see it anyway—the height of my high school rebelliousness. I went to my first and only garage band jam session wearing tennis shoes, as my mother forbade me to buy sandals—doctors had apparently told her that my weak ankles and arches required more sensible footwear—and when Joan Baez led a walk-out at my high school one afternoon, I was in the minority of students who stayed behind and went to class. These days when I hear people reminiscing about the sixties, I feel even more left out than I did back then. It's not the experimentation with drugs or sex I wish I hadn't missed out on, it's those early opportunities to exercise my political voice. I chose not to get involved in social issues, because to do so would mean going up against my conservative parents, and I was far too timid to do that.

When I left for Washington State University, the "great things" foremost in my mind to accomplish were 1) a boyfriend—handsome, brooding and romantic, along the lines of, say, Oliver Barrett, and 2) some clue about what to do with my life if I wasn't Mrs. Barrett come graduation. I had no idea that even such ignoble goals might well be beyond my reach given my ailing self-esteem. I thought that a relationship was exactly what I needed to heal the pain I carried from every too-harsh word from my parents, sister, and friends; every too-long silence; every too-dark hour alone in my room, wondering if there was something wrong with me.

After three years at WSU, a full year shy of graduation, I came away with:

1. knowledge of how to make the world's cheapest wine from yeast and a can of Welch's grape juice;

2. an appreciation for alcohol's abilities to mask insecurities of all kinds;

3. fond memories of hundreds of students—mostly male, and all buck naked—streaking down the street outside my dorm room one winter night;

4. more shards embedded in my self-esteem from an unhealthy 2½- year relationship;

5. three 'F's on my last report card; and

6. an engagement ring.

Given my growing penchant for skipping, and subsequently failing, classes, getting married seemed like the best thing to do. Particularly since the man who proposed to me following a six-week courtship was a good man, a hard working man, a well-intentioned man. He still is, I gather, from what little I see and hear of him these days. We divorced thirteen years later, having lacerated each other with nonacceptance, anger, misunderstanding, and neglect. In the last few months of our marriage, I would add an affair to my list of sins—an attempt to feel better about myself that made me feel oh so much worse. After our separation, another premature relationship made the task of dissolving our marriage with any degree of care or respect entirely impossible. My list of regrets, of pains I caused, grew longer.

But between marriage and divorce came two children and three houses in two North Idaho communities where I demonstrated how NOT to do a lot of things: cook venison, keep a clean house, raise children with patience and wisdom. If there's ever a market for how-not-to books, I'll clean up. Which is not to say I never did anything right or with love. I did. I did my best to live by the sign that hung in my writing room—*88 percent of life is showing up*—and show up, especially for my sons. I showed up for bedtime stories, bike rides, birthday parties, school carnivals, teacher conferences, science fairs, band concerts, and Fourth of July parades. I showed up for baseball, football, basketball, soccer, and wrestling. I showed up for breakfast, lunch, and dinner. I showed up, because often that was the only thing I could do. Often I was too mired in depression to do anything more.

I didn't know I was depressed. I didn't fully come to know that until my late thirties. The boys were close to college age by then. All I knew was something wasn't right with me. I didn't seem to feel joy the way other people did. The emotions I did feel—mostly anger, fear, and guilt—I couldn't control. I cried a lot. I either couldn't sleep or couldn't get enough. I'd feel the pressure of my emotions build up inside until inevitably they would erupt in a screaming tantrum. At its worst, the depression felt like dense, gray fog seeping into my brain, making it difficult to think, dimming my vision, draining the color from everything around me. I felt vulnerable, defenseless—crazy.

I never turned to drugs—that is, illegal drugs—for the simple, uncontroversial reason my only attempt to smoke a cigarette in college made me so sick to my stomach, I decided that no drug warranted the risk of feeling that crappy. Alcohol was a different matter. I thought of alcohol as a medicinal drug, like something a doctor might prescribe to settle the nerves. For a while, a doctor actually did prescribe Valium to ease my chronic anxiety.

At times the fog would lift enough for me to take a deep breath and relax in the thought that I might not be crazy after all. I'd feel energy return to my body, and I'd be able to contribute more than just my body to the events of my family's lives. But sooner or later, I would feel the fog creeping back and I'd panic, knowing I was powerless to stop it.

Still, I continued to show up, which makes me quite proud, now that I am well and know what a colossal feat that was. I doubt, however, that it's the sort of accomplishment Hal was referring to that day at Disneyland. At least, I've never looked back on those days when I managed to slog through depression like a Clydesdale through a swamp and thought, *Oh, surely that was it!*

Nothing I've done so far has ever felt like "it." Not the college degree I finally earned—a bachelor's, in journalism. Not the work I did, or the awards I won as a newspaper reporter and as a school district communications specialist. Not even the first book I got published. I always thought I'd recognize that "something great" the instant I did it. I still do, most of the time, though there are moments when I'm not so sure. In those moments, I wonder if Hal was able to foresee the impact of some small action, some passing word, in a way that I might never know for myself. At the newspaper, the reporter assigned to the police beat called me the "fluff queen" because my assignments were the feature stories, stories that don't qualify as "hard" news. I wrote about the latest fashions in school lunch boxes. I wrote about the elementary school principal who wore plastic ties with live goldfish swimming inside. I wrote about the old man who made clocks in the shape of Idaho, with real Idaho garnets marking the hours.

I didn't write the story of the man who held his wife and children at gunpoint on New Year's Eve. The police reporter did that. But I did write the story behind the story—about the wife who wanted the people of her community, especially the ones who were teasing her children on the way to school, to know that her husband's mind was damaged in Viet Nam and that he deserved some compassion. I also wrote the story of a young woman with Down syndrome who left the care of her mother to taste independence in a group home for the first time, and the history of a once-thriving town being kept alive by just one old-timer and the family next door.

I suppose any one of my stories could have changed a life in some profound way, thus fulfilling Hal's Prophecy, even if I never learn the details. But if my work in journalism answered the conundrum of my destiny, wouldn't I still want to be doing it? Would I have left newspapers to go to work for a public school district? And if churning out district newsletters and organizing school levy campaigns had been "it," would I have quit that job just eight months later, ready to finally quit dreaming, quit talking about becoming an author and start risking the attempt?

Back then, I measured the greatness of any piece of writing by the number of people it reached and the length of time it endured. None of the writing I did for the newspaper or the school district measured up to those standards. The numbers weren't bad in journalism, but mosquitoes live longer than most news stories. In fact many mosquitoes have gone to meet their maker on the rolled-up end of a morning newspaper, deceased within an hour of its arrival. As for my brief foray into school district communications—consisting largely of memos, press releases, and snippets of praise for deserving staff in in-house newsletters—I could barely remember what I wrote about from one day to the next, so I held no illusions that my work would outlive me.

I quit my job at the school district because of a billboard. For months I had been wrestling over the question of whether or not to quit my job. How I felt about the job was clear; I hated it. What wasn't so clear was whether quitting would mean failure. I asked that question of my therapist, my friends, and my family. It would probably come as a surprise to them to know this, but as with any decision I had ever made, the opinions of my family members mattered most. Which is to say their opinions of *me*. Which is not to say I tended to follow their advice; more often than not, I didn't. But I would call to solicit their opinions just the same, trusting they would love me no matter what, but knowing that in their approval or disapproval, I would either give or deny myself permission to relax in my decisions.

This time, however, something entirely different gave me the permission I sought. I was driving down a busy Spokane street, wondering whether it was more to delusion, or even laziness, than it was to good sense that I owed the thought of quitting the highest paying job I'd ever had to try my hand at writing…what? Novels? Children's books? I didn't even know the answer to that, for Pete's sake.

Then just when I thought I couldn't take the strain of indecision another second, I looked up and saw these words, plastered across a giant ad for a furniture store:

Believe Your Eyes

I have no idea what those words had to do with furniture, but in that moment I knew—I don't know how—that I risked nothing by quitting my job to start writing, even with no idea of where the writing would take me. My breathing eased. My body relaxed. All the haggling voices in my head fell silent. I drove home that night and wrote my letter of resignation. I still phoned my parents before submitting it, of course, but I already knew my decision was right, because emotionally, physically, it *felt* right.

Now only three questions remained: *Novels? Children's books? What?* I began searching for the answers by arranging my writing space. The window in my tiny home office opened onto Lake

Coeur d'Alene, a lake with moods as extreme and changeable as my own. Faced with the hardest of winters, its fluid blues would turn to a foreboding, steel gray ice. In the dog days, it would nestle in the mountains like a lazy hound and let scores of people run their boats, jet skis, and other toys across its back, though a summer storm could suddenly cause it to bristle and howl and chase all the interlopers away. But it was on clear nights, when the moonlight reached from shore to shore that it revealed to me the true depth of its spirit. The lake was the part of North Idaho that most captivated me, and so, to be productive as a writer, I knew I had to move my desk as far away from the window as I could get it. I emptied the closet, removed the doors, and shoved my desk inside.

After cleaning every inch of the house, renting every movie I had ever wanted to see—anything to delay facing a blank computer screen, and possibly, a blank mind—I finally sat at my desk one day and endeavored to begin a novel. A novel! The very idea was daunting. Who was I to write a novel? What raw material did I to bring to a story? I had lived a middle-class existence, and as far as I was concerned, middle-class was synonymous with middle-of-the-road—neither deprived, nor privileged enough to be remotely interesting. Neither the stuff of *The Grapes of Wrath*, nor *The Great Gatsby*. Still I figured that I could probably come up with something, as long as it was suitably deep and convoluted as I imagined all great novels were supposed to be.

I began work on the opening of my novel—so deep and convoluted, even I didn't know what the story was about. Gradually, I began to feel the presence of other stories crowding into my writing space, the way the fairytale characters crowded around Wilhelm Grimm's sick bed in *The Wonderful World of the Brothers Grimm*, another of my favorite childhood movies. After a while, I abandoned the novel, deciding to give myself over to whatever words, whatever stories, whatever characters wanted to come through me.

What came through me were fables—at least that's what I like to call them given that they fit the definition: stories that feature fantastic characters or situations, and convey some message about life. At first, all I knew for certain was that these stories conveyed messages to me about my life. People and events that had once seemed mundane looked much richer, more colorful to me on paper.

Growing up in the same house with my maternal grandfather, for example, hardly seemed romantic to me as a child. Grandpap ate that canned, snot-colored chow mien, and clicked his false teeth at the dinner table. He belched a lot. He made a monthly ritual of scanning the obituaries in the West Penn Power Company newsletter, hunting for the names of former co-workers the way a child might hunt for Easter eggs, then reading aloud any names he found as though we had a clue who they were. His habit of parking himself at the kitchen window became especially irritating during my high school years, on those precious few occasions when a boy brought me home from a date.

All those years later, when Grandpap showed up again in an idea for a story, the search for words to describe him revealed the diamonds in his character and in the experience of living in his presence. He gave me my first bicycle. He built cedar flower boxes and planted them with fuscias, so that it appeared to me the eaves around our house sheltered hundreds of pink fairies. He taught me, in his own style, to treat people with respect—to "never spit in a man's face unless his mustache is on fire." He showed me that a person could be old, have cancer, and still get stopped by the state patrol for doing ninety on the straight-aways.

After gathering a stack of rejection slips from children's book publishers, I took a new approach. I partnered with my friend Karolyne, a therapist, who saw in my stories, her stories and the stories of her clients. Karolyne matched my fables with excerpts from her journals and crafted tools for assisting others in discovering the richness of their own experience. The manuscript found a publisher almost immediately, though it would be nearly three years before it was ready to market.

When, at long last, the UPS box arrived on my doorstep and I ripped it open to see the first copies of my first book in print, I did know that I had achieved something great in the sense that any dream come true is truly great for the dreamer. At forty-one, I could finally call myself an author. Wow! To lift *A Weaving of Wonder* out of the box, to hold it in my hands was to witness the miracle of birth for the third time in my life. I had even dedicated my portion of the book to my sons, Jason and Joe, in gratitude for all the "firsts" we had shared together.

Again, for this book to be "it", at least in my mind, it would have to meet my greatness criteria of mass audience and longevity. Therefore it would have to be published in hardcover and attract readers in numbers large enough to put it on the *New York Times* best seller list. Alas, of the three thousand paperback copies the publisher printed in the first run, several hundred of them are still sitting in my guestroom closet.

Among the readers who found their way to the others, some have either written, or spoken to me in person, to tell me the book benefited their lives—that it sparked their creativity or gave them insights about their own natures. Hearing that kind of testimony, and seeing firsthand the creative spark ignited in the workshops which have grown out of that book, I have come to count any blessing perceived by any reader as a triumph.

I entered the new millennium with a resolve to go public with my work—that is, to risk standing up in front of people to speak my beliefs regarding the power of story. During the previous year, I had completed two novels—one for children and one for young adults—and sent out more than 250 queries to publishers. My submissions generated some interest, but no takers.

Then it came to me during a morning meditation that, if I sincerely wanted to get more of my writing published, something more was required of me in exchange. I had to stop hiding behind the written word, the little voice inside me said, and be willing to tell others face-to-face about the wisdom and guidance available to them through their own experiences, their own stories. And so I said to that little voice, "You've got to be kidding. I loathe public speaking. You really ought to be talking to someone who is comfortable doing that sort of thing, and that ain't me!"

The little voice answered, "Too bad."

I began by accepting an invitation from one of the ministers at the church I attend to read a fable as part of her Saturday night church service. Then I started teaching a series of classes on fable writing at the church, while accepting other invitations to do readings at workshops facilitated by a couple of local therapists. Each class, each presentation was an exercise in terror, bringing with it a host of reflexive torments: stomach pains, dry mouth, shortness of breath, and shaking, sweat-soaked hands. The fear felt like a sharp, spiny, lizard-like creature, pacing in my gut. I had the symptoms of an alcoholic going through withdrawal, only I was withdrawing from the safety of playing small—of staying within the limits of what I knew I could do without failing or looking foolish. I could not comprehend the logic of a God who would call a person so obviously afflicted with stage fright to speak. It made about as much sense as calling me to try out for the NBA.

I did it anyway. Each time I saw an opportunity to speak, I showed up—even if 88 percent of me was sweating like a pig in the desert. I clung to the hope that speaking in public would become second nature to me in time. As I write this, I can report it has not, though I can finally see the sense in my standing in front of an audience. If, as I've come to earnestly believe, my mission here is to encourage others to move beyond their fears and share their stories, how hollow that message would sound had I no fears of my own.

As the second year of the new millennium approached, a series of events triggered in me another long, slow—and after years of mental health—completely unexpected descent into depression. My sister was diagnosed with breast cancer and just beginning radiation treatments when our father made his passing. In answer to a prayer, God gave me the honor of being with him when he died, though when my husband, Charlie, and I made the twelve-hour drive from Phoenix just the day before, we had no idea death was so close. Not even my mother knew, and she was with him nearly every minute. I had expected to leave my father just as I had dozens of times throughout his last two years with Parkinson's Disease—with a kiss, a reminder that I loved him, and a pain in my chest at the thought I might never see him again. Only in the last years of his life could Dad say the words "I love you" as easily as he could think them, as easily as he could show them in other, unspoken ways.

There is a moment during my father's illness that stands out for the way it captured the essence of him. After a fall that had damaged a vertebra, and a bladder infection that made him feverish, unable to attach meaning to anything around him, his doctor prescribed a temporary stay in a convalescent facility. My mother, who has dedicated her life to her home and family, made the drive every morning to spend the day with him, to carry on the loving monologues she had begun from the day the Parkinson's began slowly stealing the power of Dad's own speech.

One day when I accompanied her to the convalescent home, Mom asked Dad if he would like a piece of his candy—"his" candy being the See's brand chocolate-covered nuts he liked so much. Even such a simple question could get lost along the disconnected pathways in Dad's brain, and so it took him a few moments to answer that, yes, he would. Mom pulled the box of candy from the bedside table, and as she handed it to him, she mentioned she would have to make a stop at the candy store since there were just two pieces left. Without any hesitation at all, Dad lifted the box from his lap, held it out to me and said, "Maybe Charlotte would like one." I looked at him and saw the part of my father that Parkinson's could never touch—that gentleness, generosity, and dignity of spirit that lay at the heart of him.

Months later, as I held his hand, knowing that gentle spirit had left his body, I felt profoundly grateful God had seen fit to bring me and the other members of my family together for that sacred moment. I had thought that grief would be swift and overwhelming, like a stampede, but it wasn't—at least not for me. For me, grief was a slow process, made even slower by the continuing series of events.

Less than three weeks after my father's passing, Charlie's mother died suddenly of a heart attack while sitting in her favorite chair, watching television. By the next morning we were on a plane for Oregon, where Charlie's father met us at his back door and fell weeping into Charlie's arms. Six days later, I watched Charlie scatter the last of his mother's ashes on the beach where she'd gathered shells and driftwood, watched as the waves came and carried her away. That was in December.

In January I flew back to California to be with my mother when she had a mastectomy. My sister had already seen her through two lumpectomies, both of which simply served to reveal more tiny growths. Hers was a simple mastectomy—meaning only breast tissue, no lymph nodes required removal—so she recovered quickly, with relatively little pain. Once the anxiety of undergoing surgery was over, she seemed to find more comedy than tragedy in the aftermath of losing her breast. She entertained my sister and me with stories, including her account of the fitting for her first prosthesis, and the discouragingly lopsided result.

In the months that followed, I congratulated myself that, like Tony Curtis in *The Great Race*, I had managed to walk through the gauntlet of sour pies fate had hurled at my family's faces without getting a speck on me. I was still standing, still functioning, still free of depression. Or so I thought. The trouble was, I had forgotten the signs of its approach. OK, so I felt a little tired, a little anxious, a little irritable. So what? So what if getting cut off on the freeway made me want to shoot out the offender's tires. That didn't mean anything, I told myself.

My body kept giving me subtle signs my mind was in trouble, but I kept on dismissing them, until the day my body lost patience and took over the controls. My husband and I were making yet another drive back to my hometown for my thirtieth high school reunion. My grandson Nathan, stepdaughter Hannah, and Annette—a teenager from Germany who had been spending part of her summer with us—were all in the back seat. As I looked out the window, the sunny Southern California landscape suddenly dimmed, as though a cloud had passed in front of the sun. The sound of the kids' voices from the back seat seemed to retreat to some distance place, and every object I saw—from a tree passing by the window to a button on the car stereo—suddenly seemed foreign, a symbol I had to decipher. I blinked my eyes, shook my head and took a deep breath, hoping I could force the feeling to pass, but knowing better. I knew exactly what was happening.

I somehow made it through the weekend, through the reunion, then went home and saw my doctor. After she went over the advances made among the various families of antidepressant medications (I find it ironic that antidepressants, like depressed people, run in families), I chose one to try. One of the many inconveniences of depression is that there's no blood test, no scan to determine the nature of the chemical imbalance, so choosing the right family of medications is often a matter of trial and error. The first drug I tried was both—a trial and an error. That became real clear to me the day I found myself sitting on a park bench in Disneyland, the happiest place on earth, sobbing uncontrollably—a genuine meltdown on Main Street. I saw people passing by—parents pushing their toddlers in strollers, couples riding the horse-drawn trolley, kids hustling into the Mad Hatter's hat shop—but I felt this terrifying sense that none of them could see or hear me, that if they happened to look in our direction, they would look at Charlie and wonder why he was talking to himself.

For someone who has never experimented with drugs, never even touched a joint except to pass it on, I felt nevertheless as though I were having the proverbial "bad trip."

That scene seems funny to me now, which is proof enough for me that, while depression may come, it won't stay. But for about four months there, the most I could do was to keep breathing, and the only way I could do that was to make a fist around the thought that this depression, even this hell, played a part in Hal's Prophecy. Too weak and muddled to search for my life's great purpose, I just kept telling myself that there was one. On days when I couldn't do even that, I asked Charlie and my friends to say it for me.

The next drug I tried turned out to be the one I needed to bring my chemistry back into balance, and with some counseling and a whole lot of prayer, I felt good again. Last weekend, with a group of family and friends, Charlie and I went back to Disneyland, the birthplace of my rich fantasy life as well as my personal "ground zero." I saw the bench where I had come unraveled just seven months before. It was vacant this time, too, but not waiting for me. For that I could feel nothing but gratitude.

My sister, bless her heart, humored me with one more ride together on Flying Dumbo, so I could send a new photo to our mother for Mother's Day. Our foreheads are considerably higher than in the original, and our bodies take up more space, but our smiles are the same. Karin's is still the smile of one who loves her sister enough to endure the humiliation of riding on an elephant designed for four-year-olds (though I suspect I'd be pushing it to ever ask her again). And mine is still the smile of one seeking a moment or two of pure magic—of one still seeking the solution to Hal's Prophecy.

As I write this, I know the "great thing" he spoke of is yet to be. I know because that voice inside—the one that prods me to *Believe My Eyes*—keeps telling me it is so. That is all I know. As a reporter, I was trained to answer the "who, what, where, when, why, and how" of every story. As a spiritual being, I have come to recognize what an impossible undertaking that is. Speaking strictly for my own limitations, I'm clear I lack a certain omniscience to know the whole truth behind, or the likely outcome of *any* story. I can conjecture 'til the cows come home, but the truth is, when it comes to the solution of Hal's Prophecy—when it comes to the who, what, when, where, why, and how of it—all I know is this: I am the "who." The rest is up to God.

Reflections on the Present

...I proceed around the shop until I manage to achieve a consistent, if somewhat awkward, gait—like a toddler with a loaded diaper...

My grandson, Nathan, has been having a small challenge with potty training. Some months ago, he mastered the art of "tinkling" in the potty; it's the pooping part he has issues with. So much so that he has started scheduling his poops in the evening, after bedtime—the only time he has on a pair of disposable training pants instead of his cloth, "big boy" underwear.

His reasons for this could range from the Freudian, to the fear of the unknown, to the simple possibility that there are, at least for him, infinitely more comfortable positions in which to poop than sitting upright on the toilet. Whatever his reason, he is unabashedly intent on being the master of his personal habits.

One evening when he and his mother, Kaci, were visiting, Nathan got tired before Kaci was ready to leave. We dressed him in his Buzz Lightyear sleepers and his training pants—the ones with the stars that disappear when they get wet—and settled him into the master bedroom. By the time Kaci was ready to drive home, Nathan had filled his pants.

His mother reacted with calm confusion. "I don't get it, Nathan," she said. "I know you know what to do. I know you understand the concept."

As Kaci and I set about cleaning and changing him, Nathan looked past us, into the next room.

"Do you see those letters up there?" he asked.

Kaci and I turned to look at them—three large gold letters suspended above the living room fireplace.

"Yes," his mother answered.

With the confidence of a seasoned reader, Nathan announced, "They spell, 'I pooped in my pull-ups.'"

"Actually," said Kaci, "They spell 'JOY.'"

Nathan looked at her as if to ask, "Isn't that what I said?"

As I begin these, my reflections on the present, the date is April 27, 2002, and I'm feeling an odd sense of joy despite the fact that I've been pooping in my pull-ups for quite some time now—figuratively speaking, of course.

This revelation began with a casual telephone call to a friend, a call that turned into a confrontation. The encounter fell short of being a full-fledged argument, yet it clearly reflected two very different points of view. It grew out of an earlier conversation in which I asked whether she would feel at all dishonored, or unappreciated, if I didn't come to her fiftieth birthday party. I had given her my gift over a quiet lunch a few days before, and when the day of the party arrived, I was feeling the fatigue from too much activity and too little rest. I felt the need for some self-care, especially having so recently been reminded of what happens when I neglect it.

It turns out, her assurance she was fine with my need to stay home, had nothing to do with how she felt. My choice had, indeed, hurt her. By the time I heard the chill in her voice and recognized that something was wrong, a week had passed.

The details of our communication are unimportant. There was truth in what each of us had to say. But after saying "goodbye," and after a restless, anxious night, I awoke with the knowledge this friend and I have long been engaged in a strange dance. I realized that, for years now, I've secretly judged her, maybe even condemned her, for being inauthentic. I had developed the opinion that I could never be sure if I was talking to her—the "real" her—or one of an ever-changing series of personas she presented to the world to deny…what? Human vulnerabilities? She seemed to swing like a pendulum between confessions of painful self-doubt to professions of blissful self-actualization. I had trouble keeping up. I judged her life was never really as dramatic, or as idyllic, as she claimed.

I judged. How arrogant is that? Especially considering that I happen to love this woman. Again, I acknowledge that I lack the omniscience to know anyone's truth but my own. Who am I to accuse anyone of dishonesty or pretense? Even if it were true, who am I to declare it a sin? And if deception is a sin, since when have I been in a position to point fingers? So my friend might, *might* rely on different personas to cover and compensate for moments of self-criticism. So what? How would that be any different from the wine I drink to cover mine?

I'm not a heavy drinker. I have a two-glass limit I rarely ever exceed. But I seldom go more than a week without wine, and I probably drink on an average of three or four nights a week. Except for a few times when I've given it up for Lent or when I've been wise enough in a depressive episode to stay away, I haven't gone more than six weeks without alcohol since college. This fact has raised the uncomfortable question, "Are my two glasses of wine a habit or an addiction?" It occurs to me, if I value authenticity as much as I claim, I can't write a truthful account of my life without first acknowledging this nagging question of my relationship to alcohol, and then setting about to answer it.

I've begun a three-month alcohol fast with the idea that if, at the end of that time, I'm knocking people over at Safeway to get to a bottle of Chardonnay, I'll know I'm a candidate for AA. Maybe I am just pooping in my pull-ups, stubbornly clinging to a comfortable habit. Maybe it's more than that. Either way, I want to know the experience of life without it. If wine numbs my anxieties, it must numb the joy of all that is good in my life as well, and there is so much good.

I wake up every morning next to a man whom I love without reservation and who loves me the same way. And as if that weren't enough, he makes me French toast and coffee every morning, something I am all the more grateful for since he gave up coffee altogether.

Charlie and I just celebrated our eighth, or "bronze" anniversary—meaning, I guess, the two of us are more durable than paper or cotton, though not as brilliant as crystal or pearls. We are, for each other, the second chance to have and, more importantly, to *be* the kind of partners we once could only imagine. I like to think we're becoming more brilliant at it every year. We begin each day trusting neither of us would ever knowingly hurt the other, and we go to sleep each night assured that every one of our needs have been listened to and supported. As far as I'm concerned, anything beyond that is gravy.

At an age when many of my contemporaries are motherless, I am blessed to still have my mother. She and I have long since healed any hurts we caused each other, and we cherish every opportunity to make each other laugh. In her eighties, she has earned the right to let others take care of her, but passivity is not her style. My father may have been the breadwinner, but my mother was, and continues to be, the meal planner, grocery shopper, bed maker, coffee brewer, house keeper, bill payer, and weed puller—and never more so than when her family is around. When we're not, she writes us long letters, offering her news as well as praise for all the good she sees in us. While her arthritis has never kept her from writing beautiful longhand, she has let us push her onto the internet. I can't adequately explain what a miracle it is to go to my computer and find an e-mail from my mother, from this diminutive woman who irons her dish towels, and once managed to preserve a box of raisins for more than twenty years simply because the raisins were perfect—not too sticky, not too hard—for making the eyes on Santa Claus cookies. I am so grateful that she is someone I would want to know and love, even if she weren't my mother.

I have a dog that keeps me company while I am writing, and who welcomes guests in our home by humping their arms and legs. We are working to curb his enthusiasm in this area—trying everything from banishment to a shot in the face with a water bottle—but what can I say? Jarvis is a people lover. He makes no judgments; he humps everyone equally.

Jarvis is my second chance to be the kind of caregiver I was not for the dog we had in Idaho. Poor Lady spent too many hours alone, outside, starving for affection. Jarvis is so accustomed to my attention that often he doesn't bother himself to meet me at the door when I come home. He knows I'll come to him.

I have friendships with both men and women in which we challenge and inspire each other to reach beyond our limitations. I think of them all as God's emissaries, even when we disagree.

We are, for each other, facilitators of the lessons we need to learn. I'm working at seeing my least favorite people in the same light.

Thanks to God, in Her infinite wisdom and sense of humor, I am also gifted with four children (I'm counting my step-daughter and daughter-in-law here) who, collectively, reflect back to me every single quality that I have most embraced, and rejected, in myself. One is the embodiment of the human heart's limitless capacity to forgive. Another is a picture of fearless self-expression. One is the image of a soul's search for the truth of its being. Another is a natural at the art of manifesting whatever vision the mind can hold. All are amazingly creative. They are musicians, artists, scholars, entrepreneurs, and comedians.

But there are times when one or more of them will leave me ranting to myself—or to Charlie—about how thoughtless, self-absorbed, unappreciative, conceited, moody, impatient, or churlish they can be. Yet even in the midst of my ranting, I love them, deeply. I wish I could say that with as much conviction about every thoughtless, self-absorbed, unappreciative, conceited, moody, impatient, or churlish-behaving stranger I encounter on the street.

The truth is, I have to work at loving every neighbor as myself, just as, for a very long time, I had to work at loving my sometimes thoughtless, self-absorbed, unappreciative, etc., self as unconditionally as I love my children. It is in loving them that I've learned that love does not require perfection, and it is in that knowledge that I can learn to expand my own capacity for unconditional love and forgiveness to include everyone—something that's become a little easier since the horror of September 11. I haven't been able to stretch my spiritual muscles far enough to feel genuine love and forgiveness for terrorists who willfully sent hundreds of people to their deaths. However, in trying, I've stretched them enough that I can meet the divinity in the contractor who refuses to deliver what he promises, the woman who laughs to see her child push in front of Nathan at the petting zoo, the acquaintance who consistently takes without giving anything back, the neighbor who litters our patio with his hedge clippings, and the relatives who periodically dredge up their memories of every old boyfriend of mine they couldn't stand. How trivial such offenses seem now. In the presence of my grandson, most any offence becomes altogether forgivable, if not forgettable.

My children were my second chance to protect the innocence, the purity of heart that I lost from my own childhood. Having sometimes harmed that innocence in my own children, Nathan is my third chance to claim the wisdom I was born with. He is my best, my wisest teacher these days.

Nathan finds JOY in his bowl of cereal in the morning, JOY in his cup of orange juice. He finds JOY in knowing the words to "Twinkle, Twinkle, Little Star," JOY at McDonald's where they put those great toys in with your food. He finds JOY—not guilt, not shame, not regret—in pooping in his pull-ups, even though he knows he won't be doing it much longer, even though he knows he is supposed to have outgrown such behavior.

I've outgrown a lot of things that I still do. It's good to know that I'm in such wise company.

Reflections on the Future

...Scarcely knowing how to express my gratitude for the mystery of fate, I hurry inside to buy the shopkeeper the very first copy...

My future. The task of writing about it calls to mind once again my lack of omniscience. I face my future in the full knowledge that I am neither omniscient nor omnipotent. Neither omnificent nor omnipresent. I am, however, omnivorous; put me in front of a buffet and I'll eat everything in sight. So all I can say with certainty about my future is what I want to bring into it—not the least of which is my appetite.

Aside from food of pretty much all kinds (except for tapioca pudding, egg custard, and okra), I have a voracious appetite for stories—for hearing them, telling them, writing them, reading them, gathering them. I also hunger for travel, conversation, creativity, knowledge, family, friendship, and the whole truth of what it means to be a child of God.

I used to believe the mark of spiritual mastery was the absence of troublesome human emotions such as anger, envy, and fear. Spiritual mastery was synonymous with being in a constant state of peace and joy. The fact the demons of anger, envy, and fear continued to dance in the pit of my stomach from time to time, despite my best efforts to conquer them, only seemed to serve notice, as far as my soul's evolution went, my knuckles were still scraping the ground.

What I have come to know is this: God creates nothing to be thrown away. All of our emotions are part of the palette God gave each one of us to learn with, grow with, create with, and serve with. For me to try to eradicate any one of them would be tantamount to an artist opening a full palette of colors, discarding the reds, and then setting about to gift someone with a painting of a sunset. It would be like the Disney Corporation opening the gates to the Magic Kingdom one morning, then closing down the Matterhorn and Peter Pan. (This has happened to me, by the way, and it's no fun, I can tell you.)

I sometimes feel envious when I see someone else's dreams coming into view more quickly than mine. The sharpness of the feeling only serves to sharpen the focus of my own dreams, to point me toward success.

I feel angry whenever I see what looks like injustice—someone getting what they want through force or manipulation. The heat of my anger only tempers my resolve to demonstrate far greater riches are gained through love and surrender to Spirit.

I feel fear each time I step beyond familiar limits—say, when I try out a new speech or workshop. There's no small amount of fear in writing this, in opening the contents of my soul for anyone to see. It is in seeking out that which brings me fear, stepping up to it, and acting in its midst, I fully experience the boundlessness of my strength and the fruits of my faith.

Rather than work at overcoming the more uncomfortable emotions that come with my humanity, I'm learning to embrace them as part of my divinity, as part of what I bring to the blank canvas, to the Disneyland of life from this day forward.

Besides my appetite and emotions, I bring to the future my dreams, my visions. The sign, "88 percent of life is showing up," has been replaced by a strip of paper, taped onto my computer screen that reads, "My mission is to inspire, foster, and model the Creative Spirit within all persons, and in the process, bring hope, strength, and healing to those struggling with depression." I hold this mission for my business—*Wonder Weavers, Inc.*—and for my life. In my future, twelve percent of life is showing up; the rest is creating whatever Spirit, in the quiet moments, has called upon me to create.

Spirit has called me to write. I'm clear on that point. The call came in 1964, when I felt moved to write this essay for my third-grade teacher. The essay was titled simply, "Future."

In the future, I plan to be an auther. I want to write mystery books.
In the future I may write my life story. I might draw the pictures for my books too.
If I decide not to be an auther I might be a reporter. I would write as interesting articles as I could.
I may be the reporter who writes down imformation about a robberie or a murder.

*I might help find a thief or maybe help find lost jewelry and things like
that.
But whatever I do I'm sure it will be exciting.*

Years after I'd forgotten that I ever wrote this essay (my
mother had squirreled it away in a bedroom closet), I became a
reporter. Some years after that, I became an "auther" and pub-
lished my first book. A feeling of wonderment came over me the
other day as I considered the writing I'm doing now and recalled
the line, "In the future I may write my life story."

It would seem I've also got a mystery book in me just waiting
to come out.

I have embellished my third-grader's vision over the years. I
don't just see myself writing the books; I see the books published,
on bookstore shelves, in libraries and classrooms. I see myself
reading from them, watching with gratitude and joy as my words
find their way into the hearts of the listeners, because it is for
their hearts that I have written them.

I also bring to my future my willingness to learn and grow in
those areas that still mystify me—money, for one. Money has
always been, for me, an enigma, even though I've always been
blessed to have all that I need. A tax season visit to my accountant,
or a meeting with a lender when buying a house, has been known
to send me running to my car in tears, convinced that, when it
comes to money, I'm the stupidest person on earth. Where money
comes from, where it goes, what it's for, how to manage it, how
to speak its language—these are the questions, at forty-nine years
old, I'm just beginning to answer for myself. However, I can en-
vision myself mastering the art of personal finance. I can see
myself at a dinner party someday, having glib conversations about
PMI, MMAs and ARMs. (At the moment, the only concept I'm
clear on is ATM, but that's because I've done exhaustive research.)
I can see myself completely at ease with money—both the sub-

ject and the substance—as I lay back in a bed of $100 bills and belt out, like Madeleine Kahn after conjoining with the monster in Young Frankenstein, "Oh Sweet Mystery of Life At Last I've Found You!"

Along with my willingness to open my mind and heart to higher levels of understanding, I also bring my willingness to let go of any belief that no longer serves me. This week I listened to the Rev. Harry Morgan Moses issue this directive: "Stop arguing for your limitations. Be aware they are not working for you." I've heard that advice stated other ways, the most powerful for me being Jesus' admonition, "Do not judge by appearances, but judge with right judgment."

Not long ago, a friend wrote to me her husband faced a possible diagnosis of prostate cancer. Such a diagnosis, she told me, inevitably meant a diminished life for him, both in span and quality. The doctors, statistics, and conversations with other people she knew all confirmed this to be true and, out of her fear of losing him, she actually argued for this belief, against all other possibilities—even against the power of the mind, the power of faith to heal the body. Seemingly miraculous healing does occur, she acknowledged, but not very often.

I felt baffled and frustrated by her uncharacteristic negativity. Given the choice between focusing on the limitless possibilities of God and focusing on the statistics, why not go with the only one that has any chance of producing a good result? As I've said, however, God has this way of providing me with mirrors for seeing what lurks in my own shadow. The strength of my resistance to my friend's point of view was God's way of telling me that my nose was pressing on the glass. The truth is not a day goes by I don't have to stop and ask myself whether I'm seeing each person, place or situation through my human eyes, or my spiritual eyes, because in most every instance, the view will look much different.

There was a time when my human eyes did almost all my seeing for me. When it came to my spiritual vision, I was Mr. Magoo. Yesterday as I drove down a busy Phoenix street affirming that I am a spiritual being, living in a spiritual universe governed by spiritual law, I had one of those magic moments of seeing the scenery change. I watched it go from a cacophonous hodgepodge of automobiles, traffic lights, road construction, strip malls, street vendors, neighborhoods, schoolyards, and city parks, to something akin to a particular fish tank I remember from the Monterey Aquarium. There a school of silver fish swam in a ceaseless, circular pattern—their movements at once instinctively connected and utterly protected from anything outside of their silent playground of water, plants, and rocks. Any one of those fish would probably have been surprised to learn his little fins were flapping in such perfect concert with all the others—that he was doing anything more than swimming along, living his life, doing his own fishy things. I know I felt a sense of amazement in that momentary recognition that I was divinely linked to all I surveyed. That my soul swayed in rhythm with every tree blowing in the wind, accompanied every driver en route to fulfilling our divine purpose, touched and was touched by every feature of the landscape.

My human eyes have weakened with age, but my spiritual eyes see all the better for it. What's more, they continue to see more clearly every day, in all directions—future, present, and past.

It is only with spiritual eyes that I can see the full value of my history—not only the history I inherited from my ancestors, but also the history I have created for myself. Looking from a strictly human standpoint, I once viewed the events, relationships, and decisions of my past as falling into two distinct categories: the sublime and the ugly. Giving birth to my sons fell into the sublime category, as did the time that I and some fellow pilgrims communed with a tribe of Aborigines in a remote part of Australia where our hosts fed me a live grub, painted my breasts, and invited me into a sacred tribal dance. These seemed the kinds of memories worth carrying into the future—certainly the only ones worth exposing to others.

Other parts of my history seemed more like the stuff that rots in the back of my refrigerator—the stuff that's best thrown away without daring to examine it. There were, after all, those old boyfriends. The ones I dated after my divorce. The ones my family couldn't stand. The ones whose relationships with me ended with anything but a whimper, and in one case, with the words, "Fuck you," banging in my ears.

I am grateful to these men. Each one left me with a gift I carry with me every day. From one, I learned how to be a better parent. Another believed so much in my calling as a writer, I started believing for myself. One opened my eyes to nature while another showed me the darkness which comes from having nothing to believe in. My marriage to Charlie is all the better for these gifts.

The life God and I are creating for my future requires I know, and know deeply, I already am all of those qualities that I most desire to express. I am powerful, successful, prosperous, beautiful, talented, creative, generous, courageous, compassionate, and wise. I'm happy in my marriage and other relationships. One of the most valuable lessons I learned from my parents, who taught by example rather than words, was the people most endowed with those qualities are the ones who never profess to have them. They feel no need to. They have no interest in delivering progress reports on their personal and professional goals, but revel in hearing the progress of others—a fact that makes them easy to pick out in a crowd. They're the listeners, not the talkers. When they do speak of themselves, it is from the depth and breadth of their being, from the knowledge that they are not simply perfect, but perfect in their imperfection. Like a well-crafted story, their lives show, rather than tell, the nature of their character.

My father was the most brilliant and successful man I've ever known, yet he never boasted of the last board position he was appointed to, or quoted passages from the latest economic forecasters he read, or dropped names of wealthy and famous associates—though all of it would have been true. Instead, he focused his attention on others, imparting far more questions than declarations, though he could be downright verbose on the latest episodes of the *Muppet Show* and *Sesame Street*. Dad lived from the knowing he had nothing to prove, not even to himself, and no one but himself was worth impressing.

I am evolving into the sort of person whose life speaks for itself, though I still catch myself responding to other people's progress reports with one or two of my own, lest anyone think I don't measure up or I'm stagnating. Oh perish the thought!

So indulge me, dear reader, as I report big changes indeed are afoot. For one thing, Nathan has stopped pooping in his pull-ups. Now he marches into the bathroom like a seasoned professional, as though he has been doing it all his life. He has, however, developed a new and annoying habit of questioning just about every word that comes out of anyone's mouth but his own. For him, "why" is not just a question, it's a game. He no longer asks "why" to get an answer, but to see how many answers people will offer before they realize he's only messing with them.

"What's that tortoise doing?"

"He's sitting in his pond, Nathan."

"Why?"

"Because it's a hot day and he probably wants to cool off."

"Why?"

"Because he'll be more comfortable."

"Why?"

"Because too much heat could make him sick."

"Why?"

"Because their bodies can't handle extreme temperatures."

"Why?"

It's usually at about this point in the exchange when I realize that 1) I no longer know what I'm talking about, that I'm just making stuff up as I go along, and 2) information isn't what Nathan is after anyway. It's the sport.

For a while, Charlie thought he had taken the upper hand by turning the tables on Nathan. When Nathan would ask, "why," Charlie (known to Nathan as "Goga") would answer, "Why do you think?" And for a day or two, Nathan actually found himself forced to search his own limited knowledge bank for answers. That is, until he came up with a new strategy: answer every question with another question—

"Why?"

"Why do you think, Nathan?"

"Why do *you* think, Goga?"

I, too, have found a new game. It's a question game, too, but with a different question. My game begins by asking "what?"

"What is my purpose?"

And God answers.

"What is the first step?"

And God answers.

"What is the next step?"

And God answers.

"What is the next step?"

And God answers.

Like Nathan, I like this question game. I like it for the sport. Only God never tires of answering, and God always knows what (S)He is talking about. God is omniscient and omnipotent. God is omnificent and omnipresent. God is past, present, and future. It is with God I move into the future, one step at a time.

Courtney's Shoes

In Our Shoes

Fable

Lifeline Theatre

The envelope was waiting outside her apartment door when she got home from work—a plain white envelope with her name inscribed in a fine black calligraphic hand. No stamp. No return address. No other markings except for a red wax seal on the back flap.

She opened it carefully, neatly slicing through the flap, and reached in. The invitation was made of a white velvety material trimmed in red. The kind of deep red those movie stars wear. The kind of red she would not be caught dead in; *she* was no Jezebel. The curly red letters read:

Lifeline Theatre
6 p.m.

That was it. No explanations, no directions, no nothing.

Goose bumps traveled up her arms. She didn't know how she knew, but she knew she simply *had* to be at that theater by six o'clock.

She looked at her watch: 5:45. If she took the stairs instead of the elevator, and if Mac, the building security guard, happened to know the location of this place, and if the theater wasn't twenty miles from here, she just might make it there on time. A lot of variables, but she believed in destiny.

She opened the apartment door, sat down, and was about to put on her running shoes when…

"Here you go Miss," a voice squeaked.

She glanced up into the face of a stranger. He looked gnomelike and bald except for a half circle of fine frizzy hair that reached from temple to temple. Stray tufts of hair protruded from his ears, and his nostril hairs, she noted, could use a trim. His rheumy hazel eyes were close set, and his bushy gray eyebrows competed for attention with a pointed nose graced with an impressively large, incredibly hairy wart.

She squinted in the semi-darkness at the man, at this apparition. What else could he be? He wore a red velvet suit exactly the same shade and texture of the trim on the invitation. The heavy gold buttons on the suit seemed to weigh him down.

The invitation! She had to get to the theatre!

"Here you go, Miss," the nasal voice squeaked again. This time she looked beyond the face to the bony hands—actually more claws than hands—that held a pair of bright white socks, a theatre ticket, a bucket of popcorn and a soda. What, no Milk Duds or Raisinettes? She closed her eyes and counted to three. When she opened her eyes, the little man was still there, in his Jezebel-red suit, holding out his hands, and peering at her as though she were the one who looked strange.

"Welcome to the Lifeline Theatre, Miss," he said, his mouse-like voice taking on a note of pride as he flung out his arms, spilling some popcorn.

Her eyes took in the space indicated by the sweep of his arms. She indeed stood in a theatre furnished with comfortable-looking red velvet seats, a large screen, and concessions such as those he offered in his claw-like hands. The place smelled of popcorn and old gum. She inhaled the nostalgic fragrance of spilled cherry sodas mixed with an unmistakable air of adventure, comedy, and drama.

She took the little man's offerings and was about to ask about the socks when he said, "They are for your 'now,' Miss—for your present. Put them on."

*Ooookay...for my 'now'. I wonder what that means? I'll just
put them on and go with the flow,* she thought. She pondered where
she should sit.

"Sit anywhere you'd like," the gnome-man chirped. "This is
your show."

This is your show. She mimicked his voice in her mind. *What
is this crap and how does he know what I am thinking?* She settled
into a seat in the middle of the theatre, near an exit and as far
away as she could get from "Jezzy"—as she now mentally referred
to him. She put on the socks and was about to chomp on some
popcorn, when Jezzy popped up beside her.

"Get a bell, why don't you!" she shouted. He waited for her
to collect her wits before handing her a pair of shoes.

Now these shoes were even stranger than the stranger who
offered them—a pair of pumps, but each shoe sporting an
entirely different design and color. The left shoe had a black and
white checkered pattern, while the right shoe was a solid gold
color. Both were adorned with baubles, beads and stuff, but the
right one held a smooth rock with the word "Love" deeply carved
into its surface.

She looked up from the shoes to find Jezzy still there,
patiently waiting to continue his instructions.

"The left shoe goes on first, Miss," he directed. "Just slip your
foot in and enjoy the show."

The time was now less than a minute before six. She placed
her popcorn on the floor, took the shoes from the gnome-man
and attempted to put on the left shoe. What first captivated her
as she held the shoe was a red hand, palm up, inscribed with the
word "STOP" in black letters. The toe of the shoe displayed a
picture of a green island surrounded by a blue sea. The word
"Jamaica" was printed below the island and above appeared the

initials J.E.D., written in black and white. As her eyes traveled around the shoe, they took in the pink paper chain of male figures that stretched from the left side of the toe to the black bow at the back of the shoe. The heel sported a tiny black book with the words "Holy Bible" written in gold letters.

Turning the shoe, she was surprised to see an empty needleless syringe next to a paper image of a Rolex watch. A gangly, gold giraffe galloped nearby, close to the red hand. Touching some of the objects, she felt a fleeting sense of foreboding, but *knew* she had to put on the checkered shoe. It took some wiggling, but with perseverance, the shoe slipped on, fitting like a too-tight glove. A feeling of anticipation and excitement came over her as she settled back in her seat and looked up at the screen.

The year 1962 flashed on the screen along with a picture of a baby girl. All of a sudden a dank, gray fog seeped into the theatre and ominous music began playing. She felt herself rising and falling, rising and falling and, for the first time since this whole weirdness began, she felt fear. She heard voices in the fog—voices yelling, laughing, singing, screaming, murmuring. Like a living being, the thick fog held on to her. Through the fog, flashes of light and color appeared on the screen. Events unfolded before her, around her, and even through her, as she became part of each scene in what struck her as a poorly conceived plot. Definitely two thumbs down, *way* down.

She gasped to see the shadowy figure of a man standing over a little girl. Watching, she felt a yearning like she had never experienced before. It was as though a hole opened up inside her and she craved to have it filled. Boys and men paraded in front of her then, their arms outstretched, offering emptiness. Their faces looked different, but the emptiness felt the same.

The parade gave way to two ceremonies—beautiful ceremonies in which two halves were joined—followed by a series of still shots of a woman being hit, lying on the floor, floating out of her body enveloped in a bright light, then re-entering her body.

At the right corner of the screen she saw the same little girl she had seen before, with arms above her head as if warding off an attack. The little girl screamed and cried as angry red welts appeared on her back, on her legs, across her face. The words "New World Translation of the Holy Scriptures" flashed across the screen like a neon sign.

Sitting in her lush theatre seat, the feelings of yearning grew sharper as she felt the little girl's pain.

Numbers and letters floated in front of her vision—'A's at first, then numerous 'D's and 'F's. Next she saw pictures: beautiful colored drawings and paintings on white paper. The pictures floated in front of her, but as she reached out to touch them, they ripped into pieces and fell into a fire. She recoiled, pulling back her hand. A woman in a white dress, standing at a bedside, appeared. The woman moved to stand at many bedsides before she, too, disappeared.

Without warning, a pain tore through her as though her belly were on fire, but before she fully recovered from that pain, another pain stabbed at her left wrist. Suffering and accompanying sadness were inside her and all around her. Crying out for the first time since entering the theatre, she shouted "STOP!" then collapsed in her seat, sobbing.

She cried for the little girl.

She cried for the lost innocence.

She cried for the children that could no longer be born.

She cried for the woman.

She cried for herself.

The screen went blank; the fog lifted, and light surrounded her. Tentative at first, the light grew sure and strong. It lifted her out of her seat, high above the theatre, holding and rocking her before gently re-depositing her on the plush red seat.

For what seemed like an hour, she reveled in this healing light. She felt past events and feelings leave her—felt the goodbyes of long-held friendships and beliefs. She let them go and was left with the knowledge that the life she had witnessed was not poorly conceived, but absolutely perfect. She knew the perfection of her own life.

She felt a movement near her left foot and glanced down to see Jezzy gently removing the checkered shoe. She had no questions for him now. Instead, she realized that she knew all the answers, had known all along. She had not, however, been prepared for the raw emotions, the pain, the anger, the fear, and the emptiness. With the shoe removed, her mood lifted considerably.

She hesitated a moment before picking up the right shoe to examine it. The golden shoe had colorful heart-shaped buttons glued to its toe section. Near the buttons, brightly colored initials, CLD, sat above a peaceful white dove with outstretched wings. On the right rear of the shoe, a tiny magazine entitled "Home" appeared above a picture of a contemporary southwestern style house, and an African mask and a leopard print button whispered of creative possibilities near a blank canvas. A cluster of yellow at the left of the shoe near the heel caught her eyes: a sun face shining down on a sunflower, a bumble bee, and another heart-shaped button, this one bright orange. To the left of the cluster clung a trio of tiny books: one purple, one pink, and one green. The words "Loving Yourself" were written on the cover of the pink book. A green champagne bottle stuck awkwardly to the side of the shoe's heel, while two stars glued to the back twinkled with a light of promise. White feathers on either side of the shoe hinted at the possibilities of flight.

The shoe felt so free and light with its bright gold stars and feathers. The various colors reminded her of the beautiful drawings in the fog. She felt no apprehension as she removed the "love" rock and easily slipped her right foot inside the shoe. It felt very comfortable.

At first, the movie screen remained blank. She was aware of nothing but the classic smell of the theatre. Then something about the light began to change. It suddenly felt alive, lovingly alive, as it pulsed and wavered all around, cradling her like a newborn. She heard a sound like the chirping of many crickets, and the screen seemed to open into a large room full of people. They stood clapping, their hands coming together in a rhythm that got louder and faster as a tall slim woman walked into their midst. The woman smiled as she walked confidently through the crowd.

The scene faded, the screen returned, and green leaves began to flutter down from overhead. They multiplied until the air was thick with them. As some of the leaves brushed ever so gently against her face, she reached up to catch one.

"Leaves, my butt," she laughed with sudden recognition. "Benjamin Franklin, come on down!" Before she could gather up any more money, the image of a woman appeared on the screen. The woman knelt in a garden and began tending the plants.

The scene changed, and the woman now stood among a crowd gathered in a gallery or museum—someplace where pictures hung on the walls. Even though most of the attendees wore black, it was definitely not a funeral parlor. No, the air here was charged with joy and celebration. People were laughing, drinking champagne, carousing. She watched as the woman moved graciously among the crowd, welcoming all.

A series of still pictures showed the woman creating, painting, speaking, teaching, traveling, and writing. She observed the woman reading her stories to children, sitting on the floor with them, her voice rising and falling, taking on new intonations as each character was introduced. The light followed her wherever she went. In fact she was the light, touching all she met with love.

She sensed *him* even before he appeared on screen, larger than life—a tall, loving, commanding presence that felt so familiar, like someone she had met before. She watched as he walked up to the woman and stood before her.

"I want someone like that," she thought, not fully realizing the connection.

At her thought, the man reached his hand out, and touching the face of the woman on the screen, said, "You already have me."

Her face felt the warmth of his hand and a shock of recognition went through her bringing tears to her eyes.

The screen went blank.

"Excuse me. Miss?"

She continued to stare, wanting to see more—more of her past, her future.

"Miss? Miss? Miss?"

She jerked, suddenly aware of Mac, the security guard, speaking to her through the open apartment door.

"Miss, Miss, are you O.K.?"

Embarrassed that she'd been caught daydreaming, she blurted out, "I'm fine, Mac. I was about to come downstairs to talk to you. I just need to put on my shoes."

She reached for her running shoes and picked up a mismatched pair of pumps—one checkered in black and white, the other painted gold. Inside the golden shoe, the face of Benjamin Franklin offered a knowing smile from a crisp, one-hundred-dollar bill.

Reflections on the Past

...She felt past events and feelings leave her—felt the goodbyes of long-held friendships and beliefs. She let them go and was left with the knowledge that the life she had witnessed was not poorly conceived, but absolutely perfect...

The first time I got married I knew what I was doing, or so I thought. I do remember walking down the aisle smiling at the boy waiting for me at the end, and asking myself, "What the heck are you doing?" Maybe I asked, "What the hell are you doing?" I know for sure that I did not say, "What the fuck..." I was a good girl then, and good girls did not use such language. I was twenty-one.

The second time I got married, I knew what I was doing. I did a mental check before I walked down the grassy slope under the cottonwood tree and assured myself that this was right...for now. I had no illusions of forever. I was thirty.

I was eight or nine the time Daddy returned to Jamaica from one of his visits to the United States. I had missed him so badly it felt good to see him. The feeling was so unfamiliar; I had no words for it. It started in my gut, shot all the way up to my heart and made me light-headed—a strong feeling, and so unlike the fear I normally felt whenever my daddy was around. Unsure of what the feeling meant, I ran away and hid. He had brought me back a multicolored ball as a token of his love—one of those small balls you can get for a quarter in a round glass machine near a check-out stand. The next day, full of idle curiosity, I bit the rubber ball and it split into two.

For the first part of my young life, my father, a policeman, spent long periods of time away from home. He became an almost daily fixture in my life around the time our family began studying with Jehovah's Witnesses. Always a stern disciplinarian, he became even tougher after his conversion. Determined that

we would all survive the end of the world—"The Great Tribula-
tion"—as a family, he held many family gatherings at which he
drilled into my siblings and me the importance of staying in "The
Truth," as the religion is called by insiders. My dad talked, or
rather preached, a lot about sex during these meetings, where I'd
pass the time by breaking my own record for holding my breath.
I remember writing a letter to my cousin, venting about Dad
going on and on about his "fave" subject. My dad found the
letter and another lecture was born: another twist on the evils of
sex before marriage and on making light of a heavy topic. Sex
before marriage was a subject matter Daddy was very familiar
with, having fathered many children with many women. He was
just telling us in a roundabout way of his own experiences with
the commodity. I suspect he knew firsthand the emptiness that
sex could not fill, but was unable to explain fully to us children
what he really wanted to say. So at practically every family meet-
ing—of which there were many—he would go on and on about
waiting until marriage to have sex. Those lectures cultivated in
me a curiosity about sex, but I managed, with all my groping and
body cavity exploring, to stay away from the dreaded "sex before
marriage." I wanted to be a "good girl," to wait for the big night,
the wedding night, the "we know what you are going to be busy
doing tonight" night.

On that night, eight months and one week after my twenty-
first birthday, I remember lying in bed, incredulous. "This is what
I saved myself for?" I asked. "This is what the whole fuss was
about?"

I had expected explosions, fireworks, a culmination of all the
feelings I had kissing the boys of my youth. I had expected my
husband and me to be transported to a space above ourselves
from which we could see eternity, a place where we would merge,
become One, and know each other completely. Instead all I ex-
perienced were the ridges of the condom that felt like an old-time
washboard inside me. "Ribbed for her pleasure"…definitely not.

I learned how to French kiss around age eleven. Maybe I was younger. I didn't keep notes then. The person I learned from wasn't your typical "boy next door" type. Oh, he was next door all right, but definitely not a boy. He was an adult, a friend of my parents, a father, and a grandfather.

By my eleven-year-old standards, Mr. S. was an old man. He had skin the color of dark chocolate that had been left on the stove too long. His lips, too, were dark and his bottom lip, which drooped toward his chin as if he was in the habit of tugging on it while in deep thought, had an area of bright pink that spread unevenly toward the edges. He smelled of stale cigarettes, sweat, and axle grease. Mr. S. was a gentle and quiet man, the perfect foil for his wife who chain smoked and shared her opinions easily with folks on her veranda or across the street. On rare occasions, Mr. S. would raise his voice to call his daughter, my best friend, home for dinner. He occupied the rear of the house, tinkering on cars while his wife reigned on the front porch, seeming to see and know all.

I search my mind now to explain how it happened. Just how did I end up in a musty old maid's quarters at the back of the house, being felt up and taught to kiss by a man who was older than my father? That rainy day and many days after, I was educated in the ways of what I thought was love. Mr. S. was insistent, however, that we not have sex. "I don't want to hurt you," he said. But hurt me he did, by introducing my young mind and body to experiences not fully understood and by opening a place in me better left closed until I could consciously decide for myself how to experience that opening.

The relationship continued until I got baptized as a Jehovah's Witness. With my newfound pre-teen righteousness, I decided not to see Mr. S anymore. I remember the day I refused him. He stood at the corner of his house beckoning me furtively and I kept shaking my head. I was pure now, having gotten a new start on life through baptism, and I intended to stay sin-free.

Was it weeks or months after I refused him that I caught him with my sister? She was younger than me by about four years. I had gone in search of her and something told me to look for her at his house—specifically to look in the dining room at the back of the house. I know this is not possible, but I remember seeing them behind the door through the wall. They were standing slightly to the left of the door. He had his back to the wall, his left arm around her waist and his right hand up her dress. Was I really seeing them or was I merely remembering? I do remember opening the door only to have it shoved back in my face with fearful adult force. Did I call out my sister's name then while I pushed my slight body valiantly against the door? When I gave up pushing, the door shut and I went home to wait. When my sister came home a little later, I told her, "He did the same thing to me. Don't ever go over there again." She and I both were looking for love.

My decision to stay pure lasted until I kissed a boy close to my age—a friend of my brother's. Of course, I did not stop with him. I was hooked on the high, the feeling of "almost sex" and did not want to stop. The floaty high helped me feel better, less empty. I went on to kiss many boys in my teens, so many that I have forgotten most of their names and faces. Recently a man with whom I had gone to high school reminded me of an incident after school that involved him, an empty classroom, and me. I had no conscious memory of it. "Knowing me," I told him, "I bet it involved kissing and groping." He acknowledged that it did and I felt disturbed by his revelation. I had been seeking the fullness of a feeling without seeing the human at the other end. I repeated this pattern many times, in my marriages and throughout my single life.

My yearnings were answered by unattainable men, half-baked as though they had been pulled out of Life's oven too early—fully formed, but not quite done. I invited them to bring their uncooked selves into my life in attempts at becoming the "one big whole" religion is so fond of talking about. In each man-boy, I kept trying to find the piece of the puzzle that fit, the other half that would make me whole. Instead, I found men who were looking for the same thing I was, men who held up a mirror to me saying, "I am you." We were all drifters blown together by karmic needs, then blown apart by the lessons learned. I did not understand it at the time. Slowly the pattern of my life emerged: I had been attracting the same man over and over—same dick, different face. The energy was always sexual, as I had learned as a child of eleven to attract from that place, and I knew of no other.

The day I killed myself dawned like any new day. My young husband visited me in our trailer at around four o'clock that evening. In his anger he slapped and pushed me while I accepted the blows with the same non-resistance I had demonstrated as a child. Compared to my father's beatings, my husband's hands felt like feathers, and in my martyred mind I thought I deserved such punishment. After all, what man would not be justified in hurting a wife who not only slept with another man, but also had the nerve to get pregnant by him?

I had no one to turn to and no one to talk to. The laws of their religion prohibited my parents from talking to me unnecessarily. I remember telling my mother, "I'm pregnant."

Her only response was, "Oh my."

At that time, I had lived in the United States for about five or six years. I knew nothing of welfare and even less about bearing and raising a child alone. Although I was disfellowshiped for my adulterous behavior from the only religion and support system I had known since around age ten, I still felt a part of it and it strictly forbade abortion. So it was while I was in this spot between the proverbial rock and a hard place that my husband entered our trailer, yelled at me, hit me, and left. After he left, anger arose in me, anger that had been simmering for over twenty years.

"I'll show him," I thought, "He'll be sorry he hit me."

The plan was born then to kill myself and, in doing so, kill the fetus and "make" my husband feel guilty. I drove my white Ford Escort to the closest Rite Aid pharmacy, purchased a box of sleeping pills, then to a drive-through liquor store where I got some hard liquor. Once home, I took the pills, drank the alcohol and then decided to clean up the trailer so that when my body was found, no one would think me a terrible housekeeper. As I washed dishes in the sink, I began to feel woozy, so I dried my hands and made my way toward the bedroom. My weak, rubbery legs took me as far as the living room where I collapsed near the hallway. I still remember my final rational thought as the soothing darkness wrapped around me: *So this is what death feels like.* The darkness intensified and I gave myself up to it. I awoke sometime later, my stomach heaving and contracting. Vomit spewed from my mouth onto the carpet and coated the side of my face. I was aware of the room but could not move. The darkness took over again as I lay in my own vomit. I do not know how long I remained like that, but when I finally came to, I purposely got up, cleaned up the vomit, took a shower and went to bed. There were no longer any thoughts of suicide. By the next morning I had made a decision to have an abortion. The girl who had taken the pills was not the same woman who got up from the vomit-stained floor.

In my mid-thirties, I mentioned my molestation to my father. I'm not sure what I expected him to say. How my father reacted, what he said, told me volumes about him. It told me he was just a man, not the god I had once thought him to be. It told me he really tried to take care of and protect his family and was disappointed by his inability to fully do so. It also told me that he knew what Mr. S had been—had known all along with the intuition of a policeman and parent—but did not think any of his children would be, or had been, his "victims." The energy behind his words also told me that he blamed me for what had happened.

Without raising his voice my father asked, "Why didn't you tell me?"

Simple words, but they said so much more. As I casually mentioned my sister's experience, driving another nail into the coffin of my father's impotence—his inability to protect—I felt him shrink before me, a little man with the weight of the world on his back.

I write this not to get pity, but to show how predatory old men can and do entice young girls like me, the young girl I was. How did I get involved with my neighbor? How did I attract such a predator? I can say with certainty I desired attention, craved feeling special, needed to be needed, and wanted to be loved. I was taught the fundamentals of manners, math, science, and literature but had the natural love and self-esteem beaten out of me with electrical cords, belts, and fists…ironically all in the name of love. I was reminded to brush my teeth but not reminded how special I was. Intellect and obedience were valued over creativity and individuality. Adults were not to be questioned.

So when someone came along, someone who acted kind, who listened, who gave me the attention I craved, I took it. There is a saying in Jamaica: "Screw face know a who fi fright'n." Literally translated it means, "An ugly person knows who to scare," and the basic meaning is that an opportunist knows the perfect opportunity. This man knew instinctively that I would respond favorably to him. He knew that my sister would respond the same way. Cut from the same cloth and wanting desperately for fatherly attention and love, we sent out distress signals that he answered readily. I went back repeatedly, voluntarily. It felt good to be wanted—however inappropriately.

I took this early lesson of unacceptable behavior and translated it into a still improper, but more socially accepted, behavior as an adult. I dragged the void into both my marriages, a black hole of insecurity and longing that neither husband could fill.

The men between and during my marriages could no more replenish me than the boys of my childhood. I went through many men thinking that the next one would be "the one," the fix I needed. I feel no shame in wanting to be loved. My "shame" lay in forgetting my magnificence, forgetting my inherent worth, and seeking it in another. It was not until my late thirties that I realized that there was no one "out there" who could make me whole, although many attempted.

During this time of searching I knew that having a child would be disastrous. How could I mother when I had not been mothered? I could only teach what I had been taught, and most of the lessons I had learned were based on fear, not love. Four times in my life I cast out souls that desired to be born through me. A journal entry dated September 1992 reads:

Why do I need a reproductive organ as useless as the uterus? I have, more than once, rejected its fruit. I will not have children. I was not brought up to have children. A hysterectomy—yes, a complete removal of my womb will make me whole. Vomiting, headaches, and bloody discharge will be things of the past. I'll save at least forty dollars per year in tampons—not stemming non-existent flows. I am a woman, but not in deed, dropping children at will…and enjoying the slavery of crying needs. And I never will be. My womb serves no purpose—maybe I'll store some thoughts inside it, make it useful for something.

On September 8, 1997, I had a partial hysterectomy. I had never wanted children. Indeed, as a teenager I declared as much to my father. About three days after my surgery I was in Bisbee, Arizona, with my best friend, Sara, a fellow nurse, celebrating my "uteruslessness" with a bottle of champagne. The following Saturday, an incident occurred that ultimately saved my life.

Never one to let physical challenges keep me from the things I love to do, I was on the back porch that day tinkering with a large piece of glass into which I had sand-carved a roadrunner and chili peppers. A friend, John, had come by earlier to look at the carved glass, and he suggested that the figures would look better without color. I looked all over for the acetone-based nail polish remover he suggested I use to remove the color but since we had moved into the new house only days before, I was unable to locate the bottle. When John left I finally found the nail polish remover and cleaned the color from the glass. During this time something kept nagging at me—a warning—but I did not listen. Finally, when I was done with the color removal, I picked up the glass and my world changed forever.

There was no sound, no sensation. Time stood still. I found myself facing 180 degrees from where I had been standing and staring at a gaping hole near my left wrist. As I wiggled my fingers in fascination, the tendons moved like white worms through a red river. I looked into my body under the skin and observed it with clinical detachment. When my wrist refused to respond to the command to flex, fear hit, and sound returned bringing with it pain and panic. The nurse in me took over and I called 911, called Sara, as she was the nurse on call for the operating room, and cleaned and wrapped my wound. I was trembling in fear but had the presence of mind to leave the cell phone at home in case my husband returned and wondered what the bloody mess was all about; we did not yet have phone service. The blast of adrenaline would not let me stay still and I walked down the road to meet the ambulance. The surgery was a success, thanks to Dr. Padilla, Sara, and the rest of the surgical team, but it was not until days later that I was able to reconstruct exactly what had happened. The large glass panel I had been holding had hit a pole, shattered, glanced off my watch and cut my wrist. I took this as a warning to "use it or lose it."

During the time off from work for physical recovery I was guided onto a path of self-discovery and spiritual recovery. Julia Cameron's book *The Artist's Way* had caught my eyes a few months before. I had thumbed through the book, but when I saw the references to God, I hastily placed it back. God-shmod. I wanted nothing to do with God. The God of my childhood, the God who thought I was a whore, the God of vengeance, the God of judgment, the God of anger, the God my father shoved down my throat for over ten years. I could still feel that God, stuck in my throat like dry bread, cutting off my breath. His anger was my anger. I felt physically sick as I exited the bookstore leaving the spiritual way to higher creativity in its proper place on the shelf.

But the book refused to leave me. After my "glass meets wrist" accident I saw the book once again. Sara and I were in a bookstore and I pleaded with her to buy it for me. I do not know why I did that as I had my own money with which to purchase the book. We ended up getting books for each other that day.

After a false start I began the course in earnest on December 1, 1997, the same day I returned to work at the hospital. Four weeks into the course, I noticed many changes. I became softer and less angry. I drank less, partied less, and began to question my marriage more. I also tentatively accepted the creativity I had grown up with. I took myself on artist dates, alone to special places, as the book suggested. I wrote my morning pages almost every day and sometimes wrote more than required. I cut my time back at the hospital to three days per week and began to explore my artistic side more. I also began to meditate.

I noted on 12/25/97: *Do I believe in guardian angels? Do I believe in a protective spirit? Do I believe in God, the Great Creator? Do I believe in me...and my ability to effect positive changes in my life and others? A tentative "yes" now might become resounding later—I think it will. It's been a short month and here I am. What if I keep learning, doing, discovering for a year? For the rest of my life? I'll discover that there is a God who loves me, who has protected me for His purpose and who will soon reveal what that purpose is.*

On 12/27/97: *I have changed so much in these four weeks. I could not believe a course could change anyone so much. I am less afraid, more trusting of myself and my talents.*

The person who emerged from the pages was like a newborn chick that needed to be protected yet allowed to roam free. I nurtured her as she reunited with the God of her birth, a God she now knew as Love, Spirit, All That Is—a God she had never been separate from.

During my marriage, I was concerned by my husband's lack of faith in my artistic abilities. I wanted so much for someone to believe in me, to tell me how good I was and how great my talents were. I remember writing letters to him, angry letters in which I stated the love I have for works of the hands, letters begging him to let me do what I wanted to do. Thankfully, he ignored them. At the time I was struggling to find my voice, struggling to find me. I had a lot more growing to do. In 1996, I wrote him this letter:

I have been dissatisfied for some time with my situation. This is not a marriage but more like bondage…economic dependence. I didn't marry you for your money. You asked me to marry you at a time when I was very vulnerable and I, despite my better judgment, said "yes." Marriage seemed to you an assurance of "forever." Neither of us was ready, as you demonstrated a few weeks later while claiming that I forced you into marriage. I don't want to be married. I was quite content to just live together and I still am. Marriage does not assure anyone of anything but a lower tax base.

Your claims of believing in my dreams are all bullshit. But I think the important thing that I have refused to focus on is that I don't believe in myself. I have been using your lack of belief in me and your lack of support to reinforce that lack of belief in myself. There has been a pattern to my life that needs to change and only I can do it. Two years ago I wrote you a letter about me not coming into the marriage whole…remember that? I still feel that way. If you can find the letter now, please read it again. Read between the lines this time and hear what I was saying.

All my life I have been repeating patterns learned from my parents. I know I am but find it difficult to stop. At least I realize that, and that is the first step...

Although you claim that you hate this "yours" and "mine" talk, you stated so eloquently last night that I shouldn't expect any of YOUR MONEY...

I think it fair that I pay half of all the bills that are held jointly in both our names. If you want me to pay for insurance on the vehicles, then they need to be in my name. You can do what you want with them. They are of course yours. I would like to be taken off your credit cards, so if I mess up along the way, your precious credit won't be affected. I don't want to screw up your life with my quest for happiness. I know you worked hard to build and keep your credit status.

You mentioned the five years that you "supported" me. Give me a bill for the food, clothes, and shelter and I'll give you one for emotional support, cooking, cleaning, decoration, landscaping, washing, and sex. Of course the fees will be higher during times of crisis or high stress such as: while you were in San Diego; the FEB (Flight Evaluation Board) the WIC (Worldwide Intelligence Conference); not getting promoted; the move to and from Maryland; and finding a job. I'm sure you'll agree that I have more than "repaid" you...

Years after those letters, I began to get in touch with who I am. I began to believe in myself and in my creative abilities. I began to love myself. Until then nothing anyone said about how good I was really mattered. True, I felt good when my creativity was noticed and praised, but until I really *felt* creative, until I *believed* I was creative, the feelings stayed on the surface.

I left my husband in September of 1999. I wanted more for my life and realized that by beginning to believe in myself, I had to let go of my anger over his lack of belief in me and also let go of him. I was no longer the girl he married. I did not leave my husband for the proverbial "other man." I had enough sense to know any other man I attracted at the time would be as half-baked as I was. I needed the time and space to heal, to fully know and love myself, so I left him for the "other woman," the woman I had become. It took me a few more years to begin to let go of anger and blame, to honor my checkered past, and to own my power of creativity in all aspects of my life. Now I can clearly see the cause and effect in all my dealings. There is no blame, just responsibility. And it is from this place that I approach all relationships.

August 11, 1999, was a date more important than the dates of my pre-teen baptism, my two marriages, my graduation from nursing school, and even my birthday all combined. I had received the date of August 10 in meditation the week before and had been anticipating something wonderful for that day. Indeed, for days before, I felt the sureness of "something coming." Dreams, meditations, and intuitions gave me the certain knowledge that what was coming was so much more than I had experienced before.

The day of August 10 came and went—a normal day. I spent most of the day with my friend April and her five children. Later that night, when April left on a date, I stayed with the children giving them Reiki (a form of hands-on therapy) and watching movies. I got home the next morning at 1:10. It is said, "God may be late but He never forgets." By mid-morning I was experiencing uncommon warmth that began in my sternum and spread to my entire chest. The exquisite energy burned yet did not hurt. I can only liken it to a "runner's high," the burning that one experiences after a long run. As my heart opened fully, I floated blissfully throughout the day allowing the feeling to embrace me. Wrapped in the warmth of this love, I had the total knowing and acceptance of self and knew myself as Love—the love that fills from the inside and flows outwards, the love that always is. This was the love I had been vainly searching for in the darkness outside me, in all the faces and in all the places. On that day, and with that one intense experience, I realized that I needn't search anymore—that the love I looked for, the wholeness I sought was inside me and had been there all my life.

I look back on my past, clear-headed and without reproach or guilt, not feeling like a victim. I have forgiven myself for looking for love in all the wrong places. In the late eighties when the names and faces numbered around fifty, I stopped counting. When I decided to look inward at my emptiness and stop trying to fill the hole from outside, I became celibate. I stopped the clock after having sex one night in November of 2001. That time something was different. It was not a matter of feeling empty and wanting love. I was feeling horny and wanted sex. I held no illusions as to my partner's role in my life or in my bed, and when he left, I started keeping time by a new clock.

Reflections on the Present

"Sit anywhere you'd like," the gnome-man chirped.
"This is your show."

I sold my Rolex today. It was a symbol of status given to me at a time when outward show was important. But for one split second on September 13, 1997, the watch ceased to be a status symbol and became for me a lifesaver, protecting my left hand from certain paralysis and possible amputation, and launching me into a journey of self-discovery. I told the buyer about the watch—a little of its history—but I did not point out the quarter-inch dent in the stainless steel clasp, which was visible, but only if one looked closely. It was a dent I could still feel when I ran my fingernail across it, even though the folks at Rolex tried their best to buff it out.

The buyer might have reduced the price.

While sitting in the jewelry store, my mind went back to the day of the accident. I'd had a hysterectomy just five days before but was feeling invincible. From the evidence it seemed an edge of the 30-by-30-by-¼-inch piece of glass I had been holding hit against a pole on the back porch. The old glass shattered and a shard hit the watch clasp dead on, glanced off and cut me, totally severing three flexor tendons in my left wrist, and slicing halfway through a few others. It must have been a big piece to have left such a visible dent in stainless steel. Thanks to the watch I survived with no handicap.

I had worn the watch daily for over eight years and the band was old and shabby, flopping like a lifeless thing whenever I took it off. With its band stretched to the limit, the watch no longer sat on my wrist but threatened to slide down and off my hand. It was time to let it slide. I woke up this morning knowing I no longer wanted or needed the watch and the memories associated with it. I sold my Rolex today and bought a ten-dollar watch at Wal-Mart that suits me fine.

I have been slowly letting go of possessions of my former life, also letting go of people, attitudes, and belief systems that no longer serve me. I am at a place in my life I never thought possible: a place of total trust in the generosity of the Universe. Well, my trust is not absolutely total, but I am working on it. I have moved beyond mere words into action, asking and receiving graciously, and tasting and seeing that all is indeed good. The many recent leaps of faith I have taken come back to me now: quitting nursing, leaving my marriage, moving to a big city, and setting up an artistic sandblasting business. During these times I have never been forsaken nor have I been hungry. I have been afraid and unsure but always received guidance through dreams, meditation, spoken words, the written text...

When I moved to Phoenix in July of 2001, I knew that I wanted a home-based business but ignored my knowing and yearning to instead set up two separate places—one to live in and one to work from. Where and when did I lose sight of what I truly wanted to do? When did I decide that having a separate place of business that would dazzle my clients was really my soul's desire? It may have been an attempt to impress, rather like my Rolex. I even went so far as to look down my nose at those who worked from home. I had a "real" business and they did not.

After rediscovering what I knew to begin with, I set energy in motion to create it. I quickly got what I wanted, a house on five acres from which to work; however, I had to let go of everything in my life I did not want. The unwanted reality dissolved perfectly without my actively doing anything. Business dried up and I could no longer afford a place to live and a place to work from, and yesterday I arrived at the shop to find the locks re-keyed.

After the initial feeling of heart-in-stomach, I drove around back to get comfort from my neighbor and friend who operates a machining business behind mine. I felt no shame or embarrassment and blamed no one. For weeks I had imagined the scenario of getting to my office and the key not fitting. I had daydreamed often about a place where I could live and work. I was the one responsible for the reality I was living, and it took a lot of focus to concentrate on what it was that I wanted, not on what I was getting at the time. My friend not only comforted me with hugs while reminding me of my power to create, he introduced me to a young couple who was seeking to lease or sub-lease a space in the same area.

It was incredible how the energies worked to bring me exactly what I wanted. The couple loved the space, although the young man was a little indecisive. I did not push but kept declaring to the Universe, in my mind and out loud, exactly what I wanted. I told myself that if they are not the right ones for the space, the right ones will come along. I was sure of this. God has Her own timetable, though, and sometimes waits until the last minute to scoop one of Her children out of seeming danger. That totally pisses me off, but I'll get over it. I know all will show up at the correct time for me.

Physically my neighbor looks like a kid—a short chubby-cheeked Italian kid who often jokes about his "stubby legs" and his other chubby body parts. I can tell that he likes me. I did ask God for "6-foot-5" but I think God misheard me and gave me 5-foot-6.

God, you and I have to talk. Being 5 feet10, I have only just recently become comfortable enough with my height to wear heels as high as three inches. As a teenager, I stooped sometimes and wore shoes as flat as possible to avoid towering over the boys. Classmates called me "string bean" in high school, but I felt more like a giraffe, ungainly and knobby kneed. My father slapped my back if I stooped while sitting. He declared that he did not want a daughter shaped like a "capital C." I am now very grateful to my father for doing that. Now, even with my short friend, I stand tall, proud of the woman I am and proud of the place I am in my life. The difference in our heights is teaching me not to conform to another's expectations, to be myself despite what others may want me to be, and to see beyond the physical into the very Spirit of the human.

My friend is definitely aware that he creates his own reality and it was one such creation that caused me to look at him differently. He had declared that he no longer wanted to do small mechanic's jobs but wanted larger machining accounts. Recently he showed me a purchase order for a very large amount. At that moment I felt so proud of him. I felt the pride of a parent, of a teacher, of a friend. He was surprised and touched when I told him, "I am proud of you."

The prosperity he created was the most powerful and personal example of manifestation through focus, outside of my own experience, that I have ever known. He is coaching me just by being. We have a synergetic relationship where he teaches me about business and I teach him about relationships. Once upon a time, in my arrogance, I thought people in my life were there only to learn from me. I have come to accept that others show up in my life in order for me to learn from them. I know my friend is not "Mr. Right," but he could be "Mr. Right Now." He provides a supportive space for me to grow, expand, and to relearn trust. That, more than height, is a sacred and important element in this relationship.

The human part of me sometimes worries about my future and the worry, like a snake in my belly, threatens to overcome me. Knowing, as I do, that I get what I think about, I return my focus only to the thoughts of what I want and let go of the thoughts of what I do not want. The "worry snake" has not been active much lately, as I do not feed it with thoughts of things I do not want. It has taken a lot of faith, self acceptance, and a knowing that I am indeed the creator of my own life in order for me to have gotten to this point. As I hold tentatively to my newfound position, to my new trusting and to the "peace that passes understanding," I shine a light for others who also wish to change their lives.

I am letting go of my need to control an outcome. I have a vision of my life that extends beyond the current boundaries of my belief in myself. I can also see the woman I am in service to other women. Sometimes I ask to be shown a bridge, a visible link between what I am experiencing now and what I know I will experience. God has yet to show me the bridge. I guess I really do not need to see it. It's such a human thing, this wanting to walk by sight.

I stand now in the present with white socks on my feet. Socks symbolically decorated with feathers and soft pom-poms, both pink and blue, representing both sides of me, a balanced human child ready to fly. Gulls glued on both socks illustrate my favorite book by Richard Bach: "Jonathan Livingston Seagull." I am now that seagull, having defied conventional "oughts" and "shoulds" to stand in my own power, in my own knowing. The masked faces of mother Africa that are positioned below the gulls are like the faces which come to me now in the stillness. This is my present, capped by sparkly golden halos of light, a present rife with possibilities complete with dancing shoes and a dove of peace.

I am working from home now writing this, and the feeling of "rightness" is delicious. I move from this apartment into the home on five acres this weekend and I absolutely know it is exactly where I am supposed to be. I tell my customers that I am "in transition" and the words take on new meaning as I transition from old limiting beliefs to new, expansive ones; from lack to abundance; from wishing to knowing; from two places to one; and from old relationships to new. I feel my life changing and the directions are clearer now. I celebrate the changes and welcome them into my life. I also welcome new spiritually-minded friends who live what they believe. Despite the "reality" that I am locked out of my workspace and do not now have access to my tools, I feel great. My computer is here, I have forwarded all my calls to my home, and the cats have gotten back into their old routine of jumping into my lap while I write. I really missed this life and, along with it, the feeling of wholeness that comes from working where I live.

I sold my Rolex today. I may use the money to cover part of my lease that's due. But then again, maybe God has other plans. Maybe She'll give me the paid vacation I have been envisioning.

Reflections on the Future

…The light followed her wherever she went…she was the light, touching all she met with her love…

I've "seen" things and "known" things most of my life but managed to convince myself that everyone saw or knew the same things I did. There is a certainty that has followed me since birth, and that is the certainty I will always be taken care of. This knowing has manifested itself in bouts of seeming recklessness at times and downright craziness at others. I was really, really stupid, people shouted, when I left my job as a nurse to grow fully into the artist I know I am. My husband declared artists do not make any money and, even with a combined income of over $100,000, we could not afford for me to quit. I quit anyway. I was crazy, some said, for leaving my last husband. Who will take care of you now? They wouldn't do that if they were in my shoes. I knew that leaving could possibly plunge me into poverty and that my "hobby business," as my ex-father-in-law called it, may not be enough to sustain me. I left anyway. I survived these changes while holding tightly to the knowing that there was something bigger for me, that I had been born to a greater calling.

I look back on my life and see the person I have been.

I see the little girl growing up with an abusive father and an abused, shrinking, silent mother.

I see the little girl declare that she will never become like her parents but go on to become the very essence of them.

I see the years of "love" addiction—the yearning to become whole through another.

I see the despair that led to my death and to other attempts at death.

I see the faces of my unborn, all four of them.

I see the women that have come into my life, and I also see myself as every woman who has lived and who will live.

Choosing to be healed, I help others, especially women, who wish to heal. For this purpose I was born. For this purpose I lived as I did. And for this purpose I have been born again. I do not set myself up as a leader needing followers, but as an example to other women as to how life can be fully lived.

How could I feel disgust for a woman in whose shoes I have not walked? With my life experiences I have strolled beside her if only for a moment. How could I judge my sister for the very thing I have done? I would condemn myself as well. What right do I have to cast the first stone? My yard is littered with boulders. Having walked my life's path I can truly say, "Been there and done that, Girlfriend!"

I see pictures of myself traveling the country speaking before large audiences of women. I walk strong and tall, with a strength born, not from arrogance, but from love. I feel lives changing, as each woman realizes her inherent worth and accepts herself fully based on her own love, not on the judgment or opinion of others. I see the children born of these women; children who will not forget who they are but who will grow up knowing their importance. These children teach me as I teach them and they are aware that the love they seek is the love they are. While Barry Manilow writes the songs "that make the whole world sing," I write the books that make the women and children of the world look at themselves in a brighter, more loving light.

I also see myself painting and creating for pleasure and profit, transferring the images I receive in meditation to canvas. In my volunteer work with children, I encourage them to do the same, bringing the love from inside them and expressing it appropriately with words, movement, paint or other means.

As I learn and grow, I allow into my life the male expression of the love I am. He is tall (6 feet 5 inches), dark, and handsome. Yes, most wish for that, but I have seen him and he will come.

My home in Santa Fe awaits and I smell the pinion fires that burn on chilly fall nights. There is an almost physical yearning now as I think about Santa Fe. That city calls me home and soon I will answer the call. My home in Arizona, filled with sunny winter rays and built on the land I love, is also waiting for me. All my homes will be built with straw or adobe, with a north/south exposure, and have gardens filled with fragrant flowers and fruit. The water used in these homes will quench the thirst of the trees and flowers, and Earth will yield Her best for me as I in turn honor Her.

I will live the life I was born to live, the life I have always known, and the life I have had glimpses of. This life is being created by my every thought, word, and deed now. As I create and fine tune this life, I look forward in anticipation to the woman I am becoming, while celebrating the woman I am, and fully embracing the woman I have been.

Jami's Shoes

In Our Shoes

Fable:

One Woman's Trash

I've skulked these alleys far back as I can remember…always watching, always looking, always searching, sometimes wanting, sometimes finding. Finding's the best—I mean, I see the fancy folk in their fine clothes—furs and feathers   flaunting their happiness like one more expensive trinket from them "too high" places downtown—the ones that charge more than's necessary just 'cause they can.

Anyway—as I was saying—findin'—cast-offs, throw aways, dust bin droppin's—in lots o' places ain't much—but in these alleys sometimes out right Treasures—with a cap-i-tol "T"—appear.

Like these shoes I found one day—tossed in the trash like so much spoiled trout! Beautiful, they were—different from one another—but clearly a matched set, too. I mean they were these basic black pumps like everyone knows the fancy women have to have. But they'd been messed with—each one in its own way— not so's you couldn't tell they were shoes, or a pair, but rather so's they invited me in, like they had a story to tell.

I scarfed them shoes and high-tailed it down to the pier at Downey Lane all the way to the boathouse where t'was empty and I could really check 'em out.

First the right one—lined in a rainbow and sportin' eggs inside. I set those on the shelf and slipped my foot inside. Like a glove! Snug, bit stiff and confining, but those rainbow colors ran right up my leg—ticklin' and tinglin' and settin' it to tappin'.

And off each side of the toe—these white doves fluttered, lifting my cares. And I swear if I'd have put the other shoe on right then I'd have flown right off into space!

But I kept my left foot firm on the ground and watched while this lizardy thing scurried across the toe—back and forth—back and forth—like it t'was agitated and wantin' to climb my leg or get inside and chomp my toes!

And all around the bottom, these green stones flashed and beckoned and I just *had* to watch. I mean I couldn't look away—like I was hyp-no-tized!

And I felt this green fog start swirlin' up around me and—I know this sounds weird—but I swear I was all of a sudden like swept into that world—the one I watch behind those windows, inside those carriages. It was me with them fancy folk, laughin' and dancin'—twirlin' all about and eatin' too rich food and drinkin' too much wine and spinnin' and spinnin'—

And out of the corner of my eye—on this mantle—them three eggs I told you about. Like every time I turn, there they are. And they're not covered in green fog. They're crisp and clear, and callin' to me, stronger than the fog.

And when I finally reach for one—I'm back in the boathouse with one funny shoe on and its mate settin' there like off to the side.

So I'm holdin' this egg and that lizardy thing's still wanderin' and them green stones don't glitter so much. So, I—well—I cracked open that first egg and nothin' but a bit of green smoke came out—a little, tiny tornado that danced along my hand and up my arm and then—sssssss Pop!—into my right ear!

And I started to imagine…the pain behind the laughter, the empty behind the full, the wantin' behind the havin' and Lord, I got so sad…

I grabbed another egg and cracked it open and a pink swirl floated up and settled soft around my shoulders and I saw sweet peas noddin' in a field. I never before saw such loveliness—gentle and soft and sweet. Mm—Mm—Mm.

That third egg—the blue one—I *had* to know. So I tapped it real gentle and pale blue stars rose out of it and I swear they tinkled! And then got quiet—so quiet!

And I could hear everything. Not all at once—but when I thought about somethin'—the sea, the birds, my own heart—well, I could hear!

And I thought about that other shoe and I heard it callin'… "C'mere, c'mere, come here, COME HERE!" So, I went…one big basic black pump (and the tale already told) clumpin' over to another, similar, mirror image, very different mate of a shoe— for my left foot.

Oooh, it took so long to finally wiggle my toes over the doo-dads and past the feathers to stand up right in this pair of not-so-basic-black pumps.

And in a heartbeat the green fog slipped to a memory and the pink swirl stopped and the blue stars settled and the feathers took to flappin'—inside and out and I was floatin' on the breeze, slippin' in and out in patent leather heels and what you see me in right now!

But it wasn't places and things I was passin'—it was Time! I was soaring over the past—I mean the looonnnggg past! And I was spiralin' to the future and I tell you it was amazing!

There was gods and goddesses and kings and queens! And then One Shining One—and then all the Shining Ones!

And then that damn lizard! Run right up and bit me and I fell down here—well back at the boathouse—and the shoes were gone and so's I just come back home—to these alleys and I watch and I look and I search.

And maybe someday—soon—maybe…

Reflections on the Past

*...First the right one—lined in a rainbow and sportin'
eggs inside. I set those on the shelf and slipped my foot
inside. Like a glove! Snug, bit stiff and confining, but those
rainbow colors ran right up my leg—ticklin' and tinglin'
and settin' it to tappin'...*

A blank sheet of paper and an empty screen beckon me toward self-examination: a past replete with blessings and awash in tears; a present rife with opportunity and muddied with doubt; an open-ended future in need of designing, hinted at but not promised. All await free expression of the whispers in my mind illumined by imagination.

These shoes depict a desire to see my childhood blessed with extraordinary intervention. That's the mythology I clung to then and grasp now. I choose to see the rainbow and doves rather than the rain and the resignation that rooted my parents too long in a past of their own making.

All the colors of the rainbow welcomed my arrival in human form that Sunday in 1952. I brought with me three gifts designed to hatch and grow throughout my earthly existence—empathy, comfort, and vision.

Setting sail on the currents of time, God's hand firmly at my back, brilliant gold stars to light the way, my parents gave me roots and wings. Their guidance grounded me in practical needs for money, work, shelter, food, and water. Their love urged me to develop the talents that were uniquely mine. Their desire to keep me safe gifted me with caution, doubt, and worry. Their wish for my success graced me with courage, hope, curiosity, and fierce determination.

Our first home in West Lawn had living, dining, and sleeping space above a dank basement where suppliers delivered coal for the furnace through the window to the spidery bin below. My father built rough, wooden shelves along the wall to hold the fruits and vegetables my mother canned for winter meals. In the center of the room—away from glass jars and coal dust, illuminated by weak rays of light filtered through the filthy window—stood a wringer washing machine that "could crush my fingers" and, on more than one occasion, threatened to flatten my mother's forearm.

I am the younger of two girls. My parents said that when my sister Merrie was born they raised her by the book. When I arrived they threw the book away. When she was a toddler they would put her in the back yard and tell her to stay close to the house and she did. When it was my turn and they'd say, "Don't leave the yard," I would ask "Why?"

"Because there are cars in the lane and broken glass in the street. There are snakes in the field and it's got holes and rocks that you can hurt yourself on."

Trusting that I understood the admonitions, they'd go back inside and then check on me a few minutes later to find me picking bluebells and violets in the field, or walking up and down the lane waiting to wave at the few cars that bothered with the bumpy passage.

There must have been quite a neighborhood picnic for Labor Day in 1951, for in our little neighborhood, four of us were born within weeks of one another. My best friend, Susie, lived next door. Her much bigger house had two magical places to play.

Inside, the coffee table with four leaves that hinged up or down had holes carved in them that made perfect side rails for our make-believe wagons, buses, cars, spaceships, and prisons. Two small children could easily hide underneath and a third could sit on the top and spin fantastic journeys to mythical shores.

On rainy days our mothers put us in the screened-in porch, thinking us safe from the world beyond. I wonder if they knew that even that spacious prison could not contain our imaginations. We defended pretend castles and staffed hospitals. We ruled as queens, fought as soldiers, performed miracles as doctors, won awards as actors. As Indians we defeated cowboys; as pirates, walked the plank. We morphed into an entire zoo full of animals. For me, pretending to be "special" was a defense against feeling alone.

I got sent home one day because I told a lie. Hoping for extra attention, I said I was wearing a sweater because I had been sick the night before. Susie's mom wanted no part of whatever germ I might be carrying and walked back with me to tell my mother so. When my tale failed the truth test, I lost porch privileges for more than a week.

Some months later, Susie's little brother Billy (no, the names have not been changed) came to pester me at the edge of our yard. I was busy acting out by pulling up the little decorative metal fences my father had placed in the ground around our shrubs and trying to make them hang inside the bushes. Billy wanted to play as well, but I wanted no part of him. So I tossed a teeny tiny pebble at him thinking to shoo him away. It hit him in the face, split his lip, and cost my parents a large enough doctor bill they forbade me from playing with him ever again. I won my freedom from the pest but lost access to my best friend.

A few weeks afterward, Susie got permission to come to my house and play quietly indoors. On our wonderful hardwood floors you could slide in your stocking feet. So we started just gliding elegantly about. Then boredom set in. We escalated our efforts. A challenge erupted—run from the hallway, slide through the living room, make a sharp left turn, and stop on the edge of the dining table. The first heat I won. Second heat, Susie. Third heat—neck and neck until suddenly Susie's feet were up in the air and her face was on the floor. She bumped her chin not once but twice. No little touch and go, she split her chin wide open. Blood streamed. Susie screamed and sobbed. I tried hard not to laugh—and succeeded after one look at my mother's face as she came through the swinging door from the kitchen.

Six stitches and another doctor bill later, our parents separated Susie and me for good and all. Years later I heard my first best friend had grown into a strikingly beautiful young woman who'd been diagnosed with diabetes and died of complications in our twenties—a noticeable scar marring the chin of that lovely face.

Not what I had in mind when dreaming of making a mark on the world.

I don't know why I thought I was so different as a child. Somehow I just didn't feel like I fit. Mostly I wanted to fit, but I also wanted to be special. Every awkward attempt at normalcy made me cling ever tighter to the opposing, arrogant notion that I had been born to do something extraordinary.

Posing on my tricycle at age four, dance classes at eight, sashaying around pretend stages in backyard shows for the neighbors at eleven, longing to follow in my older sister's footsteps to star in school plays at thirteen, I just knew I was capital "I" capital "T", IT! Yet shame assaults my senses even decades later.

Seems I've felt ashamed as far back as I can remember. I don't recall the first time shame swept over me, but occasionally I am still haunted by humiliation suffered on the first day of sixth grade. We'd moved to town just the day before. So, day one, my mother took me to register. Classes were divided according to grade points. Scoring 'B's and 'C's in math at my previous schools, the principal thought I'd do best in the middle section, that the smarter kids might be further along than I. The scene has not dimmed with age—my hair frizzed from sleeping in the pin curls Mama so painstakingly wound the night before. A new long, black raincoat to "grow into" over the homemade pleated skirt of washable cotton in shades of yellow and orange. Hem brushing below the knee above my high-gloss saddle shoes. Entering the classroom late, my arms full of books and forms. Facing the crowd of strangers—my peers—my friends. Hopes of passing into acceptance shattering as my plastic pencil box full of new implements and erasers clatters to the floor. Drowning in derisive laughter.

Even months later, my parents, thinking me too young to follow my peers' fashion tastes, refused permission to wear nylons, lipstick, earrings or even Capezios. Looking like the child they hoped I would remain, I sealed my fate by daring to get all 'A's.

"You messed up the curve!" they snarled.

"It's good she's smart, since she's so damn ugly," taunted others.

"She's not so smart if she can't fit in," rang the pedestrian truth of puberty.

Self-conscious ineptitude, smothering me in plain sight of the howling pack, worsened one day at recess. Chosen pitcher for kick ball, each attempt spun farther afield, triggering escalating jeers and mockery so overwhelming that I heaved the ball one last time and fled. Tears streaming, feet pounding I streaked toward home.

Gasping for air, I arrived home. My mother refused to let me in the house. She was frightened at the illegality of my actions. "You're required to stay at school!" she reprimanded. I stood stunned and shocked at the absence of much-anticipated solace and safety. Grabbing her jacket and my hand, Mama turned me about and marched me straight back.

My teacher, Mr. Warner, had clearly chastised my classmates for their rude behavior but let me know in front of them and in no uncertain terms that I was wrong for leaving. He wanted me to say something, to "explain myself." No recollection remains of my mutterings that day and all these years later I still doubt my ability to discharge that duty—to explain myself.

Blame it on being born a Leo on the Cancer cusp. Rationalize it through an un-raised consciousness. Fault my gender, hormones, un-sophistication, soft heart, thin skin, flat chest, wide hips, or bad attitude. My continuing sense of shame defies explanation and dims only in the face of maturing self-acceptance.

Relationships with family, friends, and strangers generate the experiential collage of my life. Music—instrumental, song, and dance; words—books, magazines, and letters; radio—records, drama, and humor; movies of every genre; television and theater sweeten the mix and bridge painful gaps forged by human conflict.

Before my first days in school, Grandpa—Dad's dad—played fiddle and called square dances. My folks liked all music. Songs in the car gave way to hymns in church. "I Love to Tell the Story," "The Old Rugged Cross," and "Blessed Be the Tie that Binds" trigger flashbacks to both my earliest spiritual yearnings and the backside numbness that accompanied sitting too long on wooden pews.

The Little Golden Books, Reader's Digest, Ladies Home Journal, McCall's, Saturday Evening Post, Look, Life, and eventually *TV Guide* cluttered the counters and toilet backs in every home of my youth. Family legend has it that during potty training my parents found my sister seated on the porcelain throne, holding the *Digest* upside down. Visiting my paternal grandparents meant a chance at solitary inspection of Grimm Brothers' fairy tales and Mother Goose—tools my mother used to teach us the alphabet before we entered kindergarten.

During my first years of public instruction, music, mystery theater and radio comedies took a back seat to television. My family sang along with Mitch Miller, danced with Arthur Murray, and spent Saturday evenings with Lawrence Welk. Sundays were reserved for Ed Sullivan. Mama, Merrie, and I would sit on her bed and watch Shirley Temple movies and the Miss America Pageant and I would just know someday—one day—I would be famous and beautiful and rich. I would walk that runway in Atlantic City. I would shine on the silver screen. All this artistic input and pretending allowed me to keep the loneliness at bay.

I practiced for hours to the record player (with a setting for 75s) that scratched out "Winkin' and Blinkin' and Nod," then graduated to Perry Como's yellow vinyl version of "Catch a Falling Star" and Andy Williams' Christmas Carols. The little suitcase turntable retired with the arrival of a console stereo—long the nicest piece of furniture in our house. At 33 RPM, my folks played big bands, Fred Waring and the Pennsylvanians, and organ music. Much to their dismay, I memorized lyrics, created choreography and enjoyed a "Lovely Bunch of Coconuts" with Danny Kaye over and over and over again. I was in fact quite the star of numerous backyard bonanzas.

Pearl Bailey ac-cent-tu-ated the positive notes in my early popular music education. A Smothers Brothers comedy album remains a favorite. I can still remember most of the words to "Map of the World," all of "The Streets of Laredo," and the entire routine entitled "Chocolate."

In Junior High, hard-earned babysitting money purchased my own first 45s—"Lemon Tree" and "Love Potion Number 9." The overture to my adolescence included tracks from Herman's Hermits, Tommy James, Gary Lewis and the Playboys, the Beatles (I'm still a Paul girl), the Animals, and the Monkees. (Since clearly Davey was both too short and taken by at least a million other teenyboppers, Mickey, Peter, and Michael took turns haunting my dreams.)

My sister had parts in every school play that came along. We both sang and took dancing lessons for a year, and I *had* to mimic Big Sister. In so doing, my love of live performance deepened.

The drama teacher didn't much care for me and speaking roles were few. Clarinet in the Marching Band sufficed until senior year, when I won a spot on the color guard. My licorice stick was traded in for the glamour of wearing a skirt and twirling a six-foot pike—that's a large show flag.

For recreational listening my sister favored the Beach Boys and Elvis, but my high school music score featured blues by BB King and the soulful sounds of The Impressions, The Intruders, and everybody Motown. For a brief span I cherished the white bread rhythms of The Association, The Seekers, and The Searchers, but as older classmates missed college, leaving on jet planes to fight and sometimes die in Viet Nam, Joan Baez, Bob Dylan, and Peter, Paul and Mary sang my sad torment.

Occasional school and summer trips to New York provided tastes of the extraordinary: Cleavon Little, Sherman Helmsley, and Melba Moore in *Purlie*; Henry Fonda as the Stage Manager in *Our Town*; and good seats for *Jacques Brel is Alive and Well and Living in Paris* and *The Me Nobody Knows*.

Crosby, Stills, Nash and Young singing of "four dead in Ohio" frightened my parents that summer before my freshman year at Valparaiso University. Indiana was too close for comfort to the slain Kent State University students. *Woodstock* hit the big screen and rocked the nation; however, in the dorms, Sweet Baby James, Carly Simon, and Carole King soothed the homesickness and burrowed deep into my consciousness. They supply the longest running strains in the soundtrack of my life.

After a year on campus with only minor parts in *The Marquis de Sade*, a Frederico Lorca one-act and a grad student's showcase, I returned home, funding my life in the Coffee Shop at Montgomery Wards and feeding my soul in Community Theater.

That first fall back my mother put my name in for the local preliminary to Miss America. I approached it as a joke, at first, skirting the rules every way possible. My first choice of a sleeveless floral pattern for the evening gown competition gave way to the *required* solid pastel chiffon. Initial refusal to spend money on a hairdresser resulted in the mandatory pre-pageant portrait showing my limp hair, freckles, and crooked teeth. I even arrived at rehearsal the day of the pageant with my regulation peau de soie shoes un-dyed.

But something happened between the judges' dinner Friday night, the rehearsal Saturday afternoon, and the pageant that evening. My competitive spirit rose up and I knew I *wanted* to win! Preparing at home for the long night ahead, I showered and shaved my legs, ripping roughly six inches of skin off my left shin. Sobbing on the side of the tub, I vented all my frustration at being less than the typical contestant. I'd be going on that stage with the daughters of doctors, corporate chiefs, and lawyers. "And, and, and…" I hiccupped, "My shoes don't match my bathing suit!"

Mother soothed my histrionics. Daddy got the styptic pencil to staunch my leg wound. Meanwhile, Merrie, my Big Sister, my champion ran to the drug store for a bottle of dye. By the time my breathing and bleeding slowed, she saw to it that my shoes were the same egg yellow as my suit—the same color my feet would be for days after the competition.

Not music, but drama led me to win the local title. I interpreted part of a one-act entitled *French Gray*—essentially Marie Antoinette killing rats the night before she lost her head. Oddly appropriate. The first runner-up was six inches shorter than I and twirled a baton to patriotic music.

Let me confess, I hate baton twirlers. They're perky and popular and doing something in which someone who has twirled a six-foot pike has trouble seeing the artistry. Years of Miss America pageants had produced a bevy of baton twirlers who never won but always placed. It only seemed logical to me that batons—flaming or not—were the kiss of death.

In between the October win at home and the state contest in Hershey, I got pregnant. Over Thanksgiving I was house-sitting for my former high school drama teacher. My then boyfriend and eventual first husband went with me to feed the cat, water the plants, and roll around on the floor. My generation knew the disgrace of unwed motherhood. Unwilling to weather that storm and not wanting to get married because I wanted to be a Star, I drove with him to New York on St. Patrick's Day and when I came home, I wasn't pregnant anymore.

That June, I placed fourth at the Miss Pennsylvania Pageant and won a talent award for my acting. Among the higher placing finalists were a baton twirler, a tap dancer, and the winning concert pianist. She placed second in Atlantic City. I don't remember her name. Terry Ann Muesen won the crown that year with her version of "He Touched Me." Only now, as she hosts the *700 Club*, do I get the religious implications and the irony.

In my mid-thirties Merrie confessed how much she had hated me as a child. "I was a princess until you came along," she sobbed. Boxes and boxes of old black-and-white photographs bear witness to her "pre-me" royal status. The rosy-cheeked cherub gave way to the golden-haired toddler and just as her baby cuteness started to fade into grubby-kneed childhood—Ta-Da! A new baby arrives.

My sister, my protector, my role model, eventual mentor and tormenter made a premature entrance to the family four years earlier. Weighing in at less than five pounds there were serious concerns over her survival. A heart murmur, scarletina, and asthma all contributed to escalated concerns as childhood diseases—measles, mumps, whooping cough, and croupe—made their inevitable rounds.

Trust me. My sister survived, and in the first-born spotlight and the adoring shelter of my parents' love, she thrived. Pictures show our Precious in wide-brimmed bonnets and darling crinoline skirts, lumpy snowsuits and mittens, ruffled swimsuits, and hand-smocked jumpers. Here she is in her crib, there on a swing, spaghetti-covered face grinning from a high chair, and cake encrusted bliss at the birthday parties.

There's even a newspaper clipping of her and my mother at the Easter Parade the year before I intruded.

My mother's first-born arrived too early, too small and sickly, so you can imagine Mama's anxiety during a second pregnancy. I not only gestated the full nine months, they had to use instruments to get all nine-plus pounds of me into the world. This traumatic process resulted in many stitches for my mother and a literal black eye for me.

When the proud parents brought me home, my sister reportedly went door to door through our neighborhood telling everyone the doctors beat up her baby sister.

Despite her pronouncements thirty years later—she loved me then.

I don't know how long it took the resentment to take root. Clearly the demands of a newborn stole time and attention from the housebroken, responsible, big sister. After all, they'd promised her a playmate but brought this squirming, squealing, smelly thief of affection instead. Accompanying my shiner was a gout-like goiter in my neck. On doctor's orders, my mother used to stand at my crib and rock my head back and forth until I fell asleep. Eventually the mass dissipated but the rocking did not.

My trek into childhood resulted in fewer, but just as cute, photographs—just not the portrait, stellar, headliner quality of my sibling's early years. Furthermore, most of mine have her in them as well. I always thought we were bonded, close, uniquely related.

We had more than our share of fights. Despite heroic efforts to parcel out love and hard goods equally, my parents were constantly settling the "she got more than I did" and "she's on my side" disputes. As I learned to walk, my sister learned to hide. As I learned to talk, my sister learned to play deaf. If my parents left the two of us alone, for even a few minutes, we'd be snapping and swatting and picking and poking each other, and when one or the other of the adults returned, we pouted and cried and on more than a few occasions out-right lied.

My mother sighed and sent one to a nearby corner and the other to our bifurcated bedroom. My father yelled and spanked or—in worst-case scenarios—sent one of us to get his belt off the door handle at the end of the hallway. That was the longest walk of all, down and back. The punishment worsened, however, when we returned with the strap. Instead of suffering a few swift blows, we endured what seemed like hours of lecture while he snapped the belt in his hands.

As we grew, such occasions brought my sister and me closer together. In the wake of my father's anger, my mother whispered and hugged and reminded us that we started it. For a short while we would make up and realize we knew each other in a way no one else ever would.

That became even clearer in the ensuing years. My father's anger simmered constantly. He not only lashed out at us for fighting, but in the long dark hours after bedtime stories and late night bathroom trips, he argued with my mother.

As an adult I realize it took the two of them to fight, just as the sibling rivalry required both my sister and me to stay ensnarled. As child, however, his voice, the sound of the slaps, and my mother's pleas for somebody to help her frightened me most.

As my parents climbed a few rungs higher on the social and financial ladder, we got a house with enough bedrooms for my sister and me to each have our own. More money did not make us happier.

Lying in my bed miles away from the sister who, when the thunder rolled through the house from outside or within, used to welcome me under her covers, I put my fingers in my ears and rocked back and forth, back and forth until the fighting stopped, or he came to yell at me or I finally fell asleep.

Make no mistake, my parents' angst did not reduce the haranguing between my sister and me. As we aged, our arguments grew pithier, meatier, meaner. Oddly, we fought about our parents. Odder still, she seemed to always be defending my mother. I took Daddy's side. I thought he had all the power and if I could win him over—well, to the victor go the spoils.

I still hear my sister's words on the Marvin Gardens-sized fight of all. Our sniping about which parent was worse and who started what escalated over more than an hour. She saw our mother being abused emotionally and physically. I saw our father being ignored and manipulated. Suddenly my sister yelled at me—"You think he's so great?! Well, he tried to get me pregnant!"

Shocked in my prepubescent confusion, I stopped cold.

"What? How?"

She mumbled something about how he could touch you in a way as to open you up and you would get pregnant. I'd never been so scared and disappointed. I felt betrayed—by her, by him.

From that day on our conflicts rumbled less frequently and at lower decibels. It took years for me to understand what she'd told me. Years longer to heal from the knowledge. And another generation to challenge him, threaten him with repercussions, and finally forgive him.

In my forties my sister said she didn't really hate me. She just wanted things back the way she remembered, when she was safely sheltered and adored. There is no other person with whom I share my personal history on such a profound and intimate level. There is no one whose memory is clearer than mine of what went on in our childhood homes. To this day, whether we're playing Scrabble, watching TV, looking at photo albums, or swapping reminiscences, no one else occupies such sacred territory.

She is vanilla and I am chocolate—our perpetual choices for ice cream on those Sunday drives. She is the child who gave my parents grandchildren. I am the child who gave them grief and adventure. Together, we gave them a fuller expression of family and more than a little input on changing times and tastes.

Through my twenties and into my thirties, my musical potpourri acquired dashes of the Eagles, Elton John, Billy Joel, and Paul Simon, with repeat performances by Barbra, Liza, and various Broadway musicals. I played "Lucy" in *You're a Good Man Charlie Brown*, had a substantial supporting role as a gun moll in *Anything Goes*, and brought the house down as Joanne in *Company*.

My first husband had a theater degree from Penn State and wanted to direct but did not realize his dream until after we parted. Still, our first Christmas together he gave me tickets to see *A Chorus Line* on Broadway with Donna McKechnie. They were good seats for the weekend of his birthday in February. We filled the week after with other shows in cheaper seats.

Only one experience topped *A Chorus Line*. We purchased half-price tickets to see *Equus* with Anthony Hopkins just moments before matinee curtain. Great seats, midway in the orchestra, center stage. As the lights dimmed the traditional "no cameras or recording devices" announcement began—except it started with an apology: "Ladies and Gentlemen, we regret to inform you that Mr. Anthony Hopkins will not appear this afternoon..." The air went flat with the hum of disappointment. After a lengthy pause the announcer resumed very slowly "The role of Dr. Dysart will be performed on script this afternoon by

Mister—Richard—Burton!" I let out an ear splitting scream and nearly fainted from lack of oxygen. When the raucous ovation finally waned, there he was, script in hand. Thunderous applause rolled on and on, with only the barest acknowledgement. He took a step back and began.

I finally understood what all the fuss was about. I'd seen *The Sandpiper* and a number of his television appearances and thought him handsome but not anymore special than dozens of movie stars. But even with the script in his hand, he had more potency, more vitality, more authenticity than any performer I'd ever seen. In years to come I would witness Frank Sinatra, Mikhail Baryshnikov, Nureyev, and Edward Villela in solo performance. Although each was gifted, none had the intensity or charisma of Burton.

When I left him—my first husband, not Richard Burton—I pretty much exited the theater. I began what would become two decades in broadcasting and entered the foyer to the world of the rich, famous, and infamous—newsmakers, movie stars, sports celebrities, and recording artists. I took my place on the dial at a station featuring the "new" country music. Elvis was still living, Willie Nelson was just beginning his vocal career, and crossover country was being born.

I met the Oak Ridge Boys and saw Loretta Lynn live. Crystal Gayle turned brown eyes blue and Dolly Parton swore she would always love you. Tanya Tucker married Glen Campbell and, while the First Edition launched his career, Kenny Rogers made it to the top courtesy of country.

Don't get me wrong, I didn't sing or even spin records. Besides, records were about to be displaced by carts (pre-timed loops of audio-tape inside plastic cases, which have since been replaced by CDs). No, I made use of that innate need to question. I became a "newsperson." I cut my teeth reading wire copy—back when it came off teletypes from both AP and UPI.

On my first job in an AM/FM combo station, the AM day timer played old-fashioned country music and went off the air at sunset. The FM carried automated soft rock. When I arrived in the morning I'd record a newscast for FM and do the AM casts live—that is if I arrived early enough to sound awake. If I didn't, I scrambled madly about to do the first live cast, then record the FM and get it into the machine before time ran out. More than once, time won.

In a matter of months I'd split from husband number one and, for the first time in my life, got fired. Though they blamed my lack of experience, I knew that the Program Director, who had asked if he could "pat my butt" and at whom I laughed as I emphatically told him "No," had put me out of work by the end of the week—quite a shock for someone with a sterling employment history and absolutely no concept of sexual harassment. In 1976, nobody talked of such things. Some things *have* changed for the better.

The radio bug had bitten. I needed a trade to take me to New York to study theater. I just knew I could do this well. On to the next gig, larger market, more money, and a boss who wanted to play Svengali. At his direction, I became one of the first chatty newsreaders on radio. We dumped the sounders and turned off the teletype machine. I wrote chatty questions for the jock to ask me as a lead-in to the news.

On one occasion—one of the first years of the "Great American Smoke-Out"—I wrote a question regarding the event. The jock on duty asked that question, listened to my answer, and then said he didn't smoke, but he did have a weight problem. "Maybe they could have a day like this for people like me," he said. "They could call it the Great American Eat..." and he stopped cold, suddenly aware of the unfortunate sexual connotation in what he was about to say. (The phrase "eating out" has a double meaning.) Like a deer in the headlights he stared at me, hoping I'd save the moment. Too late. I'd collapsed in giggles, gasping for air and unable to continue. He hit a commercial. The seeds of a talk show host had been planted.

Over the next two years I worked for a Top 40 station across the river. The day Elvis died I announced his passing on my own station, then, knowing the teletype machine was off most afternoons, called my former boss, Svengali, and asked if he'd heard the news. He hadn't. In a matter of weeks he offered me more money and a title of News Director, so I crossed the river once again.

In a matter of months I fell in love with the overnight jock, shacked up, got fired again and moved to Kansas City for another radio news job. My new love came along and stayed sullen in part-time positions while I excelled. He finally grabbed at a job in Washington, DC, at one of the first rockin' country stations there and fairly bolted out the door taking the good stereo equipment and a wonderful coffee table my mother and dad had when they first married. I miss that sound system and table to this day.

When TV news anchor Christine Craft got fired from her job in KC for being "too old, too ugly, and not deferential enough" to men, her boss called and offered me an on-camera job. Though I accepted, the general manager at the radio station refused my resignation and asked me to at least consider staying with his company and working for their TV outlet. They topped the ratings, offered me the same money, and soon I launched a fairly successful stint in television news.

The week I turned thirty, my former DJ came to visit with an engagement ring and a proposal. I accepted, but within a month jumped ship. Seems while we shared an apartment in KC, my DJ had a fling with one of my best friends. The real pisser is that I knew, and I knew that I knew, and at the time, they both vehemently denied it. He stayed in DC, I in KC where I anchored television news on weekends and returned to radio as the first female, full-time, weekday talk host in the market.

I loved it. I could read and write and play a little music, interview the celebrities and become a minor celebrity myself. I even had a shot at returning to the theater. I was cast in a supporting role for a professional presentation of *Cabaret*. Unfortunately the theater changed the run dates, and I had to choose between that role and a set of heavy commitments I'd already made. This was one of those "I wonder what would have happened if..." eras of my life scored with great jazz, Kenny Loggins, movie soundtracks, show tunes, generally sad songs of every ilk, and the first strains of New Age.

I spent eight years in Kansas City; met Oleta Adams when she played the Sign Board Bar in Crown Center; saw Andreas Vollenweider in concert; covered President Carter, President Ford, and President Reagan during their visits to the Heartland; interviewed a very young Michael J. Fox, the aging but vital Charlton Heston, hysterically funny Tim Conway, the irascible Mickey Rooney, and the lovely Mary Hart. I briefly made friends with Mitzi Gaynor and her husband Jack, got an exclusive with then Secretary of Defense Caspar Weinberger, and won top awards for a pioneering, twenty-part radio series on child abuse and neglect. I also twice weathered the sale of the radio station before realizing it was time to move on.

During a station-funded trip to the Radio Television News Directors Association conference in 1985, I unknowingly made an impression on a man who would later move to Phoenix from his award-winning work as a News Director in Boston. The very day I released word I was ready to leave KC, I got a call to send a tape and resume to him. Six months passed before the follow-up conversation...but finally in 1986 I flew to the desert southwest and auditioned for my own talk show.

Despite all my questioning, I can be a very slow learner. Waiting at the luggage carousel the day I arrived, I answered a page to the infamous passenger white phone. The station program director called to tell me that he and his wife were on their way to a movie so I should grab a cab to the hotel and spend that evening listening to the station.

My luggage didn't arrive with me and by the time I filed a claim, found a taxi, and got to the hotel located some twenty miles from the radio station, my confidence was badly shaken. I had very little cash and no car. I had no fresh clothing, no toiletries and, worst of all, no make-up, hair spray, or curling iron. I had no clue that the warm chocolate chip cookie left on the night stand during turn down was as good as my career was going to get for the next three years.

After two days of on-air auditions and a three-on-one contract negotiation in which they scored most of the points, they hired me. I moved from news to music to talk in twelve short years.

Shortly before my initial two-year contract expired, I met the man who would become my second husband. He showed up among a group that came to my house for a coaching session on fund-raising for a fledgling charity. I tried to get him to stay but he had a date. Two weeks later the fund-raising session convened at his office. I loaned him some materials that he promised to return, and two weeks later he called on a Friday evening, purportedly to apologize for being so long in getting them back to me. I reassured him it was not a problem, but as he began to respond with a second apology, he stopped mid-sentence. "This is bull," he said. "I actually called to see if you'd have dinner with me."

"Sure. When?"

"How about tonight or Sunday?"

Now everyone knows Saturday is date night. Besides I was licking my wounds over a failed relationship and had already rented my sad movies and nuked my popcorn for the evening. If I wasn't good enough for dating prime time, I sure wasn't going to miss out on a good cry.

"I already have plans for tonight, let's make it for Sunday."

Sunday morning a friend with a traveling massage business came over to get me all relaxed for the evening ahead. Throughout the session she waxed poetic about the great guy she had gone out with the night before and the great movie (*Stand and Deliver*) they'd seen. I got a very funny feeling but said nothing.

At six on the nose he arrived to take me for sushi—a sophisticated choice I thought. Over chopsticks we took the first tentative steps in the mating dance—until he started to tell me about the great movie he'd seen the night before. Need I say more?

Actually, yes. I still had a great time and my competitive spirit stirred at the thought that there might be someone else eyeing this sweet, sexy, smart, straight, and available man. I saw him at an event Monday evening, talked with him for several hours on the phone on Tuesday, and went to his apartment for dinner on Wednesday.

As he offered a warm, increasingly interesting and delicious kiss, I pulled back. "I make a great friend," I said. "I have gone down too many roads too quickly and I'm not interested in casual sex. I want either a clean, straight-forward, platonic friendship or a committed relationship, nothing in between."

I'd played house once, been married once and, like Mary Tyler Moore's Mary Richards, had too many dates in my thirty-something years to dally any longer. Besides safety became an issue. Our generation broke the abstinence rules, rolled through the sexual revolution and slammed into the age of STD's (sexually transmitted diseases for the uninitiated.) Now sex outside of marriage not only threatened pregnancy, an experienced, unfaithful partner could kill you.

Instead of blanching or fleeing, he asked what I wanted in a committed relationship and then listened to my answer. He told me he knew what he was looking for and I just might be it. Over the most garlic-laden Caesar salad I've ever eaten (before or since) we talked seriously about how to proceed. We decided to take the rest of the week off and each would write a list of everything we desired in a committed relationship. We promised to be truthful and not write anything because we thought the other wanted to hear it.

We met at a restaurant for dinner on Friday and swapped lists. I handed him four typewritten pages. He offered one and a half, hand-written on a legal pad. I read through his and saw only one problem—the physical description. He'd envisioned a redhead no taller than 5 feet 7 inches. I'm a heavily highlighted brunette, nearly 5 feet 10. I suppose it's not a big deal, unless one has already gone through a relationship with someone nearly your own height who swore he didn't mind I was taller, but later hated me in high heels. No, thank you. I had no desire to walk that path again.

Formulating my concerns as he re-read my treatise, I noticed my disappointment and impatience. *Might as well get it over quickly,* I thought. He folded the pages and set them aside then simply looked at me with a smile.

"Well?" I asked.

"That's me," he said, indicating my pages. "What do you think?"

"I think I need to know how attached you are to a five-foot-seven-inch redhead."

"Not very," he responded as he took the legal pages and scratched out the physical terms he'd written long before we met.

I explained my history and concerns and was sufficiently reassured. "What now?"

"We get tested."

Good thinking. "It'll take a couple of weeks to get results."

"I can wait," he said.

We waited about a week and then trusting our instincts, consummated our relationship. Within the month he proposed and I accepted.

We married in November—eight months after our first meeting and during a radio ratings period. In order to get a weekend off for a honeymoon, I suggested we broadcast the wedding. My boss agreed and even sold sponsorship to a major coffee company. At least it allowed both sets of parents, who were unable to travel, to listen to the exchange of vows down the telephone line.

Within a few months we had a "day." First the station manager announced my contract was not being renewed. My job would end in June and the non-compete I'd signed would keep me off the radio in this market for six months. Next my husband got word that his father had been diagnosed with lung cancer and had very little time. Then a realtor called and said my house—where we'd lived since shortly after his proposal—had sold and we had ten days to move. The house he co-owned with his previous significant other was rented.

Funny how priorities re-arrange themselves. At noon that day I'd been livid and relieved over the pending job loss. Two hours later I sat grieving for his loss. Another two hours and I moved into action.

He went to Ohio to be with his dad. I found an apartment and talked with a lawyer about suing for release from my non-compete. When my father-in-law, whom I had never met, passed away, I took two days to go with my beloved to the funeral. My attempt at release from the contract cost me dearly. When my final paycheck arrived from the radio station, I'd been docked two days pay. That wasn't the expensive part.

The station owner was a mean putz. When the better news/talk station in town called to check my interest in a position and my non-compete status, the inquirer said to call him when the six months was up. Even he had no desire to wrestle with a snake.

The putz then instructed his lawyers to drown me in paper. Finally my attorney advised me to settle. Not only did I sit out the six months, I paid half the putz's attorney fees.

The better station did eventually hire me and there I learned a number of valuable lessons. A sign on the bulletin board above one of the producer's desks captures the first: "Never mud wrestle with a pig. You get dirty and the pig likes it."

Shakespeare best expressed the second: "This above all, to thine own self be true…" That one took nearly five years to sink in.

The move from the underdog station to the giant in town brought less money, more restrictions, and a profound sense of failure. The people-pleaser in me warred with my rebellious side and I crossed the line often. I kept trying to fit—to be what I thought they wanted me to be—while also attempting on-air authenticity. Truth is, I am opinionated, stubborn, and intense. I've been told that, as a large woman with a deep voice, displaying those characteristics is threatening. Although, I never meant to insult or cause harm, I reportedly triggered memories in others of mothers, schoolteachers, bitchy ex-girlfriends, and nagging wives.

My circadian rhythms suffered mightily during this stint. I first worked from midnight to four in the morning, then moved to produce and host weekends, then made it to my own mid-day show, then to co-host morning drive—5:00 a.m. to 9:00 a.m. when most listeners are on their way to work—radio prime time. I had to get up between three and four o'clock, in the dark, shower and dress in order to sound even marginally conscious when we hit the air at five. This last move undid me.

Since the studio had been designed for a single host, I could no longer turn on my own microphone. My co-host, moving up in the world, made more money than I. I hit the glass ceiling and got moved, maybe not to the back of the bus, but certainly to a seat on the aisle.

After the first year, when we garnered double-digit ratings, the numbers slid a bit. The general manager left and a new program director came on board. We were oil and water from the first moment and when he finally decided that a former TV anchorman could revive the ratings and rid him of my threatening presence, I quit.

I stopped reading newspapers, listening to radio, and watching TV news. I took a job with a brilliant, unrealistically demanding woman. As I neared the end of my ninety-day probationary period, my sister called and said I needed to start making plans to come east for my mother.

My mother dealt with physical crises as far back as I can remember—at least into my pre-teen years. Circulatory troubles required multiple assaults on leg veins and arteries. Those were discovered when the second toe on her right foot had to be amputated because gangrene set in after months of useless doctor visits and pills.

One night walking up the stairs of our house in West Lawn, she felt a sharp pain in that toe. It turned black-and-blue, then black, then black with red streaks up her foot.

Since my dad traveled a lot for work, a neighbor who was also a retired registered nurse took my mother—who never learned to drive—to her weekly doctor visits. Each week Mama left the office with her blackened toe and another prescription to add to the pill collection that filled a kitchen cabinet. She took dozens of pills each day. Not only did they not help her rotting digit, they weren't helping her feel better or even feel nothing at all.

The neighborly nurse politely watched the scene repeat and quietly kept a close watch on that foot until the red streaks appeared. The following week, she picked Mama up for her appointment, but they "took the scenic route" as she called it. It led to the neighbor's doctor—an old fashioned General Practitioner—who took one look at the toe and the streaks and put my mother in the hospital. Two days later they took the toe. The resulting legend I remember is, if she had waited another week, she would have lost her foot for sure, maybe even her leg and possibly her life.

In the following years, she would have a number of lumbar sympathectomies—sort of a roto-rooter approach to unclogging blood vessels in the legs. These slowed her down somewhat, but never dulled her sense of humor or desire to make friends with whoever crossed her path.

Her good friends in the Circle at Church created a sunshine basket for one of her prolonged hospital stays. It included a box of what Mama took to be those soft, pastel colored, light as air, creamy butter mints. The night nursing supervisor had been a grump during Mama's stay, so when she came on duty the night the basket arrived, my Southern born, utterly gracious mother offered a mint to the midnight grouch. The nurse accepted and as she took a bite, Mama also sunk her teeth into one.

Within seconds, both were frothing at the mouth, foam spewing as they gagged and coughed and tried to spit out the remaining pieces of soap. Yep, they'd both eaten not mints, but those dainty little guest soaps so perfect for use when hosting the bridge club.

My mother said only the fact that she, too, had taken one saved her reputation. The night nurse was prone to believe everyone had it in for her. Perhaps many of the staff that nearly wet themselves with glee upon hearing of the incident did—but not my mother. Years later, she still stifled her own laughter about it.

In my teenage years, Mama had one of the very first heart by-pass surgeries. She was supposedly comatose but told the story of hearing her doctors—arguing over whether to take a chance on something so experimental with a young mother of two.

Mama said the debate went on for hours (I suspect it was a matter of minutes—but this is her tale). Finally she could stand it no more and forced herself to open her eyes. "What are my chances if I have this surgery?" she asked.

"Less than 50-50."

"What are my chances if I don't have this surgery?"

"You will most certainly die."

"Do the surgery," she ordered, then closed her eyes and did not regain consciousness until after the procedure. My dad reluctantly signed the papers for them to proceed.

In my memories, she is healthiest during the years that followed, although I can't quite reconcile the time frame for our most strident era of conflict. What I mean is, I don't know if it was before or after the heart by-pass that she went through menopause as I entered puberty. I do know we found it impossible to connect across the chasm through which rivers of hormones and torrents of emotion raged.

She was unprepared to explain what was happening to her and thought giving me the clinical explanations of the changes occurring in my body should suffice. I realize now that her beloved mother's death when my mom was so young left her in an oh-so-proper atmosphere of tight-lipped Southern gentility. No one had talked to her. How could she talk to me? Even if she could have found words, I didn't have the ears to hear. This was after all my "muuu-ther," so named in my arrogant, pubescent sarcasm.

We would not recover ourselves for several years and rebuilding our relationship took at least a decade. It was time well spent. From my late twenties into my mid-forties, I took the opportunity to heal myself and got to know my mother, as a woman and as a friend.

One of my favorite memories of her in later years is of her sitting at the kitchen table in my cousin's home talking with my aunt. These two women had married brothers within the same year. Their husbands both worked for my grandfather. They started families together in the same small town and nurtured a friendship that lasted the rest of my mother's life.

My aunt's husband—my father's brother—was an alcoholic, given to disappearing for months at a time, then returning home long enough to clean up, take whatever money was available, and vanish once more. Eventually, she divorced him. In the wake of what my dad's family thought scandalous on her part, she and my mother remained linked only by spirit and what is now called "snail mail." Then, in that modest kitchen decades later, they reconnected before my eyes.

In their reminiscences, the years fell away and, for a brief moment, I caught a breathtaking glimpse of my mother as a young woman fully engaged in life. That shimmering image still shines in my mind's eye.

Nothing could have prepared me for the sorrows, lessons, and miracles that came from walking with my beloved mother to the end of life as we know it. Despite the many ills and the excruciatingly slow devastation visited on her body by sclera derma, arteriosclerosis, and congestive heart failure, her gracious spirit and sense of humor expanded visibly in those final weeks.

She suffered the indignities of helplessness lightly. An infection caused by the urinary catheter was creating discomfort, so the home health care nurse said she had to be washed several times each day. It took two of us to move her without causing pain. One afternoon my sister and I were on duty with washcloth, cortisone cream, and powder. As we struggled to complete our task, our mother piped up with, "I don't know why you have to keep it so clean. It's not like I'm going to be using it any time soon." Tension shattered, and we laughed until we cried.

Bedridden and in great pain, she welcomed visitors. She listened with her whole self, asking questions about their well-being, their families, jobs, and projects. A musical group known by the neighbor across the way paid a visit in order to lift my mother's spirits. These people from a very different religion expected to witness to my mother with their music. Many of them attended her funeral and made it a point to tell the family how much my mother had blessed them that night, how they'd been lifted by her kindness to them.

When finally she laid her physical form aside, only her friend the minister and I were in her room. I knew she left. I just didn't know how huge the void would be. Suddenly the body that had been my doorway to life closed to further contact—no hugs, no smiles, no tears—nothing. Suddenly I stood closer to the front of the female side of the genealogical line—only my sister precedes me. Suddenly I had only one parent left—the one who frightened me more than a little bit but whose value just as suddenly increased dramatically.

After five weeks away, I returned to my husband. I sat on the patio reading murder mysteries and smoking. Dreading the holidays, I said I wanted to find a Christmas Eve candlelight service.

I chose the church that would become my spiritual home after hearing an ad on the radio. I left my husband at a party and entered a packed house. Not content with the isolation of the Quiet Room, I opted to stand along the wall until a woman caught my eye and leaned forward in the pew to give me a cheek's worth of space.

"Has anyone here seen the face of Christ?" asked the minister. One voice in the back said, "Yes." Hundreds of others sat breathlessly still.

"I suggest you look around." We did, cautiously meeting strangers' eyes, looking for signs.

In the pew in front of me, about half way down, sat a dear friend I'd not seen for several years. His brown eyes glistened and I started to cry. Every song, the candle lighting ceremony, the joyous conclusion filled my soul.

After the service I connected with my friend's wife who had sung in the choir. They had lived in another state for the intervening years, but as we embraced, time and distance evaporated.

"What have you been doing?" she asked.

"Caring for my mother who died in September. You?"

"I'm healing," she said. "I spent five months taking care of my mother who died in May."

After many years of ontological conversations and transformational experiences absent any sort of regular spiritual practice, I knew I'd come home.

When I returned to the party, my husband asked, "How was it?"

"I'm going back. I'd like you to come with me, but it's OK if you'd rather not."

He came. We stayed. I cried at every service for months, cleansing the grief over my mother's death, my own aging, and the end of my broadcasting career. We joined the church six months later and have each gone on to volunteer in a variety of ways—deepening old relationships, cultivating new ones, and creating a sacred space within our selves and our lives.

Expanding our awareness of God's presence did not make circumstances easier for us. I did some free-lance work, but not enough to sustain our financial well-being. Eventually my husband and I both tired of the credit card shuffle and declared personal bankruptcy.

Soon thereafter, on the pretense of wanting a regular paycheck and health care benefits, I took a job with the state. Each task assigned to me offered a platform for personal discovery and spiritual growth. On the job I could look around and choose to see the face of the Christ and learned to recognize when I was making a different choice.

Instead of stabilizing our relationship, the income seemed to drive an existing wedge deeper between my husband and me. When the opportunity arose to go on a spiritual journey to Greece, my heart leapt. He said he wanted me to go but had no interest in going with me.

The last weeks before I left were excruciating. We weren't fighting; we were sniping. We weren't playing; we were taunting.

As he left me at the curb the day of departure, I told him to take the next eleven days to decide whether he wanted to continue in this relationship with me. I spent a fortune in long-distance charges cleaning that one up.

My return to our house didn't feel like coming home. Within the month I'd found an apartment and moved out. It would prove to be the greatest gift I'd ever chosen for myself or granted to him.

Reflections on the Present

...And I could hear everything. Not all at once—but when I thought about somethin'—the sea, the birds, my own heart—well, I could hear!...

Comedic, cathartic, comforting validation calls me to these weekly confabs. Yes, I love alliteration, its lyrical lines sounding the sweet refrain...our shoes and stories differ, our paths diverge, but our experience as women is shared.

Wonder Weavers wound us together in this tapestry of telling our truths—triumph and tragedy alike. Childhood circumstances chose us. Here we choose our characterizations—calling forth chapters of then, now, and what's next.

We are different shades of time and type. We are jeweled facets flickering across the full spectrum of womanhood at the turn of the century. We've fought and won, battled, and been defeated. We have been crucified, dead, buried, and reborn count-less times—the expressed essence of the Eternal. We are women.

We wear patent leather pumps, traditional tennis shoes, clogs, flip flops, and Birkenstocks. Sandals, sling-backs, slippers, and slides adorn our feet as we stride, shuffle, swagger, stomp, and sashay along the way. Imelda Marcos and Sarah Jessica Parker seek such safety from the shoes stacked in their closets, but such shoddy indulgences miss the mark. It's savoring and swapping and snatching the stuff of our souls that makes these soles inter-esting.

What we write only hints at the "her-story" unfolding within and all around us. Each tidbit triggers the tiny time pills trapped in memory. Timeless treasures taught by our ancestors are un-earthed in the conversation that follows. Jewels of womanly wis-dom are revealed in what we say to one another after we read ourselves into existence. We are abundantly wealthy with the lapis of laughter, the travertine of tears, the diamonds of decisions and discoveries, the rubies of ridiculousness, and the sapphires of salvation.

Walk with me a while longer as I tell you more of my tales and if the shoe fits...

In addition to my families of birth and choice, here and now revolve around my job, my church, and aging.

After months of ridiculously long days filled with challenging assignments, at last I can relax into a sense of accomplishment— at least for this moment.

I serve as Communications Director for a state agency that coordinated efforts to create and fund a world-class genomics research center. My part has been to generate and guide the public conversation about the project. I have written editorials for others' bylines, crafted dozens of news releases, scheduled hundreds of interviews, and invested untold hours explaining genomics and biotechnology to reporters who really just want answers in thirty seconds or less.

Some days the sheer number of tasks, coupled with the inevitable interruptions, left me frustrated and discouraged. The day it came together, I paused regularly to silently thank God for the opportunity and the outcome.

A scant five months ago, my boss listened to a very bright co-worker suggest something like this might be possible. She then enrolled the governor, the mayor, the university presidents, and a number of philanthropic and business leaders in pursuing a vision. Political, academic, scientific, economic, and charitable interests all came together to design and build a new future for generations yet to come.

They caught a vision of life that includes the physical limitations of being human, yet expresses something more. They set aside pure self-interest to see a future that will outlive us all. They and I dedicated these months to putting foundations under a castle built in the air. It is not a bricks and mortar castle, rather a mansion richly appointed with ideas, commitment to discovery and action.

Every ounce of talent and experience given me came into play, and I know I fulfilled my God-given role, holding nothing back. This business of pretending to be special is part of my yearning to have my existence in human form matter, to act in accordance with the highest and best I could imagine. On those days when my own human form felt too tired, too anxious, too irritable to go on, I went on—for, with, and by the grace of God.

Few will know my name in relation to this project. It is enough that I know. It is enough that I have good news to share with my families. It is from and for them the desire to be used for something greater than myself arises. I have always wanted to honor those who came before and those who will follow.

Doing my best, using everything I am and have, brought me to this project, to this time when the possibility of a healthier and more humane future is born. It has been my privilege to assist in this midwifery. It will be my great pleasure to watch it grow.

My volunteer work at my church contributes to my stamina and focus. Knowing that God is always present within and without doesn't keep me from encountering challenges. It allows me to recover more quickly when circumstances shift, hormones rage or emotion floods through me unbidden.

Five years' worth of keeping my chaplain agreement to maintain a personal prayer life offers access to a deep well of peace and gratitude. As a creation of God granted free will, I sometimes forget to drink from the cup and find myself stomping about, snarling in frustration, missing the forest for the trees. Here's an example:

Half a century of living hasn't prepared me for this—living apart from the man I love most in the world, working ten-hour days in state government, and volunteering at my church nights and weekends. I thought I'd have it figured out by now, be rich and famous, or at least slender and fit.

What notoriety I've achieved up to now pales in the face of knowing that I am more than half cooked. I won't say the best years of my life are behind me, yet it is one of my fears. I won't say I haven't achieved my dreams. Certainly many dreams of my youth have slipped away, awakened to a different reality or remain dreams by choice. Those dreams that I have made real are no longer the pliable chimeras enticing me onward. They have ceased to be "dreams." Perhaps that's the encroachment of my peri-menopausal state.

So much has changed since turning forty. On that anniversary of my birth, I joyfully shed the baggage of ballerina dreams and stepped confidently forward in my career. I was a local media celebrity: happily married, smart, funny, opinionated, and attractive.

Today's fifty-year-old body carries different baggage: fewer promises and dreams, more wrinkles and pounds; less dancing and more crying; smaller dreams and larger memories. My once fair, freckled face bears the scars of shingles that flared eight months after a premature facelift. Age spots dot my hands. My hairdresser keeps the gray at bay with highlights every six weeks or so as finances allow. My baby blue eyes squint at the regular size print as the floaters swim into view. I have moles and acne and flaky shins.

My mother is dead, my father now faces physical challenges, disease and treatment both chipping away at his heretofore abundant vitality. And I know that someday, too soon no matter how long it takes, I will take another big step toward the front of the line.

I live three thousand miles away from him, my sister, and niece. My nephew and I aren't in communication. The rest of the biological family is scattered hither and yon and the guilt is relentless.

My weight drops if I smoke, but in this belief system smoking is very bad for me. I serve as a chaplain but labor at finding time to pray and meditate. I believe in God and know that (S)He believes in me…but I don't know what all the believing does if everything is out of focus.

The anti-depressants balance the mood swings, but limit the experience of exultation. The lack of sex saves time, but what good is time without the delicious anticipation of seeing and being with someone? What good are all these questions, if there are no answers? Oh hell. It must be getting close to that time of the month. What good is menopause if there's this protracted state of discomfort to swim through toward the end?

My tee shirt says it all: "Inside me is this really skinny woman trying to get out. I can usually shut the bitch up with chocolate."

Tirades like that can last a week, sometimes longer. They frighten me, so does the reaction I get from others when I forget, and then forget to remember, the illusory nature of "reality." I now know that this fear is part of what had me move into a place of my own. I didn't know how to keep from "falling in the black hole" as one good friend puts it, and I grew tired of feeling resentful because I couldn't seem to extricate myself from either the hole or my expectation that *somebody* (i.e. my husband) would pull me out.

The gift for me in living apart is freedom to hibernate in the black hole and freedom from both the shame of inflicting myself on others and the resentment over their inability to fix it for me. I can leave dirty dishes in the sink as long as I choose and not blame anybody for them or the clutter or the dust. I can just let it be and trust that I will remember. I find it funny that as I grow more tolerant of these episodes, they grow shorter and I consciously choose to focus on my blessings rather than my flaws.

Now, when I go down for the count, I indulge myself, honor

my resistance to magnificence, and grow bored with it fairly quickly. For many months, I spent time every week with my beloved husband—not out of obligation but because we love one another, we have fun together, and I was authentically interested in what was happening in his life.

What's happened for him since I moved out appears miraculous to me. After the initial shock and resulting anger passed, he began moving out into the world and back into his music. His business expanded, money began to flow from his efforts, and he indulged his love of keyboard and guitar. He now writes music, sings with an ensemble, wants to produce a show, and admits to falling asleep with music running through his mind.

While spending time together, we would talk and laugh and go places, affectionate and safe with one another once more. Then eight days after my fiftieth birthday, he announced he was tired of the celibate lifestyle and ready to start dating. I told him to file for divorce. It's now final.

As a child, being different was thrust upon me, like it or not. Inexplicable it was and unembraceable too. Now, I am what I am, and I am that I am—perfectly flawed, perfectly free, gratefully so.

Reflections on the Future

…And I was spiralin' to the future and I tell you it was amazing! There was gods and goddesses and kings and queens! And then One Shining One – and then all the Shining Ones…

"The comfort of what has been—or at least what I say has been—is insufficient to my nature. I want to do more than record what was or even what I think is now. I want to create a future that is sufficiently matched to the magnitude of existence.

The dramas and triumphs of my past and present pale compared to the yearning for what might be.

It begins with wanting. I want to have money and things and health and passion. I want freedom.

The problem is that wanting implies absence...and I know that I am free. I know that my longing for belonging is illusion, that I am not now nor have I ever been separate from that which calls me forth.

The whispers meagerly translated into words speak volumes of possibilities: a lean, fit, energetic body; passionate, familiar intimacy; wisdom beyond token manifestation of product or project; acceptance of and security in the achingly sweet mystery of being both human and divine.

Beyond this personal potential, the small still voice urges me through self-indulgence and independent isolationism into a collective consciousness that we have more than enough of all that we need to be all we can be—or better yet, all that we are. Recovery from personal wounds is not enough. My wellness contributes to the world, to all of Life.

The paradox is mind numbing enough to allow my heart to open and sing in exultation at the very notion of little me, whose stories you've read, participating in nothing less than the restoration of the planet, the creation of safety, the nurturance of awareness that God, by whatever name, is ever-present, unconditionally loving, compassionately available, and unerringly interested only in blessing and informing Life.

I cannot help but revert to my habit of questions. What if the reality I recall and observe is not Truth, with a capitol "T", but the result of free will? What if the events I witness are *all* part of a divine plan that always leads to a happy ending? What if there is no free will? What if the choices I think I make, I actually made long ago? What if I didn't make them at all? What if the things

I've worried over and doubted and feared are all illusions? What if "reality" isn't real at all—but simply the story I tell myself to keep the brilliant future at bay? What if what we perceive is misperception, or at least myopic? What if "reality" is acquiescent, fashioned by consciousness and choice?

All these questions are merely cheap entertainment, relatively speaking. I think we each and all stand at the crossroads every moment. I think all the second-guessing I do prevents a future complete with accomplishment and abundant compensation. It's avoidance of this sort that delays the inevitable realization of what will be. At any moment I can imagine a future where every life is cherished, every child loving, because each is confident of being loved.

I can imagine living on a beach or in the mountains or in a penthouse or a shack. I can hibernate in air-conditioned sterility and find my world in the words of others. I can author my own screenplay and experience it holographically. It can have whatever twists and turns I need to forestall boredom. I can envision anything I choose, from desolation to jubilation, for myself, for my world. What will be in this malleable mold called "future"? Whatever I choose.

I choose love. I choose joy. I choose peace. I choose safety. I choose health. I choose deep knowing and full expression. I choose to learn and experience and rest in the shelter of that which made me. I choose to be inspired and to awaken fully to the sacred nature of Self and Oneness. I choose Life.

In so doing, I remain fully human. Not frail and defeated, but vibrant and yearning toward new possibilities. I claim my power to birth the ideas of my mind, express the empathy of my heart, experience the patience of my soul, and be awed by the sweeping, assorted beauty of my ancestors, my contemporaries, and my heirs.

I have a responsibility to be authentic but not selfish, to own my irreplaceable uniqueness and honor the divergent expressions of humanity all around me. I must remember our unity and celebrate the full arc of our diversity. I do that which is mine to do, that which fills my heart with joy, that which is congruent with the singing of my soul.

With balance, harmony, poise; an inescapable intention to be encouraging and compassionate; willingness to serve, to be used for something greater than myself; certainty in abundant compensation; and absolute assurance that Life is unfolding and all roads lead to good, I stand on faith, knowing I am not now, never have been, and never will be alone. My life has purpose and miracles abound.

Ramona's Shoes

In Our Shoes

Fable

What's in a Name Anyway?

One grey November evening Rachele Brasseur went for a walk. She had left her eldest daughter, Cassandra, in charge of the three younger children, Marita, Ramona, and Lois Joyce. That name, Lois Joyce, it didn't fit but what could she do? It had been another girl. Who could blame her for not being able to cope with having to name yet another girl? The girls were born so close together—less than seven years from start to finish. Exhausted and incapable of thinking, she had turned to the doctor in the delivery room and said, "Sacre bleu, another girl. You name her, Doctor."

At first the doctor declined, but eventually he gave in to Rachele's insistence that he carry out his duties; he had brought the girl into the world after all. Doctor Coldiron, exhausted himself, rubbed his temples and tried to think. Why not name the baby after his two daughters, Lois and Joyce? Only hours old, the baby wailed to hear this lackluster choice.

On hearing Lois Joyce's name her father, Arnie, had laughed and laughed and said to her, "Well, well, Lost John and here you are." His rude awakening had come; there would be no sons. Wanting solace—namely a stiff drink and a few laughs—Arnie had kissed Rachele on the forehead, walked out the door and headed for the Amazon Bar and Grille.

Rachele believed it necessary to care for one's health and this included a daily walk. At this time of year, she took her walks in the evening. On this particular night, a thick fog rolled in as Rachele walked, making it impossible for her to see more than one or two feet in front of her. She shivered, tightened the belt on her coat, and yearned for Montreal. She hated this rotten miserable weather in Cincinnati, the never-ending drizzle.

At Ritty's Corner, she passed Mrs. Jones who inquired about the girls.

"How are your lovely daughters—Cassandra, Marita, Ramona, and Loith Joyce? Forgive me, Lois-s-s-s Joyce." A spray of spit escaped as she spoke her name. "It's a difficult name to pronounce," she said, embarrassed. "Like Peter Piper and that peck of pickled peppers."

"They're fine," Rachele answered, as the two women passed each other in the fog.

Rachele bowed her head. The sidewalk reminded her of wet pewter. Lois Joyce's sixth birthday was this Saturday and Rachele knew the name distressed her child. Lois Joyce couldn't say her own name without stumbling over it. Arnie called it, "Dr. Coldiron's revenge," and blamed Rachele for shirking her responsibility.

Rachele stared at her feet, at the strange shoes she had found on the front porch next to a bright blue envelope dotted with white stars. When she opened the envelope, a white card with gold lettering had fallen out.

The card read, "These shoes are for your walk, and it is important for you to wear them. With love, your daughters."

Tucked inside the toe of one shoe Rachele had found a pair of white socks—their cuffs glittered with small gold stars. These socks had appealed to her more than the plain, rather drab, pair she had been wearing. She didn't hesitate to take off her shoes and socks and put them on. Rachele stretched out her feet admiring the sparkling socks. They were so unusual and seemed almost magical. Looking at all those glittering stars, she could believe anything possible. She chuckled at this thought for this was definitely not her customary way of thinking.

Rachele had been unsure about the shoes—she had never seen such an odd pair, one black and one red. They hardly looked fit for walking. Besides having high heels, they were decorated with all manner of odd things. The toe of the black shoe held a white bird—its wings spread as though it were flying—red and blue crayons, and a pretty red feather. A pink baby carriage and a blue toy train sat on the feather, while a clock and a measuring tape tied in a bow nestled beside it. A row of objects ran along one side: a dollar sign, an X, another white bird and a pretty blue feather, and another dollar sign. A large, blue striped star with a red anchor in the center clung to the back of the shoe.

From the toe of the red shoe grew a large blue feather with a red egg stuck to it. Alongside the feather, the word "love" snuggled up against a red heart. Rachele didn't recognize an odd square object stuck to one side of the shoe. *Perhaps it's some kind of television*, she thought. Next to the odd television appeared the words, "New York Times Best Seller." Perhaps, in some way, the two were connected. Like the white socks, the red shoe sparkled with gold stars. Inside Rachele saw the words "Strength & Vision."

"These are the real necessities of life," Rachele thought. Strength and vision were traits she often prayed she would instill in her girls.

The shoes were the weirdest she had ever seen, but since they were a gift from her daughters, she felt compelled to try them on. The girls were always whipping up some new creation.

After seeing how they fit, Rachele tried to take the shoes off, but they wouldn't budge. After a few tentative steps, she decided to wear them on her walk. They were surprisingly comfortable— possibly the most comfortable shoes she had ever worn.

With her head bowed, mulling over the girls' gift, Rachele didn't see the lamppost. She bumped against it and slipped, grabbing for the post to keep from falling. She managed to hook her arm around it, but momentum propelled her forward, spinning her around. With effort she regained her balance.

Rachele clung to the lamppost until her legs stopped shaking. She noticed that the air around her had begun to clear and she could hear a hissing sound coming from somewhere overhead. Looking up, Rachele saw tubing with mist spewing out of it. Except for the mist, which matched the fog in coldness, the air had warmed considerably. Rachele removed her coat and tried to make some sense of her surroundings.

Rachele heard voices and looked around. A short distance away people sat at tables eating, drinking, and talking. Never one to put much stock in the supernatural, Rachele decided she must be dreaming. She rubbed her eyes, but nothing made the people go away. It appeared she would have to wait this dream out.

On the wall above the tables, a red neon sign glowed with the words, "Baby Kay's."

"Kay," Rachele sighed, "Another uninspired name for a baby. Why do parents do such things?" If only she hadn't been so exhausted after Lois Joyce's birth. She had thought up excellent names for the other three. If a child wasn't given a carefully considered name, could it make a difference in her future? Rachele began to worry that it might. Her intentions had been good, but now she needed to fix it. The child couldn't start school with that name. She would be tormented by the other children and marked for life—just like that boy in Marita's second grade class, Robert Allen Turner, initials RAT. The other children taunted him mercilessly. Marita swore that his pointed nose sometimes wiggled. Then there was that gynecologist, the one her sister used: Harry Roach. What were *his* parents thinking? Their faux pas made her carelessness seem miniscule. The poor man's name cost him potential patients—including Rachele and other people she knew. Silly, of course, but that's the way people are.

Through the mist Rachele saw another neon sign: "Children of the World." She stopped to look at the colorful masks in the shop window.

A voice behind her demanded, "Mother, I want to talk to you. It's this ridiculous name, Cassandra."

Rachele turned to see Cassandra standing there with her hands on her hips. No longer a child, Cassandra appeared to be a middle-aged woman.

"Why did you have to name me after the Greek Goddess of Disaster?"

Nothing made sense right now, but she somehow recognized this woman as Cassandra, so she explained, "The Goddess Cassandra felt so torn up over the murder of her mortal lover that her tears and rage turned into powerful storms reeking havoc on mankind. Such intense love, it touched me."

"Well, Mother, for your information, it cursed me."

"Is that why you've been married five times?" Ramona emerged from the mist next to Cassandra.

"Five times!" Rachele's neck began to ache. "Holy Mother, where did I go wrong?"

Ignoring her mother's comments Ramona said, "Get off the Greek Goddess bit, Cassandra. You're no more a Goddess than I am. I know. I looked it up. According to Robert Graves' book, 'The Greek Myths,' the name Cassandra means 'she who entangles men.' I'd say that's pretty right-on."

Rachele looked from one daughter to the other; they were middle-aged, attractive but nonetheless middle-aged, and still bickering. She had hoped for better.

"Girls, girls! Stop bickering or you are going to have to kiss and make up."

"Jesus, Mother. That's still disgusting."

"Ramona, do not take the Lord's name in vain!"

"Chri…oh, damn!" Her mother's wagging finger in front of her face got Ramona's attention. That finger served as a warning—a warning that meant, "Shut up or you'll get a slap across the mouth."

"Fine. Let's talk about *my* name. What an abomination. Why did you name me after a book with such a twit for a main character?"

"Ramona was not a twit! She gave up everything for love. Such an incredible story." Rachele put her hands over her heart.

"She grew up with money and everything! Only a twit would reject that life, marry a penniless Indian and live in a hovel. Okay, he had looks, but it takes more than that."

"Love conquers all," Rachele declared.

"The hell it does! Me, I agree with that old adage, 'Love flies out the window when poverty walks in the door.' But you…you had to fill us with romantic nonsense. No wonder we're dysfunctional. Now Papa thinks he's being really funny when he says his girls are the marrying kind."

"How many times have you been married?"

Ramona dreaded answering that question, but she could never lie to her mother. "Four."

"Holy Mother, how did this happen?"

"What?" shouted Ramona. "You have to ask? Don't you remember the time I asked you how I would recognize true love, and you said I would know when he kissed me?" Ramona began to sing, "How will I know if I love him so? It's in his kiss." Then glaring at her mother she added, "Well, it's in his kiss, and *his* kiss, and *his* kiss, too. The possibilities are practically endless if you have a strong libido. Mother, that's lust! There *is* a difference."

"Ramona, love is the most powerful force on earth and it does conquer all."

"That thinking is just plain fucked."

Before Rachele could slap Ramona across the mouth, Marita appeared beside her mother and gave her a big hug. "Oh, Mother, it's so good to see you. How have you been?"

After a few pleasantries Rachele said to Marita, "Get it over with, what complaints do you have about your name?"

"Absolutely none. I chose to come to earth and be given this name."

"Sister Moonbeam has arrived," said Ramona.

"Probably her astral projection," Cassandra giggled.

Marita either didn't hear or chose to ignore them. "What's to complain about? It's a beautiful name. I know you made up the name because you wanted to name me after your sister, Marie, but thought that too ordinary. However, Mother, I'm only one of many Maritas here. Coming from Montreal, you hadn't heard it before."

"By the way," said Rachele, still hoping to get her bearings, "Where are we, and what is that hissing tube? Is it causing all this fog?"

"We're in Phoenix, Arizona, Mother, and that tubing is called a 'mister.' The mist cools the air, some."

"That's a big relief. What with the extreme heat and considering all the marriages and the foul mouth, I had begun to worry." Rachele rubbed her neck, prepared for the worst and asked, where's your baby sister?"

"Right here behind you, Mother." Lois Joyce answered.

"Hi, Loith-h-h Joyth-h-h."

"Yuck, Mother, you spit in my eye. Call me LJ like everyone else."

"LJ? I don't think I like that name any better than the original, though it is easier to say."

"My biggest problem is that everyone thinks I'm a man until they meet me. Sometimes it works in my favor, sometimes not. You see, I'm a lawyer, and LJ Brasseur is a pretty good name for a lawyer."

"We're going to have to talk about that lawyer thing later, but first, don't tell me you never got married."

"Oh, I've been married twice. I'm still married to the second husband, but I use my maiden name professionally."

Rachele supposed the fact that LJ stayed married to the second husband came, in a sense, as good news. "It's not too late to find you a better name," she said to LJ.

Cassandra, Marita, and Ramona had gone into the "Children of the World" shop. When LJ and Rachele joined them, they were admiring some wall plaques made of large gold letters. Each plaque spelled out a word: LOVE, HOPE, and JOY.

Rachele wanted to go home, or wake up—whichever would get her out of here and back to her daughter's sixth birthday. She wanted to give the child a new name, as a birthday present.

Rachele's daughters led her back to the lamppost near the neon Baby Kay's sign. Marita instructed her to grab the post and spin around. In a matter of seconds she had returned to Ritty's corner. She hurried home clutching a package under her arm.

The name change wouldn't present any obstacles she couldn't handle. Lois Joyce would now be called "Joy." They'd simply tell everyone it was a nickname for Joyce. Then before Joy enrolled in elementary school, Rachele would write the government and have the name changed legally.

On second thought, maybe not. All the effort she'd put into the names of the first three girls—had that made their paths easier? Rachele shrugged her shoulders. She had done her best. Besides, LJ would be a good name for a lawyer someday.

Reflections on the Past

...Love is the most powerful force on earth and it does conquer all...

In Warsaw, Poland, it was the afternoon of August 30, 1939, the last day of peace the people there would know for a long time. Half a world away, I was arriving during a hot, muggy dawn in Eastern Kentucky. The following evening at eight o'clock, German SS men dressed in Polish military uniforms staged an attack on Germany. Hitler had created his propaganda excuse for invading Poland. The morning of September 1, German tanks rolled into Poland crushing any resistance. World War II had begun.

In the first five years, eight months and eight days of my life, forty million people were killed. That kind of atrocity is something I don't understand. I know entering the world at this time shaped my life, affected my sense of safety, as did having a mother who embraced a harsh, unforgiving religion.

On that steamy August morning, with the sun in Virgo and Virgo rising, the moon resided in Pisces, the sign of the dreamer. It could be said this is what saved me. I prefer to credit my stormy, irreverent father who embraced no religion, but had his own experience of God through nature. Daddy taught us, by example, to dream. I spent my childhood creating stories and fantasies of the life I would live.

The memories I have of World War II are much like snap-shots, moments in time with no before and no after. Perhaps they are implanted memories—tales told when I was so young I re-member the image but not the source. That is my belief. My mind still works that way, creating images to go with whatever I am hearing or reading.

We left Eastern Kentucky before I turned three. I don't re-member living in the hills of Kentucky, but I experienced that life through visits to my grandparents. Daddy found work in Cin-cinnati, Ohio, where we rented a small house on the Kentucky side of the Ohio River. How did I feel about this move, about leaving my grandparents behind and the new life we were em-bracing? I have no idea. Not one glimmer of a memory exists in my mind.

The war raged in Europe and America had become involved. Fear the war might come to American soil prompted the need for preparation, including air-raid practice drills. Mother, who felt fearful without any outside help, became terrified during these rehearsals. Black shades had to be drawn over the windows and the lights turned off. Mother huddled with her daughters and cried as the warning sirens wailed.

Like the shades over our windows, the beliefs of Mother's Southern Baptist religion cast a gloomy shadow over my entire life. Mother dragged us to church whenever the doors were open. Because children were not protected from the hellfire and brim-stone sermons, the message, "Repent and be saved or burn in hell forever," seared my innocent mind. The minister, my mother, and the adult church members told me, in order to be saved, I must adhere to the Baptist way. Everyone else would be turned away at the pearly gates. Hell, the eternal human barbecue pit, undoubtedly would be crowded. You couldn't be sure you were saved, and this puzzled and upset me. You might think you were saved, yet without even knowing it, still cling to the world in your heart, and therefore be doomed. I knew I would never be saved according to the Baptist's beliefs. I could never believe anything on faith alone. I had to question and analyze everything, and then make my own decision. I felt damned.

"Hellfire" sermons were not the only assaults on our psyches from which we children received no protection. Daddy read the newspaper aloud to us every day. There was no escape. Why the news didn't bother my sisters as much as it did me, I don't know. I felt affected by, and a part of, everything that happened in the world.

With the atomic bomb, the term "ground zero" entered our consciousness and our language. So did the notion of being vaporized if you happened to be at ground zero. Pictures of Hiroshima and Nagasaki—taken shortly after the United States had dropped the bomb—burned images into my brain that I will never forget. In my young mind, these pictures merged with the images my imagination created of Hell. Plagued by nightmares, I developed insomnia by age eight. Most nights I dreamed of Hell, or of being bombed and hearing people screaming in fear and pain.

Often when I couldn't sleep, I would sit gazing out the window, trying to make sense of the world. More often I created stories in my mind to entertain myself. Many went on for days, and some I still remember. My stories were always happy ones where wonderful things happened. My heroine encountered conflict, but in the end triumphed.

On the day the war ended, all normal activity came to a halt as people took to the streets shouting, cheering, and crying in euphoria. From where we lived, we could hear the sirens from the fire station and the whistle of a train passing through on a nearby track.

An event which occurred a year or so after the war ended brings back the first memory I know is mine. My mother, my three sisters, and I were at Union Terminal in Cincinnati waiting for a train. A soldier in uniform stood nearby. One of his arms had been amputated. Looking back, I believe he was on his way home from a veteran's hospital. I watched in awe as he lit a match with his only hand, and then lit his cigarette. I remember thinking that I had never seen a man as handsome as this. At that tender age, beautiful men already attracted me.

Despite the exposure to certain harsh realities, Mother, nonetheless, maintained many comforting routines in our daily lives. Mother loved flowers and the outdoors. At the white, four-bedroom Cape Cod house we lived in for a time, she planted flowers bordering the sidewalk. She created flower beds along the front and sides of the house, and in various spots around the front and back yards. She chose her plants in order to have flowers blooming from early spring until the first killing frost, which usually didn't come until late October or early November. Inside the house, plants and freshly cut flowers filled every available space. We lived in a profusion of color and perfumed air.

Saturdays Mother spent baking. The aroma of baking bread and sweet rolls would fill the house. My sisters and I gathered in the kitchen to be given warm bread as soon as the first batch came out of the oven. I can smell the fresh cinnamon rolls and remember their taste as if it were yesterday. Mother thought no dinner complete without dessert. Pies, cakes, cobblers, banana pudding, and cookies—hers were delicious and she prepared them with ease.

Mother sang throughout the day. Her music blended with the smell of baked goodies and fresh flowers. She sang in operatic style, hitting incredible heights on the scale. Our family sang together whether we had talent or not. Mother and Daddy played the guitar. Daddy, a left-handed guitar player, sometimes took Mother's guitar and played it upside down. We howled with laughter. In our house, opera and country music competed for airtime. I liked country music, but I loved opera.

In her sewing room, Mother made most of our clothes without using a pattern. She took a few measurements with her measuring tape to determine where to mark the cloth with her tailor's chalk. She crocheted and adorned the house with her handiwork. Everyone who visited praised Mother's talent. One woman tried relentlessly to buy the bedspread Mother had crocheted for her own bed.

The floors in the white Cape Cod were hardwood. When Mother polished them, she required my sisters and me to help. After Mother applied the thick paste, we buffed the floors by pulling each other across them on bath towels. When the floors became slick enough we "skated" on our socks, screaming and laughing and crashing into each other. Mother let us entertain ourselves this way, pointing out spots that needed a higher sheen. We would even get down on our hands and knees to buff a few spots. In the end, the floors always shined.

As part of our daily routine, Mother lined us up for a drill in proper walking. I don't remember when this training began. It seems to have always been a part of my life. My sisters and I took turns balancing a book on our heads while walking across the living room. Shoulders back, chest out, tummy and hips tucked in, head held high, eyes forward—all had to be gracefully done. Mother said I had natural ability, but considered Cassandra hopeless. Tall for her age and unhappy about it, Cassandra slumped in an effort to appear shorter. Mother constantly snapped at her to stand up straight, to walk as if she had some pride. (Cassandra would eventually grow to be 5 feet 10 inches tall, and I am forever envious. At 5 feet 5 inches, I consider myself short. Marita is 5 feet 8, and Joy tops out at 5 feet 3.)

Our training required that we learn to pick things up off the floor while keeping the book balanced on our heads. The trick to this is spotting the object ahead of time, knowing where it is, walking up beside it, and bending at the knees while keeping the head held high. I seldom lost my balance or dropped my book. I have only met one other person who had this training in childhood, and she claimed it is a European practice. By the time I met Bojena, Mother had died and I regretted never having asked why she had trained us to walk.

Mother usually went for a walk every day, her "daily constitutional." She allowed my sisters and me, on our own, to explore the nearby woods and to simply wander about, meeting people. I regularly visited a widow whose daughter lived with her. Mrs. Glasser spoke with a thick German accent. She told me of her life growing up in Germany where she drank goats' milk and ate goose eggs. She didn't like chicken eggs, so she kept geese in her backyard. I learned that geese, unlike chickens, have no qualms about attacking people; Mrs. Glasser said they could break my arm with their beaks. After one of them attacked me, she no longer had to tell me to stay away from the geese. Once she managed to cajole me into eating a goose egg, waiting for me to tell her it tasted better than a chicken egg.

"There isn't any difference," I insisted.

"Hooey, your taste buds don't work right," she said, but we remained fast friends.

Neighbors referred to Mrs. Glasser's unmarried forty-year-old daughter, Frannie, as the "old maid." Frannie had a boyfriend, Albert. The neighbors told Mother Frannie had been seeing Albert forever, and he would never marry her.

When Albert's mother died, he married Frannie. I cheered! The neighbors had figured that one all wrong. For some reason, I found this gratifying. I liked Frannie. I didn't see her often, but when I did, she always played the piano for me.

Mrs. Glasser's son, Johnny, served in the U.S. military in Germany. When he brought home a German bride, Mrs. Glasser reacted with outrage.

I remember thinking, *What is wrong with her? She's German herself!*

People frequently mystified me.

Life in our little neighborhood offered a variety of interesting neighbors. Next door, in a similar Cape Cod, lived Sibyl Smith, her husband, and two sons. She was a tall attractive woman with, as Daddy described them, "legs that went all the way to her shoulders." One day, walking down the steps to the basement, I heard a loud wolf whistle. Daddy stood on top the laundry sinks looking out a narrow basement window, giggling.

"Arnold, you bastard, I know that's you. Show yourself you chicken-shit." I recognized the voice as Sibyl's.

In answer to Sibyl's tirade, Daddy let out another wolf whistle and laughed.

"Goddamn you, Arnold, get your ass out here or I'm coming after you, and I'm going to kick your sorry ass."

"I can hardly wait. I get excited just thinking about it," Daddy yelled.

He jumped down from the laundry sinks and ran upstairs. True to her word Sybil came to the front door and asked to see the bastard. Mother never spoke a swear word (in English) in her life but somehow tolerated all the profanity that swirled around in our house. That day everyone wound up eating Mother's chocolate chip cookies and laughing.

Each night, before Mother put us to bed, she would play the guitar and sing quiet folksongs. Daddy never participated in this ritual. Daddy thought of childcare as the woman's responsibility. In many ways, he viewed family life in a nineteenth-century manner. Mother didn't have access to the bank accounts; she ran the household on the allowance Daddy gave her. He made all the decisions regarding important matters. When Mother didn't agree with a decision he made, she tried to persuade him to change his mind. He seldom did. Mother cried but did as she was told.

I would not describe Daddy as a mean man, but he did have a volatile temper that he directed at inanimate objects. One morning my sisters and I were sitting at the kitchen table when we heard Daddy bump into the chest in his bedroom. Something fell with a loud crash. Daddy screamed and cursed. A louder crash followed, accompanied by the sound of splintering wood. Daddy had thrown a can of Stanley furniture polish through the bedroom door to punish it for falling off the chest onto his foot. Another time he beat to pieces a kitchen chair that had the misfortune of sitting in the basement while he battled problems with the furnace. I supposed he thought he would teach the furnace a lesson by beating it with the chair. Mother always cried when Daddy lost his temper.

At some point, Daddy started going on two or three-day hunting and fishing trips. When he failed to return on the day he said he would—which happened often—Mother sat by the living room window watching for his truck and crying. From the sofa, I watched her and stewed inside. *He was an asshole*, I thought, *and I would NEVER in my life sit and wait like this for a man. One might sit and wait for me, but NEVER the other way around.*

When I asked Mother why she cried, she'd say, "Daddy might be laying dead somewhere."

"You know he isn't," I would tell her. "He does this all the time. Why worry?"

She responded by calling me "hard and heartless."

I would say to myself, *Well, that's OK, because I am NEVER going to be like you.* I developed a fierce determination to live my life differently.

Burning anger toward my father grew within in me. I detested and resented his hot temper, his callous disregard for Mother's feelings, or for that matter, for anyone's feelings other than his own. I began to voice my opinion of my father's behavior, to challenge him. He reacted by spanking me with his belt and demanding that I apologize. I refused. He hit harder, though never hard enough to cause severe damage.

We struggled in a war of wills. I never cried. I vowed that I would die before I would compromise my principles; they mattered more to me than any punishment. No one would ever control my mind. Eventually my father would back down. We reenacted this scene many times.

From an early age, I wanted to be seen as special, gifted. My elementary school art teacher once contacted my mother and asked if she could give me private lessons. For reasons known only to her, mother said "no." The teacher offered to give me lessons free of charge, but Mother's answer remained, "no." I never understood Mother's decision.

In our family I received praise for my drawing and my writing ability. I wrote plays that my sisters and cousins performed for our parents. I wrote and directed. I doubt a more tyrannical director ever set foot on a stage, even a makeshift one. Eventually no one would perform in the plays I wrote.

Thwarted first in art and then in writing, reading became my refuge. By the end of second grade, I had read all the literature textbooks through the sixth-grade level, and had started on the library. Mother had said I couldn't begin first grade until I knew how to read, so reading lessons began shortly after my fifth birthday. Mother made flash cards from cardboard and by the time school began the next year, I could read. To start first grade having already learned to read was not the norm at that time. Going over old material bored me, and my mind drifted into daydreams; occasionally I missed things that I needed to hear.

At home, in the upstairs hallway between the bedrooms, there was a huge closet with an overhead light where Daddy stored his books in bushel baskets. He read a lot, mostly pulp fiction detective stories. I liked to hide in the closet and read them. Not exactly appropriate reading for someone my age, but no one knew. In one humorous series the titles were as funny as the stories—titles such as, *Stripped for Murder* and *Three's a Shroud*. Adult themes, but I found enough there to keep me in stitches. *Stripped for Murder* required the detective to go undercover in a nudist colony. I must have been around nine at the time.

My premature adult reading ended with a book titled *The Big Bubble*. Mona, the villainess, drowned a man for no reason that I could determine other than to see him drown. The book described how Mona pushed him out of a rowboat, and then whacked his fingers with an oar when he attempted to climb back in. She beat him over the head until he succumbed and drowned. While I doubted the need for anyone to know how it felt to drown, the writer described in graphic detail what the drowning man felt and experienced after he went under the water for the last time. My imagination took me through this ordeal with the drowning man, and given that Mona was my childhood nickname, I felt somehow linked to the character in this grisly book. I stayed away from the closet after that.

My sisters and I loved our lives in that white Cape Cod.

Then in the summer of 1950, a couple of months before my eleventh birthday, everything changed. We moved. Daddy made the decision, and though Mother cried, he wouldn't relent. We left our close-knit neighborhood and moved to the country. Mother would often say, "It's only nineteen miles from the city limits of Cincinnati," but I felt devastated, as though I had been condemned to living in the middle of nowhere. I once described my feelings about the place we came to call "The Farm" for a writing class. Here is some of what I wrote:

The rolling hills of Northern Kentucky were bathed in moonlight. In a rural area nineteen miles south of Cincinnati, Ohio, small, thick woods dotted the open fields. Farmhouses, most with their lights off, were spaced about every mile or so along the road. The houses, barns, trees, and the occasional dog cast long shadows in the moonlight.

On a remote hilltop sat an old farmhouse, its white siding aglow. Woods covered most of this 130-acre tract. It produced no crops or cattle. The house could only be reached by a private driveway, a half-mile long.

In a field adjacent to the house sat an ancient barn. A small pond, overgrown with cattails and covered with green scum, melted into its shadow. In times past it had provided water for cattle. The loud croaking of bullfrogs echoed through the darkness and from the nearby woods came the baying of a redbone hound closing in on a raccoon.

Dense grass, wet with dew, surrounded the farmhouse. The air was hot and humid.

The stars and the moon appeared through a haze of heavy mist that covered the fields and woods, turning the sky into a Van Gogh painting.

The farmhouse windows were open and the humid air inside dampened the bedclothes. Upstairs a young girl propped her elbows on the windowsill, rested her chin in her hands, and gazed out at the night sky. In the heavy air, she felt as though she needed gills to breathe.

Tick-tock, tick-tock. The droning sound of a clock drifted up the stairs, a metronome pacing the rhythm for the passage of time.

The young girl sighed and turned toward the stairs. It must be cooler outside, she thought. She could slip down the stairs; she knew how to do it without waking anyone.

The sounds of howling came again and she hesitated. The hounds of Hell! She could see their red eyes glowing like hot charcoal in the dark.

She turned back to the window. The moon shone especially bright tonight. If she stayed close to the house, she'd be OK. She crept down the stairs, out the side door and into the backyard without disturbing anyone.

She lay down in the wet grass on her back and looked up at the sky. From this angle it looked different, a far-flung canopy covering her. A canopy for a birthday party. She doubted that she would have a party this year. Not in this godforsaken place. Well, that is, if God existed. She knew one thing for sure: this place had been forsaken by somebody.

Longing for the old neighborhood, Mother seemed depressed. Before summer ended, she had rallied and attempted to make the best of the situation. The farmhouse needed almost everything. It lacked central heat and plumbing. A hand pump brought water into the kitchen, and for awhile we had to make do with an outhouse and a galvanized tub for bathing. We hated the outhouse. A few years passed before we got rid of that inconvenience.

Mother set about redecorating the farmhouse and enlisted our help. We painted every wall in the house with vibrant colors, and she made curtains for the windows. Redecorating became part of our annual spring-cleaning ritual. One year Mother painted the living room chartreuse. It went stunningly with the flowered, burgundy sofa. I felt stunned each time I walked into the room. Everyone, including Mother, laughed about the décor but it remained unchanged until the next spring.

Mother couldn't drive, but unfortunately for me, she found a new Baptist church that could arrange for their church bus to pick us up at the end of our driveway. She became a soloist in the choir and quite popular with the church members. Hellfire and brimstone rained down on me again, but at least the church had a youth group I thoroughly enjoyed. This became our social outlet as my sisters and I walked great distances to meet friends. Again, Mother let us roam freely on our own.

The summer we moved to the farm, Daddy bought our first television, a console model with a nineteen-inch screen. Each day after school we watched *Howdy Doody, Captain Video* and *Mickey Mouse*. Mother loved the evening variety shows, while Daddy preferred the mystery shows, wrestling and the *Friday Night Fights* (boxing). We had already been exposed to TV for a few years, as Daddy's sister, Opal, had been one of the first in our area to buy a television. Once or twice a week Daddy would take the family to Opal's and we'd watch television, no matter how bad the reception or the programming. In the forties, television was a novelty.

My sisters and I were taught that family ties bind and, for us, they do. Cassandra is twenty-three months older than I, and Joy eighteen months younger. Marita is younger by five years. When we were young, Mother would stop my sisters and me from fighting, requiring that we kiss and make up. This truly discouraged frequent fights. On the farm, however, she threw us out of the house and told us to fight outside, which we did. Often the fights became physical. Mother ignored the fighting, and while we didn't kiss anymore, we always forgave each other and forgot whatever animosity we harbored. In a way fighting became a physical exercise, like running, as did screaming at the top of our lungs for the sheer joy of uninhibited expression.

In one favorite antic we'd climb on top of the chicken house where we would stomp and scream. This frightened the chickens and, with a lot of squawking, they exited the chicken house. This aggravated mother as well. She told us it put the chickens off their job of laying eggs.

Mother went with us on many walks around The Farm. At the bottom of the hill, along the creek, lay a meadow covered with flowers. Mother named it "Blue Bell Flats." In the summer, we went on long walks under the full moon in woods filled with maples. In the springtime, Mother showed us how to insert spigots into the trees to collect the sap for making maple syrup and taffy. She also taught us to find mushrooms, which she called "dry land fish." Later we would learn the proper name for this mushroom—morel.

Daddy, who worked for the L & N Railroad, decided to start his own business. A member of the Brotherhood of Railroad Trainmen union, he only had to work a certain number of hours a month to retain his seniority and receive a pension when he retired, so he started a logging business on the side. He scoured the Kentucky mountains and countryside for cherry, walnut, and poplar trees. He bought standing timber and took crews in to cut them down. He bought trucks, bulldozers, and whatever he needed to conduct his business. Money for Mother to use at home became scarce.

Once Daddy brought home two orphaned squirrels for us to raise. We named them "Chip and Dale" and fed them milk with an eyedropper. Dale loved to drink tea from a cup on the kitchen table. When they were grown they moved to the attic, and Dale would find her way down to drink tea. Eventually they moved to the woods, and we didn't see them again.

Later Daddy brought us another squirrel we named Oscar, who came to an untimely end by making the mistake of running up the leg of Daddy's pants. With one well-placed karate chop, Daddy dispatched Oscar to the great oak tree in the sky. Daddy had done his duty and protected the family jewels.

To make amends for offing Oscar, Daddy brought us two orphaned fox kits (pups). We didn't ask how they happened to become orphans. We named them "Pete and Repeat" for the funny sound they made—a sort of "perk, perk, perk." They were beautiful and we loved them, but they, too, grew up and took to the woods. At first they would hang around the edge of the woods watching us, but after awhile they stopped. As much as I thought I hated living on the farm, I found it difficult to be unhappy for long stretches. I loved life. I vividly recall running through a meadow, arms out, face to the sun, and thinking that life is wonderful.

Daddy continued to dream. Some came true, some didn't. Enough of them did to give me faith, but the fact he kept on dreaming, no matter what, taught me that the true power lay in the ability to dream. The clashes between Daddy and me continued, though infrequently. He spent a lot of time away from home, and I had learned a tiny bit about discretion.

Mother decreed that there be no dating until age fifteen. At thirteen I had boys chasing me but had no desire to be caught. A boy named Jim kept calling me at home. I asked him to stop but he continued. One afternoon, while Daddy sat in the living room reading, the phone rang. It was Jim.

"I told you never to call me again," I hissed. I don't remember his answer—only what I said just before I slammed down the receiver. "Go straight to hell!"

Daddy jumped up, ran into the kitchen, and shouted at my mother, "Mona just told someone on the telephone to go to hell. Now, I want to know where she heard that kind of language!"

I wanted to run into the kitchen yelling, "Where the hell do you think I heard that language? Are you deaf to the words that come out of your own mouth?" Instead I sat on the step by the kitchen door and shook with silent laughter. I didn't hear Mother's answer.

Jim wasn't the first person I had told to go to hell. The ancient barn had been built to hang tobacco, with rafters even at its highest point. I learned to walk the rafters dreaming of the day I would become a high wire circus performer. One day Daddy's brother, Bill, came into the barn and saw me walking on the highest rafter.

"Get down from there right now!" he screamed. He startled me and I wobbled.

Frightened, I regained my balance and shouted, "You go straight to hell!" My uncle told that story for the rest of his life, always screaming with laughter, "That little thing told me to go straight to hell."

Much of my life I have been an adrenalin junkie, going to the edge for thrills. Whether driving fast, learning to fly an airplane, or to ride a motorcycle, I seldom passed up a dare. After Cassandra started dating, she and her first boyfriend, Eugene, dared me to run through the woods and down the hill at night. With no moonlight to show me the way, I felt scared, but I did it. They had promised to meet me in Eugene's car on the road, across the creek at the foot of the hill. They did, but they took their sweet time getting there.

Once when my cousin Hank, his older brother, and I were roaming around on the farm, I fired my twenty-two rifle over cousin Hank's head two or three times on a dare from his brother. We screamed with laughter as Hank ran in fear.

Years later when we received the news of Hank's death in Viet Nam, no words could express my regret for that childhood prank.

Two or three years after we moved to the farm, Mother decided she wanted to learn to drive. Daddy said, "No." One afternoon our neighbor across the road called and informed me that Mother had run Daddy's car into the ditch and that I should tell him to bring the tractor to pull her out. He did. A few months later she got her driver's license.

Mother made her next move toward independence by getting a job in town. She no longer had to ask for every penny. Mother's job allowed her to take the summers off and we were happy for that. I don't know when it finally happened, but she got her name on the checking account—though not on Daddy's business account.

In high school, under Mother's guidance, I chose to follow the college preparatory curriculum (as did my sisters) and selected art as my major. I received recognition and awards for my talent—the apex being a second place award in my field in a regional competition, followed by exhibition at the national level. My high school yearbook prophesied, "Ramona Sallee is now a famous painter and paints the town red every night."

Time passed and during the summer before the start of my senior year in high school, we moved again. Daddy's business had improved and now our circumstances improved along with it. Daddy built a modern brick ranch-style house with two fireplaces: one in the living room, one in the basement recreation room. I think Mother loved this house more than she did the Cape Cod. While I know now that getting your feelings of self worth from the material aspects of your lifestyle is shallow, at seventeen this did not occur to me. In my eyes my self-worth went up immeasurably.

I wanted to go to college after I graduated, but Daddy believed that a college education for a woman was a waste of money. He believed women would only get married and not use the education. Cassandra, although she had graduated from high school, had married in her senior year. I thought Daddy would change his mind, knowing that I didn't want to get married, but he didn't. Mother tried to get me to apply to a Baptist college where she believed I could get a scholarship. The thought of going to a Baptist college appalled me. I refused. This upset Mother; she wanted me to get an education and didn't understand why a Baptist college wouldn't be better than no college at all. Joy and Marita would both marry before they graduated from high school. Marita married at fifteen and became a mother at sixteen.

Today I wish I hadn't been so stubborn, so closed-minded. Something in me snapped and my dreams vanished. All I saw were closed doors. I went to work for AT&T. I got married, even though I knew better. I had to fight myself to get through the ceremony, to keep from running. Three months after my nineteenth birthday, I gave birth to my son Michael. Eight days before my twenty-second birthday, my daughter, Michelle, arrived.

I started going on crying jags. I sobbed to Mother, "I'm a vegetable. I don't live, I only exist."

"Are you a potato or perhaps a carrot?" she asked.

To which I replied, "I'm a poor little petunia in an onion patch."

By this time Cassandra and Joy had already begun college. Cassandra attended full time and majored in education. I said to my husband, "All my life I've dreamed of going to college and now I'm going to do it."

"Where are you going to get the money?" he asked.

"Where do you think I'm going to get it?" I replied. "I'm going to write a check."

Four months after my twenty-fifth birthday, and with less than two semesters of college under my belt, I left him.

My children had the misfortune of being born to a too-young and far-too-immature mother. My son was born with mild cerebral palsy. When he was eight, I let doctors do experimental surgery on his left foot. They cut his Achilles tendon at the heel and reattached it further up his leg. This allowed his foot to drop into a more normal position, and made it possible for him to stop wearing a brace. The tendon grew and reattached itself to the heel.

In some ways, I was the worst mother Michael could have had. I wish that I could say I always treated my children with loving kindness, but I did not. At nineteen I had a skewed idea of how to be a parent. I had not dealt with the damage caused by my own childhood. On the plus side, I had a sense of humor and recognized the ironies in life. We laughed a lot.

A fighter, I believed in the rights of the individual. I fought the school when they tried to put Michael in special education classes because he had a severe hearing loss. He stayed in mainstream education. He refused to wear the hearing aid doctors had made for him, but his high IQ and lip reading lessons made up for this and he maintained an 'A' average.

Michael won his first argument with me at age five, after he informed me people came from eggs. I had taught him the alphabet at age two, and then how to spell and recognize his name along with some other short words like "cat" and "rat." I then filled in with some basic information about phonics, but I did not teach him to read. Trapped inside my perceptual box, I assumed he meant something akin to chicken eggs. I informed him, rather patronizingly, that people did not come from eggs. He argued. I wouldn't budge, so he said he would show me. He did. He dragged an encyclopedia into the kitchen and showed me an ovum. Checkmate.

Michelle came into this world in high gear. At eighteen months she had the vocabulary and the ability to carry on an adult conversation. At the same age she climbed out of the backyard, over a six-foot-high chain link fence, and made her way to a busy street. A passerby rescued her as I came running. Nothing dissuaded her from continuing to go over the fence at every opportunity. On her second foray she discovered the monkey bars at the school on the corner of our street. After that she made a beeline for those monkey bars each time she escaped.

At three she learned to swim by simply jumping into the deep end of the pool. My heart and those of a few other observers stopped, but she didn't have to be pulled from the water. She made it out by herself. She later took to riding horses as naturally as she did to water.

After leaving my husband, I faced the difficulty of supporting myself and two children. My solution, since I still wanted to go to college, came in the form of a job as a cocktail waitress. (The nude modeling came a little later.) I worked at a nightclub where I wore a low-cut satin blouse with high-cut black satin shorts and black fishnet hose. We were required to wear a certain type of push-up bra. It revealed a lot. I made decent money working at this expensive nightclub five nights per week. With that income, good child support, and the modeling gigs, we did all right.

Each semester I managed to pick up two or three classes, but a college degree didn't seem to be getting closer. I majored in art and was rather temperamental about it. I hated performing on command. What would I ever do with an art degree? I refused to teach. As for commercial art? Never. There again, I would have to perform on command.

I met "Bill" while modeling nude for a sculpture class. We became engaged.

Bill, of course, was beautiful. The sixties had arrived and with it the "sexual revolution," the appearance of AIDs still on the distant horizon. Sex with Bill lacked…something. On a scale of one to ten, he rated a three—below my usual requirement. Although he scored a ten on the beauty index, woman does not live by beauty alone, so I called off the engagement. Bill appeared heartbroken but Mother "consoled" him. How she reconciled this with her religion I'm not sure, but everyone backslides I guess.

During Bill's and Mother's "consolation" period, I drove home for a visit. Daddy informed me that Mother had left with Bill for the weekend. Daddy vented his frustration and concern.

"Don't worry," I said, "He's no good in bed." My comment must have been the result of shock, but I couldn't think of anything else to say.

"He isn't? Are you sure?"

"Daddy, a girl doesn't want to tell her father these things, but yes, I'm sure."

I heard Rod Serling's voice in my head saying, "Ramona Sallee, you have crossed into the Twilight Zone."

For a few years after my divorce, I spent my time dating and dilly-dallying with college. I survived a second disastrous marriage that only lasted a year. After moving out of my parents' house, I had openly embraced atheism, but always felt a little lost. I missed being part of a community. In the late sixties I discovered the Unitarian Universalist Association (church) and filled the void. To the Unitarians, not believing in God was acceptable. They left that choice to the individual. Once again I belonged to a community.

There have been many famous Unitarians, including writers Louisa May Alcott, e.e. Cummings, Ralph Waldo Emerson, Nathaniel Hawthorne, Helen Hunt Jackson (author of the book *Ramona*), Sylvia Plath, Harriet Beecher Stowe, Henry Wadsworth Longfellow, Carl Sandburg, Mary Wollstonecraft Shelley *(Frankenstein)*, Ray Bradbury, Kurt Vonnegut, and many more. I felt at home among the Unitarians, at peace with their tolerant views and in accord with their activism in the cause of human rights.

Michael and Michelle were getting older and their needs had changed. I decided to get serious about getting a degree. We moved in with my parents and I went to school full time. I switched to a double major in psychology and sociology. Before I graduated, Mother died of breast cancer. She died shortly after Thanksgiving, having insisted on cooking Thanksgiving dinner. All her daughters, with their current husbands or boyfriends, and all the grandchildren were there. A few days later, life without Mother began.

For a long time I would expect her to walk in the room or think I heard her voice, then I'd remember she had died. For years I dreamed she was alive, only to awaken and experience the sharp pain of loss again.

Bill, as it turns out, had not been Mother's first affair. I'm not sure how many there were, but I think she started philandering in her early forties. In my childhood years Daddy had asked Mother for a divorce to marry another woman. They had separated for awhile but reconciled. If her motivation was revenge, she paid him back in spades.

I wish I could say she had her affairs with impunity. Perhaps at the time she did, but she died as she had lived, in fear of her god. In her last days Mother felt great anger toward Daddy. One evening she asked me to take him to task, to tell him what a horrible person he had been and how terribly he had treated her. I refused. I explained to her that I believed he had done nothing that she hadn't allowed him to do, and in the final analysis, we are all responsible for our own lives. I told her it would be hurtful to everyone if I did what she asked. The next day, when I came home from school, Mother informed me that she had asked Joy to tell Daddy what a horrible person he had been and Joy had done as Mother requested. Mother called Joy her only good daughter. Joy felt justified, but I felt heartsick. Memories of Mother's last days haunted me for years. Daddy remarried in less than a year.

Sometime during all this I married for the third time. I cannot excuse the disruption to our lives and the psychological damage done to my children by this miserable choice. The abuse began after we moved out of Daddy's house. Not being the sort of woman who wouldn't fight back, I did, and we had some violent fights. I gave tit for tat. One morning the children awoke to a kitchen strewn with tomatoes and broken glass. They say I also had a black eye, though I do not remember it and can't imagine I would have gone to work looking like that. Shortly after that, I left him and didn't remarry for fourteen years.

At the end of my junior year, I had decided I couldn't accept making less money than a man for the same job. The women graduating that year complained about this inequity and related their problems and the problems of others they knew. I met with an advisor and asked if a career field existed in which a woman could make as much money as a man. Her immediate answer—accounting. I knew I could do that. I had already completed two semesters of accounting. After graduation, I stayed on and picked up the necessary credits.

I then found what I considered a terrific job in accounting with a locally based convenience store chain. After leaving the third husband, my children and I moved to a Cincinnati, Ohio, suburb—a fifteen-minute drive from my employer. While working full time, I obtained an MBA from Xavier University.

The single dating life resumed and, at age thirty-four, I found myself checking out men with Chuck, a gay friend.

"Look at the buns on that one," he would say. I enthusiastically agreed, and pointed out one who had those long gorgeous legs. "Ow, mama, you are so right.

"Give me five!" Chuck and I would turn and slap our open hands together.

"You're some kinda strange chick," Chuck observed. "We have the same taste in men, and, honey, I'm gay. You're in trouble."

I began writing what I called my "smut saga" to amuse my sisters and a group of our friends at our monthly bridge club. Cassandra and Marita were in the club for the fun, while Joy, a serious duplicate bridge player, rarely failed to take us to task for socializing and ignoring our bridge playing. So under the pseudonym Georgette DuBois, I wrote monthly installments about my protagonist, Clitorella Huntinpecker, who had more perils than Pauline. Clitorella was not promiscuous; she was merely conducting a comparative survey. I ended each story with, "Alas, poor Clitorella, will she ever find true happiness?" Even Joy had to laugh.

I was thirty-eight when Michael left for college and Michelle moved into the downstairs bedroom across the hall from mine. When Michelle graduated and joined the Air Force three years later, I was alone for the first time in my life. Euphoria set in but didn't last long. The house seemed eerie, unnatural. Downstairs, my children had watched TV and played pool in the L-shaped recreation room. They had occupied the two upstairs bedrooms ever since we moved into the house. After they left, I kept thinking I heard footsteps overhead. I would run upstairs to find the rooms empty. Then I would walk down the basement stairs, go through the beaded curtains, knock around a few billiard balls, and then sit on the sofa and cry.

I felt out of sync. A woman wasn't supposed to be alone at forty-one. I needed change, and change I did.

I sold the house and moved to Phoenix, Arizona, where Marita and her family had lived for two years. Once in Phoenix I couldn't help but notice the men. They were everywhere. I opened an account at a branch bank and the manager asked me for a date. A trip to a hair salon netted a date with the man having his hair done in the next chair. I half expected one to stick out his foot and trip me on the sidewalk just to slow me down enough to ask for a date. A dating frenzy ensued. Life alone had some advantages.

During this frenzy, my company asked me to take a visiting businesswoman to dinner. As we sat in a restaurant, drinking wine after dinner, the talk turned to men. She cried on my shoulder over the way her fifty-five-year-old boyfriend treated her. I asked why she, at thirty-five, dated such old men. She looked at me in amazement and asked what age men I dated. I had to stop and think about this one.

"Oh, my god!" I shouted. "Something's wrong with me! I've never been involved with a man out of his twenties!" I felt that all eyes in the restaurant had suddenly focused on me.

Thinking that I must be abnormal, I began looking for a man closer to my own age. When I found him, "Gary" was thirty-seven, only six years younger than me. Four years later he would say, "I've got this job offer in Boston and I'm going to take it. We might as well get married." Romantic.

I knew better but said "yes" anyway. My career choice hadn't satisfied me. It had served its purpose in supporting the children, but I wondered, "What now?" I decided I needed time off and a change. We moved to Boston and in less than a year, my fourth husband came to me and said he couldn't keep up the act anymore.

When I asked him what act he was referring to, he informed me he knew what I wanted from him because of the year we spent in couples' therapy before we were married, and while he had tried to accommodate my needs, he could no longer carry on with the act.

An act! He had been acting! I came undone. I had vowed I would never divorce again. I had told him this. He had agreed to work out, through therapy, any problems we encountered.

Still reeling from this news, I had a mammogram that showed a suspicious growth. My first panic attack came within days. I didn't realize it then, but I had begun the long fall that would crack the hard shell in which I had encased myself.

The growth turned out to be two intersecting cysts. Instead of catching the next flight to Phoenix and bidding Gary adieu, I dragged him to one therapist after another in an attempt to fix our marriage. He became more hostile and withdrawn. So I went on the attack. He had lied to me. This was all his fault.

I didn't work during the time we spent in Boston. At Gary's insistence I took the Becker CPA Review course and sat for the exam. I passed four of the five parts on the first try. I did this while falling apart emotionally and taking Valium to deal with the panic attacks. I took my first creative writing classes, which proved to be better than therapy.

The economy had gone down the outhouse and neither of us could find work. We had both made good money and between us we had substantial savings. I became a substitute teacher—there's always a need for those. Gary started a consulting business, but made very little money. After a year or so, we spent the rest of our savings and went into debt to buy an ongoing business. The panic attacks became worse and, with them, the early stage of phobias arrived. My Doctor prescribed Prozac. The business failed. We filed bankruptcy. We divorced.

My house, an old car, and my degrees were all I had left. On the bright side, the Prozac had vanquished the panic attacks.

Proving to myself that I had learned nothing, I immediately became involved with a younger and, as it turned out, troubled man my children's age. I decided to quit dating, take inventory, and come up with a plan for change. Originally I planned a one year sabbatical from dating, but it stretched into eighteen months.

After the bankruptcy was granted, I immediately landed a good job. I started as the Financial Reporting Director, but within a year was promoted to Vice President of Finance. I put one-hundred percent effort and sixty to eighty hours per week into the job. I reported to the President and COO, who handled even the smallest problems with derisive comments and often publicly yelled at employees, including me.

At first I handled the stress, but in July of 1998, Marita's son, Brian, died suddenly from an aneurysm that ruptured at the base of his brain. Three or four months after his death, a freak accident left me with a detached retina. Two operations ensued and my left eye now has a silicone band around the back, artificial fluid and dim, warped vision.

During recovery from the second operation, I made three decisions: to end my dating sabbatical, to begin developing my creative side again, and to find a less stressful job. I did not arrive at a plan for changing myself other than to hide the cracks in my shell by "redecorating."

I tackled the creative side first and began taking oil painting lessons at a small private art school. After a short time, the owner asked me to model nude.

"I'm an accountant," I said. She said I had a beautiful body and regal carriage.

That did it. I stripped. Fifty-eight years old and I was back to the nude modeling gig. One Saturday morning my daughter called. I kept telling her I had just gotten out of the shower and needed to get dressed and leave. She demanded to know why I couldn't take a few minutes to talk to her. I snapped, "I'm modeling nude at nine o'clock. And if I don't get out of here I'll be late. I've got to get dressed."

"Regressing are we?" she asked. "Why bother to get dressed?"

"I'm afraid a policeman will stop me and I'll get arrested if I don't," I said.

"Well, that one's easy." She said. "Just say, 'Officer, what's the problem? These are my work clothes.'"

She ratted me out to her brother and he told me I would wind up with nudie pics online for all my cohorts to ogle. He laughed when he said it.

The most significant romantic relationship of my life began with an online personal ad. After a friend told me about them, I checked a few sites and began picking out the men I found interesting. I met six or seven men this way. I found all of them attractive but none appealed to me. Then I met "Donald." I felt as though we had known each other forever. Our chemistry level reached the stratosphere. An illustrator and advertising designer, he had left his work and New York to pursue fine art, painting in oils, in Phoenix. Of course, he's beautiful and tall with long, gorgeous legs. I thought at last I had caught the brass ring. But, alas, I was not to find true happiness, at least not with Donald.

Initially I didn't answer Donald's personal ad because he declared he wanted a wife. A few weeks later at Marita's urging, I wrote to him. On our second date Donald said he had canceled his ad because he had found what he was looking for. I interpreted this as meaning a potential wife. I checked and the ad was gone.

Donald aroused in me feelings that were intense and frightening. I had run from other men who elicited these same feelings. I believed those feelings were a portent of impending true love and, from everything I'd seen, I wanted nothing to do with it. This time, however, I vowed not to run. It took courage, but I stayed in the relationship. Donald saw me through a stressful job search and celebrated with me when I found the perfect job.

Although Donald had said he wanted a wife, eighteen months later, he still could not commit. I didn't know it, but he kept much of his life hidden from me. Sensing that something was wrong, I became riddled with insecurity.

One Sunday at his house, Donald said he had an errand to run. I asked if I could stay and use his computer to do some research. After he left, I went online and came across something I wanted to download and print. When I chose "yes," to download, up popped a folder titled "Letters from Ann." I thought this an odd name for a download file but opened it.

Inside were hundreds of e-mails from someone named "Ann." A lot of the subjects were about love. I opened one. I read her comments about activities that Donald and I had recently shared, though in recounting them to her, he had apparently failed to mention me. Ann wrote that she loved him and called him her "wonderful man."

I had to know. I went into Donald's saved outgoing e-mails, and there they were—hundreds of his e-mails to her. I scrolled to the bottom to see how long this exchange had been going on and discovered it predated our meeting by several months. He called her his wonderful woman and issued every declaration of love that I could imagine, including marriage. But Ann, as it turned out, was already married. Donald frequently expressed his impatience with waiting for her to get divorced. She kept promising that she would soon. Donald's most recent e-mail had been sent that very morning as I lay asleep in his bed.

I tried to scream but I couldn't breathe. I'm not sure how long I sobbed and gasped for air. When Donald returned, I confronted him. He made excuses for his behavior, saying it was the most neurotic episode in his life. I went on a rampage throwing all my things over a second floor railing to the first floor. I took the books I had given Donald and ripped out the loving words I had written inside. Verbally I attacked Donald using every weapon in my arsenal. I felt destroyed. Betrayed.

He apologized, assuring me their affair had been nothing more than a neurotic game, and strictly confined to the internet. He also told me my rampage reminded him of his father and frightened him. Feeling the pull of my attraction to him, I listened and tried to understand.

Although our relationship grew shakier, when Donald asked me to move in with him and test the idea that we'd get married in a year or so, I agreed. At his request, I had the new bed I had just purchased delivered to his townhouse. I told everyone—my family, friends, personal trainer, hair dresser, and the people I worked with—our plan and made all the necessary arrangements for the changes in my life.

About two or three weeks before the date of the move Donald sent me an e-mail at work. The subject: "I cannot do this." He called off the relationship. Because of the arrangements I had put in place, I had a lot of undoing to do. I reacted with fury and sent a verbal assault his way by e-mail and voice mail. We ended our relationship and not on good terms. We would not see each other again for three months.

In the wake of the September 11 terrorist attack on the World Trade Center, where Donald lost some friends, we were drawn back together. Donald once again asked me to move in and get married at a later date.

For the next several months, I spent every weekend at Donald's place. One morning in April, he saw me off to a workshop with loving words.

That evening I returned to find his car gone and my things packed and piled in the hall along with a note. He had also left a voice message on my home phone and sent me an e-mail. The relationship didn't work for him, he said, and he wanted to be friends. I felt anger at the way he handled the situation, but I also felt a sense of relief. At the workshop that day, after an exercise that required we mold a lump of clay with our eyes closed, I had written these words:

The unexplored regions of my reality exist in my nightmares. A skinless man is stalking me. His outer layer is muscle and tissue. They are red but he does not bleed. I hide inside my stainless steel vault and listen to his banging. He is trying to destroy me. In desperation I try to remember. There must be an escape route. I notice that someone is in here with me. It's a small child. She and I are different but somehow the same person. I hug her and promise that I will get us to safety.

I must make something with my eyes closed and then write about the experience. In the darkness, alone with my nightmare, I work the clay and reflect on my relationship with Donald.

Sitting here molding this clay I think of things: what happened last night, last week, last month, last year. Backwards I travel fo-

cused on our relationship. This damned relationship, this man, this me.

The clay is soft, supple and moist, easily molded. For this exercise we must keep our eyes closed. An easy task since mine have been closed for a long time. The clay fans out in my hands and becomes a thin layer, then curls and folds in on itself. Like my mind. This damned relationship. The clay splits and I decide to start over.

Dry and brittle clay isn't easy to mold. Is that what has happened to me? I have no water to moisten and soften the clay, but think, "OK, I can make this work." Large holes and cracks appear in the clay. This damned relationship. I start over.

The wind is blowing, caressing my skin, playfully fluffing my hair and drying the clay. I keep kneading the clay trying to make it one cohesive piece again. The way it used to be. This damned relationship. It cracks over and over but I continue working with it. I wish to be as light as the mist over my childhood meadows and let the wind gently carry me away. I know that it's time.

When I first dreamed of the skinless man, my immediate thought had been that he represented Donald. But now I think the part of my subconscious that wrote "the unexplored regions of my reality exist within my nightmares," knew this man represented a reality that existed only in my own mind. He reflected the image of "true love" I formed in childhood as I struggled to make sense out of the world around me. I saw "true love" as dangerous—something that would destroy me if I opened the door and invited it inside.

I believe that having allowed myself to become vulnerable by loving Donald and then surviving the thing I feared most—rejection by the man I loved—released me to fully give and receive love.

Daddy died in September of 2000. He felt at peace with his girls, and we with him. For years he never hesitated to give us a hug and tell us he loved us. He told everyone who would listen that his girls were perfect and always had been. He bragged about our educations and careers. We had all gone on to college and three of us received multiple degrees. We all have successful careers. He joked that his girls were the marrying kind and said he had more out-laws than in-laws.

He found this hilarious.

Reflections on the Present

...Looking at all those glittering stars she could believe anything was possible...

When Charlotte asked me to participate in this writing group it never occurred to me that I was stepping into a circle of fire capable of bringing every shadow area of my life into the light. Ugly creatures I had hidden in the subterranean caves of my mind clawed their way to the surface and demanded to be dealt with. No one can hide in the circle of fire, but what emerges is not all darkness. Emerging, we savor again our climbs of the mental Himalayas, breathe the rarefied air, and bask in the sunlight of our most joyous moments. Each Wednesday night we Shoe Women have laughed, cried, and shared our lives. It has healed my heart more than all my years of therapy combined.

Much of my life has been fear based. I've hidden in terror from even the possibility of being rejected, especially having my writing rejected. I could never risk even a chance and had not submitted anything to be considered for publication until now. Several months ago I wrote about my fear, giving it form in an attempt to get myself writing and I believe it moved me forward. This is how I saw my fear:

What is that behind me? A dark form hides in the shadows. I sit and wait...frozen. A cold, gray vapor swirls around me. Fear. I hear its footsteps moving closer. I shudder, goosebumps cover my arms and the muscles in my neck tighten. Not again! Dread consumes me and fear leans over my shoulder. I feel its frigid breath on my neck.

"Your writing's not good enough," the phantom whispers.

"Go away," I whimper.

A bony finger extends from beneath a black robe; it traces the outline of my cheekbone.

"It will never be good enough," the specter jeers.

I wrench away, run into my room and lock the door. I crawl into bed and relief floods over me. I'm free. Free from sitting there and failing. Free from staring at the empty page desperate for words that will not come.

"Not good enough. Not good enough." The words echo in my brain.

"Go away," I plead, covering my ears and curling into the fetal position.

"What next?" my ego asks, sarcastic as always. "Are you going to start sucking your thumb? Whatever happened to the girl we used to be? Walking rafters and even daring to learn to fly. What have you done with her? Have you stifled her or perhaps caught her napping, strangled the life out of her and discarded the remains in a dump across town?"

"I haven't done anything to her," I insist. "It's him...Fear. Make him go away," I beg. But there is no answer.

I am alone with my fear.

I try to remember. I bite my lip and concentrate. The image is dim but I see her. Unafraid, she walks the highest rafter.

"No! I won't listen to you!" I scream at Fear. I hear my voice as

*if from a distance, and then I am running down a long corridor,
running for my life, back to the empty page.*

Looking back on my experiences has convinced me karma
exists and we often don't have to wait until the next lifetime to
receive in kind the treatment we have given others. During the
past several years I have walked many miles in my mother's shoes.
The world looks different now that I'm the one wearing the shoes.
Today my main focus is on the relationship I have with myself. I
believe true happiness will be achieved through unconditional
love for myself and others. This doesn't mean letting people walk
on me. Sometimes it's necessary to wish a person well and love
them from a distance. I did not choose to do this, however, with
Donald. Instead, I have kept him as a friend. My choice has noth-
ing to do with Donald and everything to do with the person I
want to become. In the past I have said, "Like Hannibal, if I can-
not find a way, I will make one." Life often becomes a struggle
with this approach.

It is far easier to stop struggling with a closed door and look
around for an open one. At the church I attend I have heard and
believe when one door closes, another one opens. If I am en-
countering one obstacle after the other, then I am on the wrong
path. If the direction I choose is the right one, there will be no
obstacles and all the doors will open. I have quit trying to force a
way and with love, released Donald to be who he is. How we live
our lives is between us and God. I believe we will be in some way
accountable for the life we have lived, but I don't think we're
going to get tossed on the barbie to sizzle for all eternity. We just
might have to do this all over again until we get it right. That is
now my concept of Hell.

The journey has been long and steep, but I am on the right
path. Writing has taken center stage. Oil painting is temporarily
on the sidelines, but I enjoy both.

I go out to dinner weekly with my son. Michael now has a successful career as an electrical engineer. He has little use of his left hand, but due to the success of the operation on his Achilles tendon, he walks with only a slight limp. In high school he tried to get out of the mandatory typing class with the excuse of not being able to use his left hand. The school responded by buying him a typing book for people with one hand. Today he spends a lot of time in front of a computer using those typing skills.

Michael and I have a good relationship and talk openly about most things—his career, the high pressure, and his desire to downsize as I have done. The shrinking of his investment portfolio due to the chaos in the stock market makes him think he'll have to delay his plan. I know Michael's future will be blessed.

Michelle is talking of returning to college to finish her degree. Ironic, since our troubles with her really began after she started school. Michelle was hardly obsessed with learning. Au contraire, I felt lucky to see her graduate from high school. I embraced her decision to join the Air Force rather than attend college, happy to have Uncle Sam take care of her. As part of the physical test to join the Air Force, she was required to either press a thirty-five-pound weight over her head two times, or a seventy-pound weight over her head once. She opted for the seventy pounds. At 5-feet-1-inch tall and all of ninety pounds, she pressed the seventy pounds on her first try to choruses of hoots and hollers from the guys. They nicknamed her Muscle-chelle.

She eventually went on to become an air traffic controller, a college student studying biology and geology, and finally a stay-at-home mother of three.

My three sisters live in Northern Kentucky, and I miss not being physically close to them. Marita—whose third, or fourth, or whichever number husband he was died six months after her son—is getting remarried. She has caught the brass ring in the Prince Charming game, manifesting him through spiritual principles.

These days, the cracks in my shell are large enough to crawl through, and I have emerged into glorious light. I am coming to accept that there is much about life—my own and life in general—I may never understand. And that's OK. It is enough for me to know I am simply a person who questions everything and then draws my own conclusions—I like this part of me.

I have spent a long time in chrysalis. Spreading my arms and raising my face to the sun, I step confidently into the future.

Reflections on the Future

...Strength & Vision. These are the real necessities of life...

The color of my future shoe is red—the color of power and my lifelong favorite color. The shoe is sprinkled with gold stars representing the unlimited possibilities I view as open to me as I purposefully manifest my future.

I believe we are all sent here, to this life, with a mission we can choose to fulfill or not. I believe we have free will and we came here with nothing preordained. As Deepak Chopra writes in his book, *The Seven Spiritual Laws of Success*, this mission is called the "Law of Dharma" or "Purpose in Life."

A still, small voice is telling me that my mission lay in writing. I sense that whatever purpose I served in the corporate arena is near fulfillment. I further believe if writing is the path I should take, doors will open. My fear is gone and I am seeking the open door.

In September I begin a three-semester course titled, "Structuring and Writing the Novel." By the end of December 2003, I will have written, edited, and revised my first novel. I am at last fulfilling my childhood dream.

The life I have lived has given me an incredible range of experience to draw upon— from the Kentucky mountains where we had no electricity or plumbing, to a successful career in Corporate America. Many times I have considered being born to my parents as a curse, but it is a blessing. I thank the insuppressible spirits of my father and my mother.

Spirit has always been with me, watching over me, keeping me safe. I have felt its presence and heard its voice throughout my life. Whenever danger approached, the voice became loud and commanding. I ignored the voice a lot, but never when it took that commanding tone. Something within me knew to act upon those demands.

"The voice" literally saved my life when I was twenty-six. A severe infection shut down one of the valves in my kidney. Doctors told me I needed to undergo a serious operation to replace the valve once the infection was brought under control.

One night I heard "the voice" inside my head demand, "Get your temperature taken and get it taken now."

Since the nurse had taken my temperature only minutes before, I had to plead with her to take it again. She relented. My temperature had risen to 106.

I found myself over the whole scene looking down, as a bright light shone above me. I felt no emotion other than curiosity. I remember thinking, *I might die. I wonder if I will.* I felt no interest in the white light. It was simply there.

The valve in my kidney resumed functioning on its own. Amazed, the urologist said he had never witnessed anything like it. To him it seemed impossible but undeniable.

"The voice" also brought me to my father's sick bed in time to say "goodbye."

My sister had been calling to say he had been hospitalized, but there was no need for me to come. Then one Wednesday afternoon as I left work, I stopped to apply lipstick. As I leaned forward to look into the mirror, I heard the voice inside me say, "September fifteenth, you've got to get out of here." I threw my lipstick into my purse and ran.

"September fifteenth." I had heard those words twenty years before, in a dream the day Daddy's mother died, with the instructions to remember them.

When I arrived at the hospital, Daddy seemed in great spirits and had been told he could go home Monday. Daddy acted as he always had—joking and laughing and getting angry at the mention of the Baptist religion. He even baited me; I played right into it and got hooked. He winked at Marita and laughed. I felt relieved to think the voice had been wrong.

That night, on September fifteenth, he died.

Joy, Marita, and I stood by the bed holding each other's hands as I held Daddy's still warm hand and sang one of my favorite songs: "Surely the presence of the Lord is in this place. I can feel God's mighty power and his grace. I can feel the brush of angel's wings and see heaven on each face. Surely the presence of the Lord is in this place."

Once I realized I believed in a higher power, I had slowly drifted away from the Unitarians. In time I found another church that fit my beliefs. I found a name for that power that guides me—Spirit. I've finally accepted that I am a spiritual being.

In my future I will actively seek the voice and tune in to the smallest whisper. My relationship with Spirit will become part of my relationship with myself. I am reminded of another spiritual message that I have incorporated into my life: "God within me is powerful beyond measure."

Many of the symbols on my future shoe depict my love for family, friends—for all people. It is my desire for this light to shine through me and reflect on the world through my words and deeds. On the side of the shoe are the words "New York Times Best Seller"—my dream for this book we have written.

As for romantic love, yes, I want it, but I have work to do on my relationship with myself before I will feel ready. This "now" time is for me. In the future I will manifest "Mr. Perfect for Me," and I perceive that future time is near.

Not long ago I felt that my appeal, the kind that attracts men, had deserted me, but change is in the ether. One night I dreamed of seeing an elevator being towed by a helicopter when suddenly the cable broke. The elevator began falling. I could see people in the elevator and I wondered, *If the people in the elevator jump just before it hits the ground, would that lessen the impact of their fall?* I thought that it would.

The elevator smashed into the ground. I ran to the scene to see if the people were OK. A man lay flattened on the grass. "My god. It's Prince Charming! Damn, he really is dead now." I gasped.

And then he moved. Not much but he did move.

Maybe I've lost my appeal, but I expect it to show up again soon—some Tuesday around three in the afternoon on a crowded freeway. No doubt I'll stop traffic. I'm looking forward to it.

In Our Shoes

Jane's Shoes

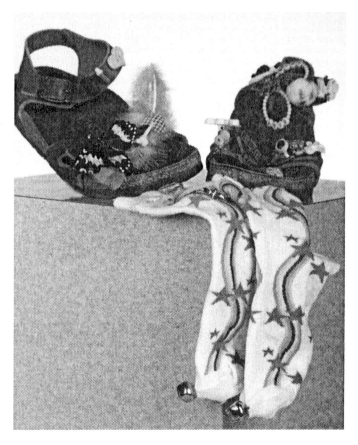

In Our Shoes

Fable

A Magical Journey

Where have I been lately? Caught in a dream, carried by breath, creating an illusion that easily turned into reality when I placed the shoes of life upon my feet.

These shoes took me by surprise. I found them hidden in my closet under a layer of fashionable, pretty shoes that are my normal everyday wear. (You know the kind, shoes for specific outfits.) I'm not certain what could have guided me to these shoes. Perhaps it had to do with the way they looked. Decorated with small charms and symbols, they appeared rich with history. I recognized their meaning immediately. A charm of a young girl with ringlets in her hair clung to the strap. The story told on these shoes began with my childhood and continued to the life that I currently lead. To someone else, they may have looked like something an elementary school child created by mistake, but I knew their reality. Childbirth, my days as a soccer mom, my growing relationship with God—these and so many other reflections of my life appeared there, witnessed on a pair of Birkenstocks.

I really couldn't fathom why I felt the need to place them upon my feet—these Birkenstocks with a history. Unadorned at one time, they had belonged to Mother. I wore them for weeks after her death, perhaps for the connectedness, to feel the closeness of the earth, to pay homage to the one who gave me birth. My grief had passed; now I felt guided.

I placed the shoes upon my feet and my soul took flight…up, up, up toward the Light. Weightless, I suddenly awakened to an incredible journey of spirit. I saw breathtaking views—canyons winding through river valleys, mountains with snowcapped peaks, white clouds yielding spirit dancers, meadows of wildflowers in all the variant shades of yellow, blue, purple, and red. I heard a melodic symphony of sounds and tones. The birds sang as if directed by a conductor. The wind caressed my face. All played in tune with my Being.

I touched the earth and mingled with the cosmos. I at once surrounded the universe and felt awed by its magnificence. I sang out with glee to feel its vastness and its closeness, both at the same time. In amazement, I saw all the faces on earth become ONE—one voice, one sea of perfection. I heard a common language spoken as love.

I knew for certain these shoes were beyond magic. I returned them to the place where I found them. In total reverence I gave thanks for the journey they offered.

These shoes will always be there waiting for me, supporting me in All Ways, directing and guiding me to the Infinite.

Was this my Mother's legacy? Just as she carried me in the safety of her womb, she shared with me the truth of her Being. She allowed me the experience of that safety once again—and through a pair of Birkenstocks, no less.

Reflections on the Past:

...Birkenstocks with a history...

My mother called me Janie or Jane-Jane from the beginning. I wasn't consciously aware of my name until I was four years old and entered the International Order of Odd Fellows (I.O.O.F.) Children's Home. The people there called me Nancy, because my given name was "Nancy Jane." Mother had named me Nancy after my great-grandmother, but thought that "Jane Nancy" just didn't sound right. As far as I was concerned, the people at the children's home could call me anything they wanted. I knew I was *Janie*.

At various times in my life I associated with characters who shared my name, starting from my first reading experiences, *Fun*

With Dick and Jane. Even though I looked more like Sally than Jane, the story of the perfect family—two children, a dog named Spot, a cat named Fluffy, and a mother and father watching over them all—protected me from my reality. It was a good read.

I'm not certain how my sister, brother and I were delivered to the I.O.O.F. Children's Home in the early 1950s. Only my older siblings, Richie and Cathie, knew what was happening. Only four years old, I was oblivious that the situation was supposed to be traumatic. I thought of it as an adventure. Fifteen months my junior, too young to be placed in the nursery with me, my sister, Mary Elizabeth, remained with our mother for the first six months. This separation saddened me those first few months because Mary and I had become dependent upon one another for comfort and support. Our mother's preoccupation with her impending divorce and with putting food on the table accustomed us to some separation from her.

I know now that our mother's divorce prompted her need for more education and income to support four children. Our father had gone away, though no one told me the reason.

Mom went to work and school with the intention of returning for us once she was on her feet. This seemed the best solution at the time. She belonged to an organization that made us eligible to be placed in the "home" as it became known. An old mansion in Gilroy, California, surrounded by huge old redwood and oak trees, it became our home for two-and-a-half years. I remember the fun we had exploring the old tower in the yard. I remember the scent of furniture oil permeating all the rooms, especially the small rooms that housed pianos.

I was fed well, scrubbed, and put to bed with prayers and stories. I fondly remember the English "matrons" who cared for me: Mitzi and the nurse, Miss Prime. A loving and gentle woman, Miss Prime treated skinned knees, tonsillitis, and generally watched out for my health. Mitzi loved my blonde ringlets, so each day she gave me finger curls and plaid ribbons in my hair. I started kindergarten as a frightened, shy, little girl, annoyed because they called me "Nancy." I can see my shyness reflected in a photo taken of me during that time, a scarf tightly covering my beautiful ringlets and plaid ribbons. The photographer evidently could not talk me out of wearing the scarf.

My brother, Richie, and sister, Cathie, were placed in the dorms upstairs. While I felt secure in the "home," the two of them struggled there. They missed their cousins and the father with whom they had formed a relationship. I don't remember seeing a lot of them unless family came to visit or take us for picnics to Sea Cliff Beach. Even then, administrators would forbid Richie to come along if he was being disciplined for fighting or some infringement of upstairs rules.

Mother visited as often as school and work allowed. We always hated to watch her leave again, especially Mary. Aunts, uncles, cousins, and a grandmother would visit also, as did members of the Odd Fellows. I can remember singing songs for them and receiving coins in a small plastic purse for my efforts.

The nurses and matrons at the home tried their best to care for us. They turned holidays into grand celebrations. I remember a Halloween party held in a dark basement room, carefully decorated with cobwebs, jack-o-lanterns, witches, and candied apples. Everyone wore costumes. I can't recall much about my costume, only the smell of the plastic mask and the stiffness of the fabric.

One Christmas Eve, a bus took us to a neighboring Air Force base where we watched *White Christmas* with Bing Crosby and Rosemary Clooney at the base theater. After the show, one of the airmen placed me on a table to "entertain" the troops by singing "How Much Is That Doggie In The Window" and other hit parade tunes. Despite my limited repertoire, the troops encouraged me to perform. While I sang, soldiers passed out gifts to all the children. I watched as girls and boys received dolls, trucks, doctor's kits, sewing machines, airplanes, and magic sets.

At last, my turn came. I could hardly wait as I looked at the large package with excitement. I imagined there must be something very special inside. Yet when I tore off the colored wrapping, much to my disappointment I found a child-sized ironing board. I had to fight back the tears.

I did not even get an iron.

Over the years, I have received other "ironing boards" that recall that feeling of dashed expectations—such as the water filter my husband gave me for our tenth anniversary.

It would be many years before I knew that my disappointment paled in comparison to the disappointment our mother felt that Christmas Eve when she arrived at the home to find that the bus had already taken us away. She had rushed over after work to spend the evening with her four children, only to learn she had missed us by only minutes. She would forever refer to this as the saddest Christmas of her life.

As a young adult, I began having a recurring dream about my biological father, Richard:

I feel the warmth from the big picture window at my aunt's house. All of us kids are ushered to the back bedroom. I can hear my mommy crying. My brother and older sister are crying too. What's happening? There is a lot going on. Mom is more than crying; she is sobbing. Suddenly someone comes into the bedroom and asks if we want to say "goodbye" to our Daddy. One at a time, the stranger brings us into the living room. Who are these strange people surrounding "my Daddy"? Something holds his hands behind his back; he can't hug or touch, only bend over for a quick kiss and to tell me to "be a good girl." I tell him, "I will be good" and then watch as he is led away. Everyone is crying, so I cry too.

In my early thirties, during a visit to my Aunt Ellie's (my mother's sister) and Uncle Dick's home in California, I learned the dream was true—that it was, in fact, my clearest memory I have of Richard, the man. My four-year old mind simply could not process all that happened that day. It was only later that I could identify the strangers who took away "my Daddy" as policemen.

Our family never discussed the subject of Richard (I don't feel accurate calling him "Dad"). Conversations included no birthday remembrances, no letters, no Richard. To this day I do not know why he was in prison. I can only speculate from the hushed dialogue I heard among the grown-ups, dialogue that suggested his incarceration was a result of his addictions and difficulties providing for his family.

Yet, despite his absence, my siblings and I always thought of Richard's mother as our grandmother and his sister as our aunt. On occasion we heard whispers when we visited our grandmother and aunt during summer vacation, but our family followed the "don't ask, don't tell rule." I do remember my grandmother introducing me once as Richard's daughter. A teenager at the time, I responded to the introduction negatively, with a scowl on my face, which probably saddened her.

Richard tried to contact us around 1964, but I wanted nothing to do with him. He had provided the biology to create my life, but borne none of the responsibility for my life beyond conception. He created the problems in his life, in part through addiction. Years later I asked my mother if she loved him. The expression on her face told me her answer—left me absolutely no doubt that she indeed once loved this man.

My father died at fifty years of age. My Uncle Dick once described him as "a lot of fun and full of the dickens." Despite his shortcomings as a father, I'm grateful to him for the role he played in my creation.

The day we left the home, the four of us knew we were lucky to be leaving. The other children placed there were orphans, but we stood waiting in the foyer for our mother and new stepfather, Art, to arrive and rescue us. (One fact that I find amazing: Richard and Art had the exact same birth date. I guess our Mom loved Cancers.) Mary Elizabeth clutched my hand. I clutched my favorite companion, a doll named "Candy Lou." Although uncertain where we were headed, we knew that a place called "L.A." had to be better than a place named after Odd Fellows. The prospect of going on this journey of hope together filled us with happiness.

Finally the Ford Coupe with our mom and new step-dad arrived, and without fanfare, our exodus began. The drive seemed long and hot—hardly the way for a seven-year-old to spend her birthday. But as I discovered early on, adults have considerable control over what happens to children.

As we pulled into the driveway on Madras Avenue, we saw "her." Standing there watering her roses, she seemed to be anticipating our arrival. When the car stopped and we emerged— weary, scared, and hungry—she found us. She scooped Mary Elizabeth and me into her larger-than-life bosoms, and hugged us like we hadn't been hugged in years. She politely shook hands with our older siblings, but focused on the two of us because she knew we would be in her care. She lived next door to the house our parents rented. Mom and Dad lived in the house for several months after moving to Los Angeles, and quickly formed a friendship with the woman who was to become our caregiver.

"Girls, this is your Aunt Nina," Mom declared. "She's been waiting to meet you children for weeks now." After the eternal hug, Aunt Nina placed us directly in front of her. She looked us over quite completely.

"You must be Mayree Beth—we have the same birthday, you know," she said as she stroked her head and hugged her again.

"And you, little darlin', must be Janie. Why you look just like Marilyn Mon-row." In just minutes, she had captured our hearts, as we had hers.

After unpacking and moving us officially into our new rooms, Mom told us that she would have to return to work the very next day. We felt disappointed; we had hardly had her to ourselves and we knew she missed us. But at least we knew she would be tucking us into our beds each night and listening to our prayers. Until then, both before and after school, Aunt Nina would be in charge. In spite of our sweet appearance, Mary Elizabeth and I knew that Aunt Nina would have her hands full! She seemed so warm and wonderful. Was she ready for two wounded, full-of-the-dickens little girls?

Aunt Nina spoke with an accent that came from somewhere unfamiliar to us, but we liked its rhythm and warmth. When she smiled, it came from her heart. Her eyes twinkled and every part of her being took on an upward motion. We soon discovered that the two of us were no match for this wise woman.

Our first morning in her charge, she allowed us to explore her garden while she worked planting fish heads and old rusty bolts into the soil beneath her roses.

"Why child, in order to make things grow, you must give them what they need," she said, sharing the first of many words of wisdom. She grew flowers, vegetables, fruit trees, and cats. They all flourished in her keeping.

Mary Elizabeth (or "Mayree Beth" to Aunt Nina) and I began our first day chasing cats. Aunt Nina had two favorites, Mischief and Itchybritches. Mischief was the mom, Itchy her wandering daughter. We soon learned that cats have sharp claws and do not like to be carried around like babies. Fortunately for us, Aunt Nina was a nurse, too. Unfortunately for us, she solved every non-life-threatening injury with iodine and merthiolate. We cried; she hugged, scrubbed, and applied her medicines of choice.

She told us, "Cats need gentle, loving care, just like all of God's creatures."

Summer ended and school began for all of us. Richie and Cathie went off to high school and junior high, respectively. They wanted little to do with their baby sisters. Mary and I could be real pests at times. Our siblings did not require the watchful eyes of a full-time babysitter like Aunt Nina.

Mary spent longer days with Aunt Nina whom she tested regularly. She learned that throwing a tantrum would never get her what she wanted from Aunt Nina, even though it worked with Mom. After one particularly tough confrontation, Mary left the room and slammed the door.

"Mayree Beth, come right back here. I want you to open and close the door quietly fifty times!" Mayree couldn't count, so Aunt Nina did the honors. On the final count of fifty, Mayree slammed the door again.

"All right, missy, we begin again, but now one hundred times." With Aunt Nina, winning was not an option unless you were playing gin-rummy.

Spring and summer, when everything around her blossomed and ripened, always found Aunt Nina at her best. She made jam from her apricot trees, baked rhubarb pies, and taught us how to crochet rag rugs using our fingers. She mixed grape and lemon Kool-aid, and made the best sandwiches in the world. The love she showered on everything showed in how everyone and everything around her responded.

I remember sitting on her back porch cradling a dying Mischief in my arms. I prayed hard for that cat to stay with me. Aunt Nina came to me and said, "Darlin', you have comforted this cat when she needed you, just as she comforted you when you needed her. She's old and needs to move on. Tell her 'goodbye.'" I did, and she died a short time later. No stranger to loss, Aunt Nina hugged and cried with me. She assured me I had no need to be afraid, that everyone and everything on this earth has its time.

Once a neighbor boy spit on Mary and me. Disgusted, we ran home where Aunt Nina wanted to know what we had done about it. "Why, we spit back," I exclaimed, thinking retaliation was the right thing to do. We soon learned different, as Aunt Nina told us a story about her daughter Linda. While riding the bus in Chicago, Linda had spit on a little boy. When Aunt Nina asked Linda why, she answered, "Because he's a colored boy."

This was clearly *not* the right answer.

At first Aunt Nina, too, thought perhaps the young boy should spit right back on Linda, but after thinking about it, she realized that to retaliate would only escalate the situation.

"Linda, apologize to this young man, right now," she told her daughter. "We have been put on this earth together. We must respect one another."

Aunt Nina once caught me on the sofa kissing with her nephew Ben. She said to me, "Janie, kissing with boys is not in good taste!"

I replied, "But Aunt Nina, it sure tasted good to me!" Benny agreed. (She recalled the story for me every time we visited, even into my adulthood.)

We were blessed to have spent time in our Aunt Nina's garden. Although not related to us by blood, we consider her a relative of our hearts. She not only planted a soil garden, she became a master of the soul garden. Our time with her was short, yet magical. She managed to imprint her wit, wisdom, and humor onto everyone she met. I often thought of her as a cross between Barbara Bush and Jimmy Carter's mother, Miss Lillian. She married a widower who lived in a nearby suburb and continued gardening into her eighties. Aunt Nina tales are stored sweetly in my memory bank, richly gaining interest, never withdrawn.

I continued "Janie-dom" into the mid-fifties. I had a mother, stepfather, sisters, brother, and a home with a dog in Norwalk, a Los Angeles suburb—one of the roughest areas in L.A. and a place that could have led me on the road to destruction. The friends I chose were not the best influence on me, nor was I on them. Another man stabbed my father during an altercation, and I can still remember seeing the blood our neighbor's head left on the pavement after her husband beat her. Mary and I looked at the spot every day until it gradually disappeared.

We had been supervised for most of our early years, but we experienced too much freedom there. Our father's work in construction kept him away from home much of the time, and our mother worked a job that demanded a long commute each day.

While I had incredible role models like my Aunt Nina, and a great, wholesome friend named John Smith, I flitted around with Jayne Mansfield in mind. I smoked at about nine years of age and went to the movies with Nancy Manning, older than me in age, attitude, and physical development. I envied her breasts. We always managed to find boys to make out with during weekend matinees of *Old Yeller* and *Davy Crockett*. Ages ten and eleven could have been my undoing because of my environment and my adolescent need to be accepted.

Our new dad ruled us with fear. Art was a hard-working, hard-drinking man who had a presence larger than life. He legally adopted my siblings and me in 1960. Legally and on our birth-certificates, Richard was no longer our father. While Art loved us the best he could, loved our mother with all the heart he could muster, and she loved him in return, he had a knack for instilling guilt and fear over the slightest infringement of his rules. He could react with little provocation, so we walked lightly. His words could sting, and being a large, strong man, when he brought out his belt or warned of a spanking, I cringed. He had a booming voice and giant's laugh.

Mostly I remember trying to "keep the peace," because that made life much easier for me. Mom spent so much of her life trying to make things work smoothly for him. She literally spoiled him rotten. Fear and indebtedness worked against her; after all, Art had rescued her children from spending their lives in a children's home. From her I learned how to be a co-dependent—how to sacrifice self for the neediness of another.

We eventually left this environment for Phoenix, Arizona—the move allowed me to slip back into an age of innocence. Life moved at a slower pace. The streets were safer and quieter than in L.A.

Though other people probably thought of us as "trailer-trash," we weren't aware of it. We were surrounded by a neighborhood that consisted of the richest of rich and the poorest of poor. This made for an acceptance of others I hold as one of my greatest values now.

I still liked to make-out, and gained an undeserved reputation as "Jane, you ignorant slut" long before Dan Akroyd made the phrase popular on *Saturday Night Live*. I believed others held this image of me, and I found it a difficult one to live with. I felt "less-than." Peers whispered and gossiped. All because of the simple fact that I dated boys, was "boy crazy," and especially loved to kiss—a practice not well accepted during my teen years. Society and parents in the sixties continually delivered the lecture, "Nice girls don't do 'it.'" I was still basically a good girl, attending church, school dances and such. Yet boys whom I never even dated called me "slut" and similar names. They judged me rather harshly, based upon false rumors. The truth is, I held out as long as I could—though kissed whenever I could—and moved out of the age of innocence as simply "Jane." I left with my internal reputation intact and knew that being "Jane" was OK.

The autumn of 1963 followed an awesome teen summer. I played. I danced. I dated with the abandon of a sixteen-year-old, knowing that going too far could end with disastrous results. (After all, hadn't my father warned me?)

My favorite song that summer was, "We'll Sing in the Sunshine." I remember all the "beach" songs that led us into frenzied dance at the local "teen" nightclubs: "JD's" and "The Armory." Dancing was freedom, music our drug. We rivaled all the beach party movies in California, and spent our summer as wannabe surfer chicks. When it ended, I felt a kind of sadness I had never felt before. Was it the end of innocence?

When my junior year of high school year started, I didn't, at least not mentally. I found it difficult to attend school, but I did anyway. I felt the need for some independence, some spending money of my own. I had always done baby-sitting, house cleaning, and odd jobs for extra cash, but now I felt the need to get a "real" job to support my '47 Jeep. It always seemed to need something— tires, an oil change…car things. I was leaping into young adulthood.

My friends were content to go to football games and hang with the "in" crowd. This did not seem to be enough for me. I found them all somewhat childish and "cliquish." They excluded anyone who didn't look like them, talk like them (groovy, you know?), or listen to the same music. I wanted to make my break from the mainstream sixteen-year-olds.

My first great career choice was to become a carhop at Dog-n-Suds Root Beer. Applying for that first job was relatively simple. I had come recommended by my friend's sister. The pay was fifty cents an hour plus tips. Wow! This was some real money! So, in taking my first steps toward liberation, I carried fully loaded trays of root beer, Coney dogs, and sundaes out to cars. Lucky for me, we did not have to wear roller skates. When the drive-in movie let out, we earned our keep.

One day near Halloween, the 1960, pink Thunderbird convertible pulled into my section of the root beer stand. Dressed like "Daisy Mae," I felt quite confident in my appearance that night. Yet I felt completely unprepared as my eyes met the bluest eyes and flashiest white teeth I had ever seen. *(Whoa...what's this feeling?)* I thought he *must* be related to Elvis. A dreamboat man with a dreamboat car. I'm certain he noticed the shaky hands that delivered his order. *(Wait a minute, I'm almost out of breath!)* My co-worker arrived, and she just happened to know this hunk. He was her boyfriend's brother. She introduced us and invited us to go to a Halloween party after work. *(Is this luck or what?)*

I could hardly keep my mind on what I needed to do for the rest of the shift. He hung around until quitting time. *(Please...I can hardly stand it. What is going on in my head, in my heart?)* Finally, we closed up the root beer stand and I was on my way to the party, riding with the top down, sitting on leather seats, next to a hunk, in a Thunderbird convertible. At sixteen, does it get any better than this?

I have no memories of the party. The hunk and I talked for what seemed like endless hours until I remembered my curfew and he drove me back to my Jeep. It was an autumn night to remember. A cool breeze, full moon and warmed heart.

That's when *it* happened. Gazing into one another's eyes and anticipating each move, our lips met—gently, breathlessly, and with ease I had never experienced when kissing "boys." I had always loved to kiss, but now I realized that I had never truly been kissed.

Finally we said "goodnight." My feet did not touch the ground as I walked to my car. I wanted to twirl around and dance, but thought better of it. I didn't want to appear childish; after all, a "real" man had just kissed me.

I wish I could write about "happily ever-after," but it was not to be. I learned that Prince Charming could be a toad after all, though memories of that kiss still linger. I've experienced the sensation since, thanks to knowing and experiencing a love that endures all. When I met my husband-to-be, Les, I learned that love and being loved has to do with give and take, not just take.

Les and I married in December of 1967. We settled into married life as most young couples do. We lived very well, buying a new sports car and enjoying "the good life." We took a trip to San Francisco to celebrate our first year of marriage, stopping in Santa Barbara to watch the sun rise over the Pacific before driving on to the Bay Area with the top down on our little yellow Austin Healy Sprite. This was more like the honeymoon I had dreamed of, and worth the wait. We ate at Fisherman's Wharf and picnicked on food from the neighborhood deli.

Upon our return home, Les went to work for a corporation that helped to subsidize his schooling, while I worked full time in a dental office. One day after work, I walked into our apartment to find a pyramid of beer cans on the coffee table. In the midst of the mess, I saw a letter with the salutation, "Greetings from the President of the United States."

"What's this?" I cried. "I thought school deferred you from the draft?" Les admitted to me that he had signed up for fewer classes that semester and it had taken the draft board three months to catch up with him. This was 1968, the height of the Viet Nam conflict. Terrified, we had only a few weeks to figure out what we needed to do. I tearfully drove him to the draft office. Even as I said "goodbye" to him at the airport later that day, we had no idea where he was headed.

He survived basic training and decided it would be better to enlist in the regular Army for three years' training as a radar repairman, than to go to Viet Nam as an Infantryman.

While stationed at Fort Knox, Kentucky, I discovered that poverty and racism not only lived, but thrived in America—an eye-opening experience for a westerner like me. There I also developed a strong distaste for a partner who drank too much alcohol while out with the "guys." This was one of the times in my marriage that I truly thought about leaving. Fortunately we were poor enough that I couldn't return "home" without asking for money from my parents to pay for a bus ticket. I had too much pride for that. Besides, I had just found out I was pregnant.

The very threat of his being sent to the war prompted our decision to get pregnant. I wanted a part of him with me in case the orders to leave for Viet Nam arrived. When I reflect on this, I have to admit that it wasn't the smartest decision that I ever made, but it turned out to be one of the best. God blessed us with our daughter, Shari.

When the orders came for him to go to Viet Nam, I can remember crying out, "Oh, God!" I could not imagine my life with him or without him.

Les moved me into his parents' home so I could spend the remaining time of my pregnancy in safety and comfort. We spent a magical time together before he left for the war. He built baby furniture and turned his childhood bedroom into a nursery and safe haven for me. We went to movies, talked of the future, and loved each other more than we had words for.

Les left for Viet Nam six weeks before Shari was born. We had been married less than three years. To this day I have difficulties watching arrivals and departures at airports. Watching him cross the tarmac to board the plane felt surreal—not only because my husband was leaving to fight in a war, but because Ronald McDonald the clown, who was boarding the same plane, walked beside him.

I began to cry so hard I could hardly breathe. It was the kind of twisted cry that comes from a place of broken-heartedness one hopes never to experience too many times in life. On the drive home, I listened to John Denver singing "Leaving on a Jet Plane" on the radio. With every word, the pain of our situation rose to a crescendo deep within my being.

Shari was born in June of 1970, after a long and difficult labor. Les's mother held steadfast in her support throughout the process, but something in me held back from giving birth. A family friend brought along a nun to hold my hand and console and coach me through the increasing hours. Finally, thirty hours later, and with a classroom of nursing students present, I gave birth. Shari looked beautiful to me, even with her lopsided head.

The mailman and I became good friends. I spent every day without Les in waiting. I could tell by how the mailman approached the mailbox whether he had any letters for me or not. Sometimes the Army would put a moratorium on the mail coming from Viet Nam and I wouldn't receive word on his whereabouts or safety. These times seemed like an eternity. When people asked if I had heard from him, I had to put up a brave front and say that I hadn't received any news for a while. I can still remember nursing the baby in the middle of the night with prayers on my lips and tears streaming down my cheeks in fear he wouldn't return.

I wrote to Les every day. I sent cookies and sunflower seeds, paperbacks, and stacks of photos of the baby and me—although Les admitted later that he didn't display the photos until she was three months old, because he thought she was funny-looking.

Every day Les's father would plot his whereabouts and the locations of the latest fire fights on a map of Viet Nam. He paced and worried.

When the baby was fourteen weeks old, the three of us managed to connect in Hawaii for a week of R&R (rest and relaxation). Just old enough to smile, laugh, and poop, Shari kept our focus away from the reality that he had to return. Les arrived from Viet Nam sick, with a fever and sore throat. We knew if he went to sickbay he would be isolated and our time together would be over. He toughed it out and we still had a wonderful time. After months of working out with weights, Les had arrived in a new package. No longer pregnant, I, too, looked rather fine. We did a few touristy things, but mostly we were content to stay wrapped in each other's arms in our hotel room.

Then came another tear-filled departure, another airport goodbye. I had planned to stay a few days longer in Hawaii, but without Les, I couldn't wait to return to the safety of home. His tour was half over now and I was a grown-up woman.

When he returned from Viet Nam, one year after he had left, we discovered the experience had changed us both dramatically. He expected to come home to his naïve young bride, but found a young mother with a child he barely knew. I sensed nothing seemed familiar to him. He kept looking around as if he had returned from a dream.

He never talked much about Viet Nam, only about the friends he had made there. He brought back some photos that we placed in an album. Some of the photos pained me, especially the one taken of prisoners locked in triangular cages barely large enough for the prisoners to sit cross-legged. A South Vietnamese guard stood over them with his weapon. While I couldn't see the prisoners' faces, I couldn't help but to view them as someone's brothers or fathers or sons.

I can't imagine all that happened during that war. Many of us who lived through the experience—soldiers and their families alike—don't talk much about it. Don't ask, don't tell. One thing I know for sure, I welcomed Les home with open arms and a heart filled with gratitude that he had returned safely.

During the late sixties and into the seventies, I saw myself as "Jane Doe"—a woman with no clear identity—while the neighbors saw me as "the granola mom" of the neighborhood—a woman who had it all together. I baked bread, made my own peanut butter, wore wire-rimmed glasses, shopped the farmers' market, and protected my children from food additives.

As "Jane Doe" I would crawl into the darkness and safety of my bed after the children had gone to school. The dishes stacked up and the laundry beckoned as I dreamed of a life of peace and serenity that I was not living. I felt as though I wasn't living a life at all, only pretending. Placing one foot in front of the other, I honored the commitments I made, but not without difficulty. I suffered with migraine headaches and severe menstrual cramps (good excuses to crawl back into bed). I don't know how I hid this Jane Doe from the rest of the world, but I did. Time and time again, she would emerge from the darkness to serve others, silently screaming out for acceptance.

Wise to my depression, my gynecologist wrote me a prescription for Valium. I never filled it. Valium did not match my granola mom image.

This was a time when young motherhood and being a "housewife" cast many women into a state that seemed to imply they really didn't matter. I had two babies, a daughter and a son, whom I determined to cultivate into independent, fear-free, confident, risk-taking adults. My goal was to instill in them all the attributes that I felt more than lacking in my own life. (It works beautifully to transfer your ideals; it takes the focus off of oneself.)

I felt fearful of everything, unable to distinguish cause for real fear (very little, in hindsight) from imaginary horrors. Believing even the slightest fever to be life threatening, I kept a standing appointment with our pediatrician. (So much for creating fear-free children!) Every bump, scrape, or conflict sent me into immediate fear of a major life crisis. I wanted their childhood to be pain-free, precious, and filled with bliss. In hindsight, I believe I had an addiction to the drama.

I felt cast into an abyss. I absolutely could not see my life's purpose, much less believe my life had any worth. Women's lib encouraged others to ask, "What do you do?" and "What is your degree in?" Though unafraid to discuss, cuss or speak out in a rebellious, *Jane Fonda* sort of way, without pedigree or college diploma, I felt I didn't matter.

The turning point came when I suddenly realized that I was unable to feel anything. For one who most always knew that good can come from most any situation, this numbness signaled a change. My husband of ten years was doing his own thing—climbing the corporate ladder, going to graduate school, taking care of the cars and yard—all while a functioning alcoholic. Blaming him for my upheaval might have been convenient, but it would not have been true. We were not conjoined at the hip; he had his issues, I had mine. And I was spiritually, mentally, and physically bankrupt.

I hit rock bottom the day of my tenth wedding anniversary. In the midst of the holidays, I could find no Christ in my Christmas. I dreaded the holidays, as they usually involved a dramatic alcohol event, too much money spent, and two over-excited, over-indulged children. Again, the over-indulgence was my issue, not theirs. I kept myself busy baking and decking the halls. On the Saturday before a week packed with Christmas programs and the frenetic rush to create my *Saturday Evening Post* holiday, everything came to a screeching halt.

I first noticed a slight backache while at a Christmas parade. I wondered whether the pain was real or imagined. After the parade, I returned home and finally admitted the pain was real. I was certain that with this amount of pain, I had to be a candidate for death. I had my husband take me to the emergency room. (Did I mention that he was not sober?)

After spending the night going through x-rays and almost dying from the x-ray dye (How ironic would that be?), it was determined that my kidneys were trying to pass what felt like a boulder through my urinary tract. By comparison giving birth was a piece of cake, and the finished product could someday grow up to be President. After five days in the hospital, I pleaded with my physician to release me for the sake of my wedding anniversary and my children's perfect holiday. Once I promised that I would call if there were any changes in my condition, such as not being able to pee, he relented and sent me home with pain medication.

I spent my anniversary home alone in bed, the same evening of my husband's office Christmas party. That night I delivered some real healthy kidney stones. The wonderful pain medication wasn't, the *Saturday Evening Post* Christmas wasn't. The spirit of children laughing with glee wasn't either. I did, however, come to a realization that I was sick and tired of being sick and tired. I knew I needed to take the steps to heal myself, body and soul.

I started attending Alanon meetings for family and friends of alcoholics. I also started treatment with an incredible psychologist who specialized in chemical dependency. I finally learned to listen. Listen to that voice within that told me not to fear, but to pay attention—the voice that assured me the crisis I was experiencing was like a phone call from God. My journey into the dark abyss was filled with lessons and did not go for naught.

I learned from Alanon that one does not cause, cure or control people who are addicted. I was not a victim of an alcoholic unless I chose to be. There is a Power far greater than self in charge. Through Alanon, I discovered the term "co-dependent," and learned that I was one. Though a master of taking care of other people and their lives, I could not do what I needed to do to take care of myself. I learned that this program is, in fact, selfish.

I also learned to separate the addicted individual from his or her behavior. I could say with honesty during this time, "Thank God for placing addicted people in my life." They proved to be the catalyst I needed for my own personal growth. My mantra became the "Serenity Prayer": *God grant me the serenity to accept the things I cannot change, the courage to change the things I can, and the wisdom to know the difference.*

Alanon threw me a lifeline.

I became a homeroom mother, soccer coach and player. I began a spiritual quest, took classes on eliminating self-defeating behaviors, went to Alanon, and joined a sorority. I served on election boards, worked on elections and campaigns, and worked with the schools to help prevent drug and alcohol abuse. I developed leadership skills I never knew I possessed. I figured out that no part of me fit the image of "Jane, you ignorant slut!" I also stepped out of the "Jane Doe-ism" that seemed to hold me in a bout of darkness and depression. I climbed out of the abyss into the light, feeling amazed at the process.

I worked in dental offices and at various other jobs over the years. While these experiences helped build the independence I needed to feel secure in myself, they did not fulfill or define me. I worked for a while in a retirement community and if I heard, "Me Tarzan, you Jane," just one more time... Yes it's true; life at times can be a jungle, but Tarzan was definitely a myth that I was not living. Once a dear friend said, "I've been married and unmarried many times during my relationship." I could totally relate. I've been married now for thirty-four years. Not always easy years, but always interesting ones.

I can state easily that being Jane, just Jane, has meant walking miles in shoes that have grown more comfortable with each step of the journey. The stories are mine to share. They are the path on which my shoes have led me. Out of darkness, into light. Stories created in an image that illuminates the Spirit within.

In so many of my favorite stories from this journey, Mary is there, reminding me of the value of sisterhood. Mary and I have walked down different paths throughout our lives, but we always manage to link up in a way that only sisters can. We have our own sorority of sorts. We have shared the same losses and many of the same laughs. We have shared cribs, beds, and automobiles. We don't share the same political views and, upon occasion, butt heads. We've fought, but we've made up. No matter what, she is always my baby sister. Mary has been a constant relationship in my life, one that has matured as I have. Our bonding shares a common thread: our mother.

Mary and I have managed some memorable road trips together. She and I look back on one in particular—the one we refer to, with a touch of sick humor, as the "trip that killed Mom." Mom, Mary, and I traveled together on a ten-day excursion that included a wedding, a reunion and reconciliation with our aunt and grandmother, and a trek on the eastern slopes of the Sierra Nevadas. We fed Mom all the wrong foods, kept her up much too late, and teased her endlessly. It was wonderful. After our return home she was diagnosed with cancer. We had a grand seventieth birthday celebration without the knowledge that the time we had left to share would be so brief. A few months later, Mary and I shared in our mother's final "road trip"—a sad, but sacred experience.

Our family dubbed Mary and me "Thelma and Louise" after a trip up the coast of California to attend another family wedding. We drove up the coast highway, stopping to see whatever struck our fancy. (Did you know the largest fig tree in the U.S. is in Santa Barbara?) We had an extraordinary time on this trip and at the wedding. Without the bondage of our spouses and children, we joyously returned to our youthful roles as the mischievous sisters. We danced, played, laughed, and dared anyone to step into that realm of knowing what only sisters know. Little did we know, however, as we left our cousin's home, what we were stepping into. To this day the whole adventure feels somewhat unreal to me, though, to quote Dave Barry, "I swear I'm not making this up!"

Our cousin lives east of the San Francisco Bay, so we started our trip early in the day. We checked the oil, tires, etc. We hugged, kissed, and waved goodbye.

Mary and I decided to drive to Laughlin, Nevada. This route offered a short-cut home to Phoenix that included a drive across the Mohave Desert. We wanted to add a day to our sisterly bonding. We took turns driving, deciding that when the car reached 100,000 miles, we would stop the car to dance on the hood.

I loved this sports car! We filled up with gas and made a comfort stop before heading into the California desert. Mary was driving when suddenly the car just stopped running...no warning, no unusual sounds, nothing. As we pulled over, raised the hood and wondered when the proverbial knight in shining armor would appear to rescue us, we remembered the phones placed every few miles in this desert. (No one owned cell phones then.) A couple in a pickup truck stopped and offered to drive us to a call box. The heat of the day approached. We jumped in the truck and rode about a mile to the phone. We arrived at the call box, called the California Highway Patrol, who immediately warned us, "Do not accept rides with anyone under any circumstances!" We had already broken Rule Number One! We motioned to the couple in the truck that we had everything under control and they could leave. We were thankful to see them go.

The Highway Patrol wanted to know the names of our next of kin. How comforting. They asked if they could send a tow truck. How perceptive. I spoke with the tow operator, gave our location and my AAA number and we walked a very long, hot mile back to the car.

While we waited for the AAA tow truck, Mary and I decided we needed another comfort station REAL quick. I am only slightly exaggerating when I say that Mary solved the Mohave Desert's drought problem that day. I shielded her from any possibility of a public display of indecency, but could do nothing about the stream that became quite apparent to Chuck, the tow truck driver.

Now Chuck was quite a sight—a big man with missing teeth— not at all the knight we had wished for. A very friendly guy, he stated that he had not met up with too many women driving alone on this road. Chuck went to work hooking my car up to the tow truck, which meant he had to bend over to reach under the car, thus revealing the Grand Canyon of butt-cracks. Now Mary and I have never been able to hide our snickers, laughs, guffaws or giggles when something hits us funny. Only minutes after watering the desert, Mary peed her pants. Fortunately, Chuck thought that Mary and I were hysterical because of the heat and circumstances.

Chuck drove us into the town of Boron, where we pulled up to Jim's Automotive, a AAA-approved garage. Boy, that comforted me right away.

As Mary and I bid farewell to Chuck, he offered to drive us to Laughlin. Thanks, we said, but no thanks.

A woman named "Nan" greeted us at the garage. Nan was pleasant enough, but tough enough to be scary. She wore a baseball cap and a t-shirt that read, "God made nipples to make suckers out of men!" (*Mary, please do NOT laugh, we are in danger here!*) Nan called Jim—a friendly, six-foot-tall, one-armed mechanic—away from his lunch to take a look at the car. We must have had a look of desperation on our faces, because after some deliberation, he said, "I can have the car ready in a few days for a couple of thousand dollars." In that moment I had to admit to myself that this car I loved was only worth a couple of thousand dollars. And I knew we couldn't fathom a two-day stay in the Boron Motel; that is, if one existed. After calling home, we decided to leave the car in storage at Jim's Automotive and return to tow it home ourselves.

Growing weary of Nan's entertainment, we asked if we could catch a bus nearby. Nan offered to drive us to the Rexall Drug/ Greyhound Bus Station, but informed us that we only had fifteen minutes before it closed at six o'clock.

A few minutes later she pulled up in an old Toyota. Struggling to keep it running by pumping the gas pedal, she hollered, "Jump in!" The contents of the car—dishes, food wrappers, baskets of clothing—told us we were sitting in someone's home, a home that only looked like a Toyota. Mary and I exchanged looks of utter amazement.

We traversed the two-lane road at break-neck speed, arriving at the Rexall in the nick of time.

"Can we get a ticket to Laughlin?" I asked at the ticket window.

"No, but you can get a ride to Blythe for the night," offered a rather non-descript (for once) clerk.

She convinced us to ride to Blythe, and then on to Phoenix the next morning. We bought the tickets and then asked, "Where is the bus station?"

"You are at it," she replied.

Mary and I knew the Rexall would be closing in a few minutes and the bus wouldn't arrive until 7:30 or 8:00.

"Where do we catch the bus?" we asked, expecting there would be a bench or someplace to hang out until the bus arrived.

"You watch for it on the highway, right out front," the clerk replied. "Be ready to flag it down in case they don't know we sold you a seat!"

Mary and I slowly descended into disbelief. Tired, dusty, hungry, and in need of some humor, we headed to the highway in front of the Rexall, sat on our over-packed suitcases and watched the Friday night traffic drive through Boron. A few people slowed down to gaze at the two strange sisters who had ventured into town on that hot summer day. Mary and I pretended we were watching a parade and waved to all who passed by. This was good practice for the Greyhound.

We were fortunate to have a comfort station available: some nearby bushes.

The bus finally arrived, and quite promptly. We loaded our luggage and collapsed into our seats.

"Hey Mary, we're headed for Laughlin," I exclaimed.

As the bus pulled into Laughlin, Nevada, the driver informed us that we could not leave our seats, as this was just a "pick-up" stop for passengers. With no fight left in us, and our luggage stored underneath the bus, we became enthralled at the thought of what great adventure might await us in Blythe, California.

In retrospect, we could have allowed this experience to turn us into fearful, angry, miserable, whining women, but we didn't. We thoroughly enjoyed our venture into Boron, even with all its oddities. I'm certain we seemed quite odd to the people there, too. After all, how often do "Thelma and Louise" drop in?

At times, life as we know it feels challenging. How amazingly funny reality can be. To be blessed with humor is one of the greatest gifts of all. Being able to share it with a sister is even more precious.

I truly look forward to many more road trips, filled with all of life's experiences. I feel equipped to drive down the road of the unknown even without a map. Whether on foot or in a convertible, I hope I am able to feel the wind in my face with every mile, or the earth beneath my feet with every step.

Reflections on the Present

*...I knew for certain the shoes on my feet were beyond magic.
I returned them to the place where I found them...*

Here I am, exactly four months away from "double nickels."
I'm midway through my fifties and quite pleased about it. Turn-
ing fifty was one of the best things that ever happened to me. I
can't exactly explain it, but suddenly I felt that I knew the mean-
ing of most of my life experiences. Would I change anything? I
don't believe that living with regrets of any kind serves me. Was I
a willing pupil in this school of life? I know that when I could stay
afloat and ride the wave, it was one hell of a ride. When I whined,
feared, resisted, and raged, I came close to sinking into the depths
of an extremely dark abyss, so I truly tried not to sink.

I now live in the present, love with an open heart, pray daily,
continue to learn all I can to enrich my spirit, and spend time in
gratitude each day. I am able to look in the mirror and love that
person looking back at me. She is wiser, funnier, softer, kinder,
more truthful, and more confident than she ever was in her twen-
ties or thirties. OK, so she's chubbier, but overall, she's in a lot
better shape.

I've experienced some painful losses—of parents, siblings, and
friends—but I'm aware that if I hadn't had these teachers in my
life, I would be lacking in some important lessons. In my mind's
eye, I can call forth these souls as needed. My mother's influence
continues to comfort and guide me. At times, I must confess, I
respond to situations much the same as she would. My losses
have also taught me about the sacredness of death. The experi-
ence has always been as sacred as birth to me. Both involve in-
tense labor, pain, and release. Birth and death are manifesta-
tions of my own belief system. During both experiences, I've borne
witness to another seeing the "Light." Both birth and death sig-
nal a completion and a new beginning. I remain in gratitude.

I've been able to learn my lessons about addictions, my own and those that affected many of the people I love most in my life. The disease of alcoholism continually knocked on my door. While I was not the alcoholic, I learned all about co-dependency and that I needed treatment myself. (The sign that you are co-dependent: When you die and someone else's life passes before you.) The disease only became a problem for me when I let it. I educated myself about the disease. I went to school to become a "Chemical Dependency Counselor" and worked in the schools on programs to prevent drug and alcohol abuse. I witnessed others choosing to go to treatment for their disease. Have we broken the cycle? I hope and pray so. Have I had to confront the role I played in this drama? Did I have to confront my own obsessions and difficulties that surfaced from the presence of these people in my life? Yes, thank you very much. The pain I experienced as a result of these people, places, and events served as my catalyst for growth.

My life continues to be blessed with abundance. I have never been in a space of lack. I've never gone hungry or been without shelter. Whatever I desire becomes manifest. I've learned that "I need" is not the same as "I want," though the two can be confused. I've learned that shopping was always a stopover, not a cure, though I must admit, having to decide whether to buy tennis shoes or a nursing bra shook my faith in this philosophy. I've learned that all I need is a relationship with God and with myself. In Spirit, all that I need is always present. This relationship blossomed with my becoming a Chaplain at the church I attend. This enriched my prayer life and allowed me the privilege of learning how to pray with others.

I just love hindsight.

My saving "grace" has been humor. I can look at situations with a sense that a joke was being played on me. When I reflect on my life, many of the situations could have played out like tragedies, but some of the most dramatic were also the most humorous (such as the time my spouse nailed me out of my own house, which does seem pretty funny now). Even during our mother's dying process, my sisters and I teased her. She wouldn't have had it any other way. Yes, we cried, but we also laughed with her. She had the greatest laugh and sense of humor in all situations.

Speaking of mothers, I can say with honesty I've done my best as one. My children can be certain that I have always loved them. They've been incredible teachers for me. I see their "light" so clearly. From the moment of their births, their spirits were fully operational. The "gifts" they have to share do not go unnoticed. I tried not to rob them of their pride in achievement. Both are high achievers and critical of themselves.

Their father and I share our gifts of organization, humor, competitive spirit, wit, and overall good nature, along with some of our less-than-admirable qualities. I have learned that my children have their own paths to follow. The lessons they must learn are their own. I'm in the process of learning to keep my mouth shut, though I find this practice difficult. Bearing witness to their challenges isn't easy either.

Things have happened along this journey that could have implanted bitterness, rage, resentment, or caused estrangement from family and friends. These are "sinking words" for me. The best lessons have been to live, laugh, love, and learn. I will continue to kiss the earth, hike the mountains, laugh at myself, pray often, and look at whatever life gives me through my spiritual eyes.

> *Would I change*
> *what I've experienced,*
> *or change the choices made,*
> *or leave the words unspoken*
> *for another day? NEVER*

I can honestly say I am amazed to declare myself as a writer, poet, Chaplain, and woman of wisdom at this age. If I cease to be amazed at this experience, then I cease to be.

Reflections on the Future

...I know for certain that these shoes will always be waiting for me, supporting me in All Ways, directing and guiding me to the Infinite...

A wise man named Bob Rizzo once told me, "all we have is today, tomorrow and the to-now." The reality is, all we have is "to-now." The future is blessed with mystery and the unknown. All the plans we make can change in a heartbeat. As I read through the reflections of my past, I fail to see the mention of any long-term goals. I find this somewhat amusing, and at the same time wonder if it is a measure of where I plan on going. There have been times in my life that when I looked to the future, I found fear staring right into my face. Times when I couldn't even face the present. Times when the darkness was more powerful than the Light. I can also remember feeling superstitious about the future. I believed if I spoke the words of something I wanted to happen, I jinxed the possibility of whatever "it" was.

Does this mean I never had goals? Of course I did. Did I ever make plans? If I failed to make plans I probably would have had ten or more children. I've made lists of things I wanted to manifest, and they usually manifested, especially if they were truly my heart's desire. I find that interesting.

During a discussion with my husband in the 1980s, the only goal I made was neither tangible nor monetary. It's a goal I continue to hold to this day. If I can make every person I come in contact with a little better for the experience, then I have succeeded in living my life the way I want it to be. I'm able to practice my relationships with others daily and be fully present in the "to-now."

I do want to hike the Grand Canyon rim to rim before I'm sixty. This is a reflection of a larger goal of touching, smelling, and feeling the earth beneath my feet.

I also hope to become a grandmother—a dream that depends upon my children. Nevertheless, I will love the children who are already present on this earth. I will love them unconditionally and look for the lessons they were brought here to teach.

I can sum up my most current list of "I wants." I want to live my life to the fullest. I want to grow into my magnificence. I want to continue to seek knowledge, and I want to share my abundance with others. As a poet and dreamer, I keep life simple.

I've learned through writing and sharing that I have a voice— a voice that is no more and no less perfect than any other voice. It has a right to be heard. I want my voice to resonate from the tops of the highest mountains, blessing and comforting in prayer those who are in need, creating an atmosphere of humor and laughter whenever possible, and reaching into the depth of my soul to remind me of my soul's purpose. Now this excites me! My dreams are filled with possibilities of magnificence far beyond any of my experiences to date.

Being in the present reflects my dreams for the future. I can see clearly and stay focused on the path before me in a state of knowing that whatever my dreams, I can make them manifest through God. I feel a sense of knowing that a collective power far greater than self is not only within me, it *is* me. In truth, the future exists and I AM living it…right here, to-now.

The shoes from yesterday
don't fit...
no matter
how I tried.
First my toes,
then my heels...
they wouldn't fit inside!
I sat upon my floor in tears,
for all they represent...
they are a compilation,
of who I am
and time I've spent.
A love lost here,
a dance or two...
wrapped up tight
in these old shoes.
Walking the path
of childhood dreams
flying kites, strawberries and cream
Carrying me to classrooms
where lessons often taught,
conform to thoughts of others
and questions go for naught.
It's past the time—
release them
they've led you on the path...
that takes you to the morrow,
a time that never lasts.
When shoes don't fit
remember...
it means that you have grown.
Into another garden
plant the seeds your
soul has sown...

In Our Shoes

Karolyne's Shoes

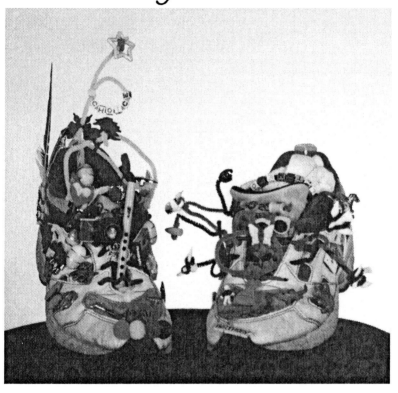

In Our Shoes

Fable

Step, Click, and then…Wisdom

She sits all morning listening to others, witnessing their pain and offering an invitation to embrace life. Her heart fills with compassion and admiration for their courage. After a long and rewarding morning, it is time for a break. She stands, stretches, and picks up the flute a Native American friend made for her. Each time she touches the flute, it brings to her a mixture of grief and comfort. Her friend died five years ago. Since then, playing the flute is as important to her life as breathing. She leaves her office, walks across the adjacent meadow, and settles into her favorite meditation spot under an enormous old pine tree. The tree is a true "grandfather" to the surrounding forest.

She plays her flute until she can feel the sound coming as much from the inside of her body as through her breath to the outside. She sets the flute aside, stretches out in the spring grass, and looks up into the branches of the ancient Ponderosa Pine tree. Light and shadow dance on the inside of her eyelids, her body and breath unite and the sounds fill her totally. Colors swirl magenta and yellow, deep purple and black.

CLICK. Her mind registers a sound.

She returns her mind to her breath.

CLICK, CLICK, *Odd*, she thinks, *it sounds like the shutter of a camera.*

CLICK. She turns over and reluctantly opens her eyes. She blinks, and then REALLY opens her eyes! *What the?*

About two feet away, CLICK, the lens of a miniature 35-milometer camera points, CLICK, at her face. The camera is attached, along with other things, to a dirty tennis shoe.

She recognizes the shoe as one of a pair she wore walking the earth in many places of the world. She recognizes the stains of red dirt both from Kenya and the Australian Outback, the mud from the lake shore at her summer cabin, barbecue sauce from a cookout, and purple stretch laces purchased in Hawaii. Other newer items attached to the shoe include: a wooden flute that looks like the one lying next to her, a pink arc full of the worlds' animals, and brightly colored wooden eggs moving as if they are ready to hatch. A white dove perches on the toe of the shoe and occasionally drinks from a small, blue pond. The pond is so clear, she sees through it to the fabric of the shoe. Something is written in the water. She blinks and moves a bit closer to read it. The word IMAGINATION shows through the clear blue of the pond.

CLICK, goes the camera; the dove is still. She notices the dove has no eyes. She leans forward for a closer look and sees her face reflected by the pond. Her face is wrinkled with remembered smiles, concentration and pain—a face gathering the wisdom of her life, the face of an elder. Behind her the branches of the ancient pine are imperfectly perfect. The sun filters through, dappling the reflection. Light and shadow define one another.

She looks up from her reflection.

Above the tongue of the shoe, suspended from a shaft of yellow light is a tree—another ancient one whose roots travel throughout the shoe. The roots support a seemingly random and chaotic assortment of words and symbols: a purple maple leaf, a castle, a saguaro cactus, Native beadwork, a feather from a flicker, a rhinoceros, books, money, a small dog, and the word CHOICE—the letters circling above the shoe, pointing it in a direction that somehow she knows is her future. Directly below the tree, held by the same shaft of light, is the world as seen from space, the shape of a new crescent moon, and a red heart.

She closes her eyes. *WOW*, she thinks. She has seen all sorts of things in meditation—colors swirling, the outlines of faces in a variety of ethnicity—but she'd never seen anything like this. She calms her breathing, wills her heart rate into a steady beat.

CLICK, CLICK, CLICK.

Feeling a little annoyed now, she opens her eyes and sits up. Another shoe, the left one. Underneath all the things attached to its exterior, it is an obvious mate to the other. The first thing she notices on this shoe is a pair of yellow-rimmed sunglasses. Their lenses are so dark, she cannot see into them, nor do they reflect. The darkness simply absorbs the light. Underneath them is a gun, a double-barreled shotgun.

Enough! She closes her eyes and thinks, *I need some time off for camping, with nothing to do for awhile.*

CLICK.

She opens her eyes. Next to the shoes, a pair of socks!

The socks are white, so white they hurt her eyes. It reminds her of a fresh snowfall, when the sun shines to reflect the perfection of each flake.

Suddenly she feels compelled to remove her office footwear and slip on the white socks. This exercise of will becomes an act of surrender as she closes her eyes and takes a deep breath. She feels a brilliant, white light radiating from the socks, surrounding her body. This Divine Light fills her body as if it were a glass vessel, illuminating every level of consciousness.

She puts on the left shoe. Her foot is held in place by two strands of words. The first reads, "help"; the second, "let me out."

As she puts on the right shoe, she notices a small container inside. The container reads "Natural Fruit—Apple Jam." She takes off the lid and out gushes clean air, clear water, good food, and health. She feels those things enter her body/mind as she settles her foot, adjusting slightly for another batch of colored eggs waiting to hatch.

Her left foot is the first to move. A flock of white doves flush from inside the shoe. "CLICK" goes the camera. The shotgun fires at the same time, wounding one of the doves. It falls to the ground. The others are caught and held in black strands coming from the lace holes of the shoe. They struggle.

"Help, let me out." The words flash from the inside of the shoe, binding her foot more tightly. The bodies of the other doves freeze, held tightly by the black strands, no longer struggling.

She stoops to pick up the wounded dove. She watches as the life drains from its shiny black eyes. The eyes disappear as the dove goes limp in her hands. The dove on the other shoe, sightless and separate from the others, takes another long drink of imagination.

The large photo album behind the camera moves slightly as the photo of the doves enters its pages. She realizes then that with every "CLICK," the camera on the right shoe fills the album on the left with images. Each step forward adds another image, another memory.

Step, CLICK. The word "Birthday" on the toe of the shoe refers to her own, she knows. CLICK: A party hat. She peeks underneath it expecting to find friends. CLICK: Only alcohol and fear under there.

CLICK: a solitary child standing alone. CLICK: fish-like creatures that slither and slide, a much loved marsh. CLICK: a dog. CLICK: a red apple and years of school. Teaching. CLICK: a baseball, athletics, coaching.

CLICK: a lighthouse with no beacon and a blue sailboat without a rudder.

Step, CLICK: a green hand, open and waiting to be held. CLICK: cards and money, gambling and risk. CLICK: an anchor recalling memories of pride in her country, the Navy, and a uniform. CLICK: a high heeled shoe. What is it to be a woman? CLICK: a golden zebra—a reminder of the white horse that flew with her in her dreams. CLICK: black-and-white photos capturing her family, recalling marriages, some of them hers. The images are devoid of color, emptying the plastic heart above them. CLICK: a baby carriage wrapped in black.

WAIT! WAIT! WAIT!

She stops walking. *Maybe there will be no more clicks,* she thinks. *Maybe this memory, this image won't happen if I stand still. If I don't take another step. Maybe . . .*

CLICK: the young son is gone through the camera, into the album.

Yes! The left shoe disappears, its remembered images settling into the photo album in the right shoe. The camera falls silent. *Noooooo!*

She sits down and cries. Her tears fall into the clear, blue pool of imagination. They ripple out, watering the roots of abundance and prosperity—the roots that support memories of all that is and all that is to come. A tree of life grows from the shoe, embracing the seasons and cycles. The sightless dove, free to fly and content to perch, drinks from the pool of imagination and, in doing so, hears the voice of the Divine. Eyes are not necessary to know that Peace is more than a reflection of what is seen. Peace begins the reflection.

The right shoe also disappears as she lifts her flute and begins to play the stories of her life. She stands in the here and now in the Light of the Divine, with a white pair of socks, cushioned by spring grass, connecting her to earth.

Reflections on the Past

...Help, let me out, doves frozen, held tightly by the black strands, no longer struggling, a solitary child standing alone, a dog, a green hand open, waiting to be held, the white horse that flew with her in her dreams...

When it was this hot, Main Street in Spanish Fork, Utah, shimmered. It looked like puddles of water stood in patches all the way to where the mountain blocked the way out of town. I knew it wasn't really water; it couldn't be, not when the bubbles that came to the road surface, black and shiny, looked good enough to chew.

I thought briefly about chewing one of those bubbles as I took off my shoes. My shoes—ugly brown things, fastened on the end of metal braces. The braces wouldn't let my knees bend. I thought about smashing the metal with a rock, like I had last month when I fell over while being pushed on a bicycle and couldn't get up. But last month wasn't this hot, and I knew I needed the shoes on the end of the damn things when I finished this part of the initiation. Braces had taught me to think swear words.

"Hurry up, we haven't got all day! If we don't hurry your mother will for sure catch us."

"Shut up, you! None of you have these damn things to take off."

The think words came tumbling out. My friends looked shocked; I felt pleased with the response and my daring. Swear words like "shut up" and "damn" were new to them. Walking across Main Street and back, barefoot, would take me twice as long as the others. My tiny, white feet turned in all crooked; they pointed at each other when I took them out of the shoes and socks. The other kids went barefoot all summer; their feet were straight and sun-browned.

Every year my friends and I did a friendship renewing initiation. The kids who were my friends were kids my mother said had sinned and therefore "were being punished by having afflictions." She forbade me to play with them. When I questioned my mother about "what a sin was" and "what an affliction was," and stated that I "was too going to play with them," my mother had become angry and sent me to my room to "think about the sin of not showing respect."

Doing all the steps of this year's friendship renewing initiation was important, maybe more important than anything else. My friends never made fun of my foot braces, my shoes, or my feet. With my friends was the only place where I had the sunshine feelings in my stomach that made me smile on the inside and out. Being with them had cost me the angry silence of my mother, but I knew it was worth it. I belonged.

I looked up at them standing around me and wondered again what my mother meant by "being afflicted." Tom was too skinny and wouldn't eat, even when his mother hit him. His legs were about as big as my wrists. He reminded me of a scarecrow. Tom was my very best friend.

Jim couldn't hear or talk with real words. He made weird sounds and hand pictures. He was the best at flying a kite, and he wrapped kite string on a stick neater than anyone. He could put together his puzzle of the United States in five minutes! Ruthie had hair that she never combed and she didn't smell very good, but she knew where all the neat sneaking places were and showed us rats at the garbage dump.

Her house sat on Main Street where the road turned off to the dump. Her dad collected and fixed dump things. Ruthie was also the official caretaker of our shared dog, Brownie.

We found Brownie lying at the side of the garbage pit where someone had dumped him. He was barely breathing.

Everyone took turns loving him back to being with them. He stood next to Ruthie, panting, his matted, brown fur hanging in shedding clumps. He looked and smelled a lot like Ruthie.

Kelly, the youngest, cried and peed in his pants a lot. He lived at the mortuary and that was the neatest, scariest sneaking place of all—even better than the dump. Sometimes the rest of us would ditch him to see how long it took for him to cry and pee.

Sometimes we would bet on it and use the nickels to sneak over to the garage and buy a coke. Coke was a sin to drink. It was against The Religion.

Katrina had pierced ears, had just moved into town the year before, and was a Catholic—an unheard of religion until Katrina. No one knew there was another religion word, other than Mormon—"the one and only true religion because of Joseph Smith," my mother had taught me. Katrina was the only one who didn't sin when she drank Coke.

Walking Main Street was the last of the steps for the friendship renewal. I was proud of not needing help on any of them as some of the others had; not even with collecting the black spiders with red on their bellies from the rich kids' playhouse.

"OK, you guys, I'm ready. Who's first?"

"I'll go first," Tom said. "Remember, you can't run."

Ha, I thought, *I have never run. I'll be lucky if it's still daylight by the time I make it across and back.*

All the kids made it, one by one, saying "ooch, oowch" all the way. Kelly made it halfway back before he started to cry and he didn't even pee. Everyone congratulated him for being brave.

Now it was my turn.

"Hey, you don't need to do this you know," Tom said. "Maybe only halfway. That black top is hot; I even got a couple of blisters. We can make it easier, like we did for Kelly and Jim with some of the other stuff."

"Shut up. I'm going to do it just like the rest, or it won't be official."

The pain started immediately. First the regular, without-braces pain in my knees. I dragged my feet into something that resembled a walk and started across the road. The new pain came as the shiny blacktop seemed to wrap around my bare feet like hot mud.

I made myself move forward using a trick I learned when, at night, the pain in my knees was so bad, it seemed to be a growing thing, alive in my bed. Or when my dad got drunk and my mother slammed the door and left for what I thought was forever and the silence rang in my ears so loud I couldn't hear anything my father said as he weaved, staggered, and moved his lips. I flew—rising above the ground, dodging the power wires, free and soaring. Watching myself, but not feeling myself.

I was aware that I made it to the other side of the road. I felt confused as I turned around and waved. My eyes were clouded with sweat and tears. I couldn't see my friends starting toward me with the wagon we all built last summer with parts we found at the dump. The squeak of the wheels sounded like a bird—a hawk maybe.

As I looked down, I saw a large clump of those black, shiny bubbles that seemed not to shine as much. I wondered why as I looked down and noticed all of the skin gone from the sides of my feet. I felt funny and light in my stomach as I looked at my feet. The skin of the sides and soles of my feet made a print, peeled off, and stuck in the top of the black shine.

I tried to fly, but I fell instead.

It was then the white horse came. The white horse I rode in long-remembered dream times. The horse that carried me from lily pad to lily pad, sometimes flying to a place that was cool and free, a place where I could run, a place even Tom could be strong.

I felt as though I was at one end of a big room where people at the other end were saying words I could only hear part of the time.

"See, I told you we shouldn't have made her. Look at her feet, they're bleeding."

"Help me pick her up. Kelly, this is not the time to cry or pee."

"We never made Tom dig, or Jim say the oath, except with hand pictures, or Kelly climb the tree or..."

"Hurry up, her mother will kill us. We're not supposed to even talk to her."

The wagon made its hawk squeal sounds as they pulled me into the shade by the road.

"Maybe we should say a prayer."

I felt Brownie licking at my feet. I could see his dog tongue go like it did when there was a carrot in the table scraps, picked up by mistake, and he wanted to spit it out.

"Is she dead?"

"Of course not."

"You kids get away from the street. Is that my daughter in the wagon? How many times..."

Everyone went into a sweaty, frozen position and looked around. It was my mother. They ran and I felt afraid.

The white horse began to disappear and I could feel the pain in my feet. I opened my eyes, hoping to be with my friends. My mother sat dozing in the chair next to my bed. I turned over and was sick. My mother held my head and a pan as I threw up. My mother didn't yell at me or say anything when she took me to the doctor to fix my feet. She told me to take the pills "for the pain."

The pills made me sick. The doctor told me that I would be in bed for a month. A week later, my mother still hadn't said a word to me about anything. She didn't say she was "disgusted" or that I had done a sin—it just felt that way. It was a not-washing-your-hands-after-going-to-the-bathroom type of feeling. My mother left the room shaking her head, and I was alone again.

The pain of my bandaged feet was not as bad as the pain in my heart. Being left alone was not new. Being sin-different was not new. Not being able to see Tom or my other friends for a month and maybe longer was a new/old pain—lonely—so I drew. I decided not to use brown because it reminded me too much of how being sick smelled. I drew how being lonely felt. I drew a dove.

It was the best bird I had ever drawn, but I couldn't sit it on a branch because of the brown. I didn't know enough yet about how to make it fly. Even when I drew another dove with its wings outstretched, it looked wrong, so I drew black around it. I wished I could draw it flying. I would have it fly all the way down Main Street and over the mountain that blocked the way out of town.

...The gun fired, wounding one of the doves...

As a child, I loved "shop words." I learned these words in my Dad's shop, listening to him and the men who worked for him. I learned early—when I was tall enough to see over a shop table—"shop words" were words used exclusively in the shop. When I used shop words around my mother, I got my mouth washed out with soap. The mouth washing session prompted my Dad's remark, "There are many things you don't tell your mother."

The phrase, "Don't tell your mother," became my favorite. It nearly always meant doing something fun with my Dad.

Guns fell into the "don't tell your mother" category. I learned to shoot in the shop, at targets in the back. First with a BB gun, next a pellet rifle, then a .22 caliber rifle. I could hit the target wherever I wanted. My Dad was proud of me. He invited his friends to bet money on me. I seldom missed, so my Dad seldom lost money.

He played a game called "taste or smell." Whoever came closest to the bull's-eye won a taste of whiskey from the bottle inside a brown paper bag; the loser only smelled it.

Once when I was shooting, a man gave me capfuls of whiskey. Every time I swallowed, even though it tasted awful and made my throat burn, he winked and gave me a one-dollar bill. Everybody drank from the brown paper bag. I liked the sense of belonging. After two dollars, I felt really happy—a feeling I captured later in my life on a daily basis from a similar brown paper bag. After five dollars in my pocket, I was sick. My vision blurred, the room spun, and I could not hit the target. My Dad lost money.

When I threw up on the floor, my Dad hit the man who gave me the money and told him to leave.

Later, guns taught me about death when I picked up a mourning dove my father shot. I saw my brothers shoot sparrows with BBs. I saw them shoot rats at the garbage dump, but I had never seen or felt any creature die. When I picked up the dove, it was still alive, quivering. I watched the bird's death in its eyes, gradually losing their shine until the bird's sight changed from looking outward to looking in.

My Dad grabbed the dove from my hands and pulled its head off. He told me not to watch the dying anymore. "Pull their heads off so they don't suffer," he said, "and you can't see their eyes."

...CLICK: the young son is gone through the camera, into the album. "Noooooo!"...

Death is an amazing teacher, the lessons always profound, at times paralyzing. Death at times sends my mind into stunned silence.

The room number is 304. My memory starts and stops. A room number is not much of a memory. A feeling of lightheaded sickness moves to my belly, my womb. My vision blurs with the rhythmic pounding of my pulse. My mouth is dry. I struggle with the truth of my life. I cannot remember. The room number is 304. I remember the room number.

Fear grazes through my memory, at first nibbling here and there. I think it is OK, and then it explodes like a cancer growing out of control, heedless of love or life. *Keep going,* I say to myself. *Touch the fear. The smell and a whooshing sound, the smell.*

When someone asks me, "Do you have any children?" I say, "My husband and my son were killed." Usually they say, "Sorry," or nothing and ask no further questions.

The sequence of events from age seventeen to twenty-four, when I started teaching school, are gone or seriously scrambled, lost in an avalanche of "almost" memory. I got married to my first husband when I was seventeen; I can't remember it. I remember some of the year prior when we were engaged and I attended college. Time, dates, the year, times tables, addition, subtraction, the alphabet, and spelling—all are scrambled. I cannot remember a phone number and even when it is written down, the chances of me dialing it correctly are iffy at best. I know about the dyslexia, although the official diagnosis did not come until I was thirty-eight and in graduate school. The other, the fear and confusion paralyzing my mind, is from trauma.

When I touch the fear in order to remember more—whether now as I am trying to match the courage of these women I write with, or in the years of therapy—it cloaks itself in a combination of blind rage and a helpless hopelessness. I have no memory of the State Hospital and very little of the year I spent in the private one. Most of these memories are associated with odors. What I discovered about the state hospital was I participated in an experimental program using electric shock therapy (EST) as a primary treatment for my non-responsiveness to trauma. The transfer to the private hospital occurred to follow up the initial treatment.

I light a cigarette, forget I have a horrible cold. My heart rate increases again. Cigarette or fear?

The room number is 304. The smell and a whooshing sound; the sound hesitates like a held breath laboring to exhale. The smell is so strong, it is a taste.

I used to believe the stories other people told me were my memory. Now I know my own story.

I spent several days looking for pictures. I found ones from my first marriage. I recognized most of the people in them. There are no pictures of my son. I vaguely remember them being destroyed, or is that another story? I make up my own stories and tell them. Sometimes they change and I don't know which ones are true.

The room number is 304, the smell is hospital smell. Not a psychiatric hospital; that smell is a different memory. My mind runs from both memories, yet they ground me in an odd way. At least they are mine. I hear the remembered sound now—a part of a life support system, a respirator.

I don't remember my son's death or my husband's. I do not remember the events preceding them. I do not remember my pregnancy. I do not remember my son's birth. I do not remember what he looked like. I do remember his smell and red curly hair. I remember stories about him. I considered writing those stories, but they are not mine. What I do have is enough, because it is mine. A room number, a smell, and a sound.

Another doctor ordered copies of the accident and hospital reports, but too much time had passed since the accident. The facts make no difference. I have heard the facts in the stories.

In my dreams I give birth countless times, all joyful, to a red-headed little boy, and when I wake up, I remember his smell. In other dreams, I experience an unbearable pressure crushing the breath from my body. I jerk and jerk and wake up with sore joints, clenched jaw, and the taste of copper pennies in my mouth.

So I calm my breathing, focus on my stomach, my womb. I grieve the loss of my memory and all it contains. I embrace the terror, my truth, and anger. They are mine.

...Above the tongue of the shoe, suspended from a shaft of yellow sunlight is a tree—another ancient one whose roots travel through out the shoe nurturing all it touches with the simplicity and wonder in nature. The roots bring light and support to a seemingly random and chaotic assortment of symbols...

The first time I ran away I was two. I do not remember my escape except through the family stories. I do remember being four. I packed a wax Santa, a doll with a black face, and two small dishes in a doll suitcase. I wanted out—out of my family, out of the place that I lived. The sense of not belonging was profound in my childhood. It became intolerable as I grew. I experienced my life in my family and community embodied in the harshness of judgment—judgment and punishment of anything or anyone that looked, believed, or felt differently. I did not feel safe; I did not feel the love that was offered. I felt isolated and wrong.

Running away at two ended with my mother finding me a block away from my house, cut willow in hand. At four, my running away ended when I needed to pee and was afraid to ask anyone to use their toilet. I went home to my own toilet.

Yet, still I ran. At first, I ran in my mind. I struggled with depression. I was sick; I manifest ulcers as a child. I cried in the beginning, then I quit crying.

At fourteen, I finally ran—literally, physically—away from home. I continued running for many years. I ran through being housed and cared for in Los Angeles by two gay men whom I thought were women. I ran through the diversity of people in other-than-Mormon country. I ran through months of weekends in jail for speeding fines I could not afford to pay. I ran through two marriages, death, and loss. I ran through suicide attempts, high stakes gambling, drugs, and alcohol. I ran through relationships: men and women with whom I desperately connected, trying to slow the pace of my running, trying to find a sense of belonging. I ran and ran. I kept running away until—

At thirty, I found the mountain.

When I experience manifesting a dream in real time and space, I forget perfection in life or structure, other than those occurring naturally, does not exist in real time and space. I do not know if this is a quote from someone else, or the truth of discovery on the day I decided to buy a house located on forty acres above an Indian mission bordering on state wilderness land.

I also did not know when I moved there full time, it was the beginning of my soul mending.

On the first visit to "the mountain," as I came to call my home, I did not notice: the cracks in the walls, (allowing the birth of baby bunnies in the bathtub); the absence of working plumbing (as the toilet had frozen and cracked the winter before); or the dog housed in one of three wrecked cars, a '39 Plymouth—a dog that bit me three times in the first week I lived there as he, not so patiently, taught me the entire north side of the house extending approximately two hundred yards was his territory. It escaped my notice that the back part of the house did not quite meet the front part. It was moving at a glacial pace down the slope (actually much faster than a glacier, about half an inch during each spring runoff).

What I did notice were the mature Ponderosa pines, Douglas fir, and Grand fir trees surrounding it. The air was rich with the smell of soil and the fragrance of spring. When the wind blew up the valley, it sounded like an approaching ocean. I noticed the fear-fed restlessness so familiar to me drain away through my feet, absorbed by the land. It was disorienting at first.

The house was huge, built on the slope of a hillside overlooking King Valley. The valley was homesteaded just off "Indian" land by the King family—an African-American family who referred to themselves as "Negro" farmers. The last of the brothers, now elders, lived below the house. Five miles away, they were my nearest neighbors.

The house had five bedrooms, a basement, small bathroom with the only interior door in the house, and a large great room— supported in the middle by a tree trunk—which served as the living room, dining room, and kitchen. The room contained a wood burning cook stove and a rusted out wood heater. No electricity, no water hooked to the house. About ten years prior to my purchase, a man with a chainsaw and limited structural knowledge built the house entirely from scrounged, bartered, used, and reclaimed building materials.

I spent years with no money exercising the skills of my history, of years spent in my father's shop learning the building, heating, and sheet metal business. I seldom had enough money for rent, so I lived in places that needed fixing and did the fixing in lieu of rent. By the time I moved to the mountain, I had built, wired, plumbed, roofed, tiled, carpeted, painted, and jury-rigged myself into over thirty different rent-free places. I blessed my knowledge and discovered a way to be thankful for my childhood.

I can count the number of words my father spoke out loud to me during his life, but I also can fix or build almost anything. My father's skills on the water, in the woods, and in working with animals also are like my second skin. The connection with the land that flows through me, speaks to me daily.

A friend and his three-year-old daughter accompanied me on an inspection of the mountain house shortly after I signed the papers. This seeing-eye newcomer noticed a myriad of things, both cosmetic and structural, wrong with the house. He shook his head and offered his opinion on how I might "get out of the deal."

As we stood on the deck talking, we did not pay attention to his daughter. She had wandered off the deck toward the north side of the house—the dog's territory. I did not notice her until I caught the movement of the dog jumping out of the wrecked car.

On previous occasions when I entered his territory, he jumped from the car, challenged and, occasionally, bit me if I did not back away.

The child noticed the dog. She giggled with delight as she hurried toward him saying, "Puppy, Puppy." She was too close to the dog for me to do anything but scream for her to stop. "Puppy," his head down, eyes up, moved stiff legged toward the little girl. Within a couple of paces from the dog, she tripped. Instinctively she grabbed for the dog. They both went down and my heart froze. I ran toward them followed closely by her dad. The little girl had both arms around the dog's neck. They were literally face to face—and the dog's tail wagged.

As we approached, the dog's tail stiffened. He lifted his head, bared his teeth and growled deeply from his chest. Her dad and I stood still. We backed up as the dog continued his rumbling growl.

The little girl was frightened now—both to see our alarm as well as the intensity dog's growl. I called to her; both of us reassured her everything was all right (a lie well told).

We said, "Get up honey, and come to us." She cried harder, although by then she was sitting up. The dog moved in front of her, between the child and us, definitely in a challenge stance, continuing to growl. The child tried to stand on the uneven ground, using the dog for leverage. The dog did not notice, did not look at her, but he stopped growling and wagged his tail.

After what seemed an eternity, she got her footing and walked back toward us. It was all we both could do to stop ourselves from rushing forward.

She walked past the dog as her father and I stood still and waited. When she had traversed approximately ten yards, we began slowly moving forward. At last her father reached her and picked her up.

The dog watched, rigid and intent, but did not move. When we were back to the deck, the dog got back into the wrecked car.

I took the little girl into the house, comforting her. Scared and angry, her father ran to his pickup truck to get his rifle. His lips pale and tight, he came back down the hill loading his rifle, a lever action 30/30. When he crossed the deck toward the north side of the house, I came out and told him to stop. He said, "That god-damn dog is dangerous! He needs to be put down! He could have killed my daughter!"

"I know," I said, "but no shooting now. Let's settle down. You are too upset to shoot well, and your daughter doesn't need to see something like this." He stopped and began to shake. All three of us began to cry. His daughter cried because we did; we cried with relief and thankfulness for her safety. Before he left, my friend made me promise I would see to it that the "damn dog" was put down.

Later, when I had time to think about what I had witnessed, when I was able to put my fear aside and replay the events, it was clear to me my friend's little girl was never in danger from the dog. I knew I had to do something with the dog, that in fact he was dangerous and unpredictable. As I sat with what I knew and what I saw, it began to come clear to me, short of putting myself in the dog's place or humanizing an animal's response, I did know how being scared felt. I understood the reactive response to fear. I decided whatever or whoever had caused the dog to react with aggressiveness instead of trust was not a child.

"Puppy," as he would henceforth be known, deserved the same chance I was giving myself to rebuild trust, to live life rather than react out of fear. I knew if I could not invite him out of his aggressive behavior, I would indeed need to shoot him.

I started the next morning with scrambled eggs. I walked toward the dog's car with the leftover scrambled eggs until Puppy jumped out. I stopped and put down the plate of food. I did that several times a day for the next month. Then table scraps gave way to dog food. By the end of that spring, I walked anywhere in his "territory" without being challenged. When I walked and explored the mountain, he followed me at a distance.

I finally packed up my few belongings and my dog (a Basenji with an aloof cat-like attitude) and moved to the mountain, an eighty-mile round trip commute from work. Puppy did not like the dog, but never harmed him. He would attack and roll him over into a submit position if he tried to chase any animal living on the mountain, especially the domestic rabbits that had been turned loose and were busily building an extensive rabbit warren underneath the already structurally challenged house.

I received as a moving gift from a friend, a young black cat. Puppy immediately protected the young cat; he followed it everywhere and sometimes groomed her by licking her fur until she looked like a bad hair day.

The first night I stayed there my young cat hunted and killed all night. My dog stayed under the covers and growled. I woke up to a dozen mouse carcasses scattered about and an exhausted young cat. Over the years, this cat honed her hunting skills, survived the many predators—specifically owls and coyotes—and proudly presented me with an incredible array of stunned and not quite dead snakes, grouse, weasels, rabbits, moths, grasshoppers, bats, etc. I learned early to listen for the infamous "muffled meow" that meant she had something in her mouth she wished to show me and then turn loose in the house. I took me six hours once to remove a wounded weasel. They exhibit nasty behavior in the wild when approached, but to have one wounded, in a house, is a daunting and humbling experience.

No matter what I was doing, when I heard the muffled meow, I promptly stopped to close the cat door before the new cat treasure arrived.

One of the first repairs was the ceiling in the main room. I repaired and re-hung a drop ceiling after locating the leaks and patching the roof. There was little insulation in the roof; the dead air space and lowered ceilings helped to a degree with keeping warm. Shortly after the ceiling installation, the mice moved in overhead. The first time I heard them in my new ceiling, I decided to try an organic mouse control device. I got the ladder, a flashlight, and the cat. I removed a panel of ceiling and put the cat in the space between the ceiling and the roof. What happened gave a whole new meaning to the words "drop ceiling." The ceiling panels literally began to drop to the floor as the "hunt" picked up pace. I had my head and shoulders through the ceiling, trying to locate the cat, trying to coax her to stop.

"Here kitty, kitty, kitty," I called softly, and then not so softly as the ceiling tiles kept falling. The flashlight caught her eyes about the time a mouse hit the side of my neck, followed closely by the cat on my head. We all promptly left the ladder and joined the ceiling on the floor. Bruises and scratches aside, I never did that again.

The mouse Indy 500 in the ceiling became part of the music of the mountain, although most evenings Kitty sat on the table and look longingly at the ceiling tiles.

I don't know which season comes first, which season starts the cycle of life. My first season on the mountain was spring. The spring rising energy starts there with the drumming of the ruffed grouse, the sounds of the migrating geese and mourning doves.

Wildflowers grow in fertile chaos: spring beauties, dog tooth violets, and trillium. Edible mushrooms—morels and others—are offered in abundance. I bought books identifying what I saw and took pictures of every square inch of spring. I filled the empty spaces of my memory with the newness.

I worked full time for the state substance abuse program, writing and implementing statewide programs. I taught in a public school system and decided to take a two-year leave of absence, solve the alcohol problem in Idaho, and return to teaching. I worked for the state in substance abuse programs for fifteen years until the state legislature, in its infinite wisdom, legislated away my job. I did what I always did when I was unemployed and insecure: I went back to school—this time acquiring a Ph.D., also known as a "terminal degree."

I always viewed myself as a teacher, still do, but I never returned to public school education as a teacher. I later substituted as a principal, later still as a consultant.

The days filled with the possibilities of great things to do in my job, limited only by my ability to imagine. The evenings and weekends filled with fixing. I never lived in a location more than two years, the length of time required to make it livable. At that point, the landlord would want rent money, so I would move to the next "not OK" place. I could hardly comprehend that, this time, I would not move as soon as this place was livable. I discovered a profound sense of belonging.

Summer is the time of fullest offering on the mountain, manifesting in the budding, blossoming and fruit of the apple trees around the house. Most of the repairs to the leaks and major cracks and crevasses to the outside of the house were coming to an end. The roof was sound. I located a spring and piped water to the house. I knew it would freeze in the winter, but the first time the new toilet flushed, I celebrated with champagne.

I gathered wood. I discovered that making cordwood to burn for heat is fun for the first cord (a cord equals approximately one large dump truck full), but after that it is just plain hard work. I lived on the mountain for sixteen summers. It took approximately eight to ten cords of wood to keep a semblance of warmth. Suffice it to say, I have felled, cut up and split enough cord wood to qualify me for having had enough of that activity.

I had many close calls in felling dead trees. The loggers call them "widow makers" because the vibration of the chainsaw sometimes makes the tops break loose and fall directly on the logger. I learned when a tree gets sawed off its stump, rather than falling in the direction that you wedged it, it can fall in any direction, including uphill. I learned you need to stand still, fighting the urge to run, until you are sure which way it will fall. This means staying put in a dangerous situation until gravity dictates the direction of the fall, making the escape route clear. It frightened me to fell trees, and I did it anyway. Under the tutelage of a logger friend, I got good at it. I learned the fear I felt cutting down a tree was different from the diffuse and permeating fear I carried for so long. It was the beginning of a "fear trade."

That summer of fullest offering I traded the fear of what my murky memory did not quite recall, for a fear that was based in the here and now. The old fear was never touchable or tangible, it did not increase my heart rate, or surge through me in the ancient response of fight or flight; it simply drained my willingness to live.

Suicide was my companion for years. It lived reassuringly in the back of my mind, coming forward with the comforting thought, *If I can not handle living, suicide will free me.* Its voice fed several suicide attempts, kept me from sleeping well, and convinced me I was not loved or lovable. The tree falling fear was real and tangible. It alerted my body and sharpened my senses. It was alive and served a living purpose. The fear trade that summer made suicide no longer an option. Letting go of it freed me to live fully for the first time. One of the best trades I ever made.

I spent the first summer getting acquainted with my neighbors—not an easy task. It took three years for them to believe I was really going to stay and I was not totally deranged. Once they did, I finally had a family—actually four families. One family owned and farmed thousands of acres. Dry land farmers, they depended upon the weather and the seasons for the moisture their crops needed.

In the valley below me, "King Valley," lived one of the King family brothers and his wife. They descended from the original "Negro" homesteaders and cleared most of the farm ground in the area. A Native American family monitored a CB base station, my only communication with the outside world (the mountain was too remote for phone service). And lastly, a family from New York building a log home and seeking peace.

Barter and trade was the foundation of my new family. For me this was a time of abundance and the epitome of the fullest offering of summer. A system of a continual offering and receiving, receiving and offering—an exchange based on trust and caring—began for me.

To the farming family, I gave time building, fixing, and repairing that are basic to farming. I drove a grain truck during harvest time; helped with burning bluegrass fields; organized annual Easter egg hunts for the kids and adults that took two days to complete. From them, I received a water line buried deep enough not to freeze in the winter; help plowing the snow drifts that got too high to ski over; the people and equipment for repairs that I could not afford. I received laughter, people to lean on, more laughter, and an exchange of meals on holidays, birthdays, special events, and "just because" times.

To the New York family, I gave the use of my shower—the only working one between us for about two years. I gave haircuts to Paul and the kids when they needed one, offered child care when the kids were too much underfoot during their building process, and helped with the labor of building a home. I received endless hours with children who re-taught me playfulness and hope the way only the young can teach. They were bright, imaginative, artistic, and mischievous kids. I loved them, and they returned my love unconditionally. While their parents and most of the others thought I was slightly crazy (which I was), the kids thought I was just "way cool." I brought them the bureaucratic discards of paper, pencils, markers, etc. They transformed them into cards and decorations for every occasion.

Paul assisted in arresting the glacial movement of the back part of my house. I had a house mover give me a bid to jack up the back of the house (which was approximately one-thousand square feet), build a support network for the upper story, knock out the walls, dig and pour a continuous cement foundation, lay approximately five hundred cinder blocks, and reset the upper story to the lower. (The back part of the house had been started by leveling out the ground on the slope, laying down some black plastic, and building a two-story addition to the front part of the house. There was no foundation to support the additions. The extended roof of the front part of the house was all that held the two together.) The bid was five times the price of the house and land. I took copious notes as he explained how this feat would take place. I spent two hours revising my notes and drawing up plans. I took two six-packs of beer to Paul's place and halfway through the second six-pack, we had a plan.

The noises a structure makes while being jacked and leveled are amazing and alarming. We cut down trees for the support structure, borrowed every heavy-duty hydraulic and house jack available for miles. We hand mixed seven yards of concrete for the foundation. After we dug and poured the foundation and laid the first row of block, Paul got a job out of the area and had to leave. In the beginning, the average time to get the proper amount of mortar, and then to place, align, and level one cinder block was twenty-five minutes worth of retries. I had five hundred blocks to lay. That summer I finished the research and the writing for my doctoral dissertation.

I laid block until I couldn't anymore, and I wrote until I couldn't anymore, and then I laid more block, and I wrote some more. The back and forth of the hard physical and mental labor chipped away at the two most difficult feats I had undertaken in either arena. First, I discovered how to apply a proper statistical application to my research data (analysis of co-variance dyslexia and all). Secondly, I got the average time per block to less than three minutes.

When I reached the 304th block, I had the first ceremony for my son. I accepted him and released him. The power of it literally brought me to my knees, but then I stood and flexed the muscles of my well-exercised body and mind, and of my mending soul.

To the King family I gave time visiting with aging ones. I re-roofed their home after Frank's wife died and he was mostly blind from diabetes. I was honored to share in the care for him in his dying process. I orchestrated the installation of an Idaho historical monument inscribed with the words he repeatedly told me he wished written honoring his lineage.

The year he died, I finished my doctoral dissertation and received a Ph.D. I dedicated my dissertation to him.

Frank gave me endless hours' worth of pictures and stories of his life. These were later featured in the state centennial publication, *Ebony Idaho*. He also gave me a pig loading lesson.

I read how-to books and discovered the gaps in the writing and the doing of things. I read in a farming magazine about the difficulty in managing full-grown pigs, especially related to inviting them into places they did not wish to go. The article gave a detailed and foolproof way to load a full grown pig into a trailer in order to transport them from point A (the place they were familiar with) to point B (a place they did not want to go, which in this case, meant to slaughter). The method involved putting a large enough bucket over the pig's snout to cover its eyes. Once accomplished, you simply backed the pig up with forward pushing into the trailer. The foolproof theory stated, "When the eyes are covered the pig becomes disoriented and docile. As long as a steady pressure is applied and maintained enough to keep the bucket in place, you can back a pig anywhere." I am amazed, as I write this, that I did not spot, or even question, the possible flaws in this theory. Frank told me many times about pig loading struggles, and I truly believed I had a solution he may not have known.

One of the first stories I heard about the mountain, or more accurately about King Valley, was about one of Frank's sisters and her hog-related tragedy. The story went something like: "Oh, uh huh, so you are moving up where those black folks live. Ya know that's where this black (except "black" is not the word that was generally used) gal married this white guy. He died and got 'et by the hogs, you know. Don't cha?" I heard that comment or something very similar, at least a dozen times before I moved there. I asked Frank about the semi-urban, semi-legend. He said his sister's second marriage was to a white man, Vern. He went out to feed the hogs one morning and suffered a massive heart attack. By the time his wife missed him and finally found him, the hogs had in fact dined on numerous parts of his body.

That story played through my mind as I arrived early on the morning that I transported the 250-pound sow that Frank raised for meat. I read the article to him and he smiled.

"Shall we try it?" I asked. A man of few words, Frank nodded and we went to locate a bucket that was suitable. I backed the truck and trailer up to the loading chute, and Frank and I entered the pigpen. The pigs were in the shed sleeping. Frank walked up to the one he wanted and shocked it with a cattle prod. The pig was not happy. After a bit of maneuvering I managed to get the bucket over the pig's snout so it covered her eyes. She got still and I was heartened. When I began the steady forward pressure described in the article, so did the pig. I was out-weighed and it was me that began to back up, so quickly I almost lost my footing ("Bad idea to fall down" flashed in my mind). I backed until I was against the fence, then sidestepped until I was in the corner of the fence and could not move. The pig continued to push until the bucket pressure on my lower chest and stomach made it difficult to breathe. Frank stepped up next to me and shocked the pig in the front shoulder. The pig let out a fierce growl (I did not know that a pig could growl) and whirled, throwing the bucket and me aside. The pig turned then and with lightening speed, ran up the loading chute and into the trailer.

"What happened?" I said to Frank

"Well," he drawled (it was the preamble to every infrequent sentence he spoke), "You should have read to the pig the part about who was supposed to back up. Otherwise it worked. The pig is in the trailer."

Fall is a shedding and letting go season in preparation for the deep contemplative time of winter. Fall on the mountain announces itself when the softness held in the summer morning takes on a cool edge. The deciduous trees change color and drop their leaves. There is one species of a deciduous tree that masquerades as an evergreen, a larch variety called "tamarack." The first year, after I observed the entire hillside of supposed ever-greens turn a bright yellow and the needles began dropping, I called the forestry department at the local university to see what dreadful diseases infested the acres of yellow trees. When I asked the consulting forester what he thought, there was a long silence. Then as diplomatically as possible he said, "You are not from around here are you?" I answered I had been living in the area for about six years and recently moved farther north.

"I see," he said, and proceeded to tell me of the species of larch that looked like a regular pine or fir tree, but is actually deciduous like a broad leaf. The next year I joined the Tree Farm Association as a tool to learn the flora and the fauna of the mountain. I learned from the tamarack that outward appearance may or may not match the innate nature of any species that holds its unique manifestations.

Along with the shedding of the tamarack and the other deciduous trees, the apple trees also shed apples. I made applesauce and juice using as many as possible, and took wheelbarrow upon wheelbarrow over to the compost area. The apples brought deer, ants, yellow jackets (a type of hornet), and ground squirrels. They also brought a species I had never experienced in the wild—black bear. Black bears, by nature, are shy animals.

I had three major black bear learnings while living on the mountain. The first learning about black bear came as a result of what must be eliminated after eating too many apples. The bear scat (or shit, as my neighbors referred to it) is formidable. The large round shape of a post-apple orgy resembles the size and consistency of a cow pie following the first spring grass. It ferments quickly and has a very bad odor. I did not make a study of bear scat, but my dog did. I came home one evening to find him caked in dried bear scat. I promptly filled the bathing tub. He smelled bad, but it was tolerable until the first ladle full of warm water re-hydrated the dry bear scat. My nose registered the smell, but was so stunned, my gag reflex acted first. My lunch joined the dog and the bear shit in the tub. Not pleasant.

The second learning came when I tried to "shoo" a bear out of the yard. They don't "shoo" well. The dogs caught wind of the bear and stormed out of the house. I read many accounts of how dangerous a mix of domestic dogs and bear can be. For starters, there's the possibility of injury to the dog. Also, if the dogs manage to anger a bear and then run back to their shelter, or worse yet, to their owner, the bear will follow.

My dogs managed to move the bear, but up the tree. Puppy had good sense with bears and all animals, but alas was lead astray by my three other dogs. This rag-tag bunch of city dogs had no sense, and when activated, they excited Puppy enough that he lost his. I think they call that a pack mentality, but in this case the smartest of the pack was outnumbered.

My housemate from Birmingham, Alabama—a woman whose wilderness experience bragged touching a cow at age twenty-five—was "helping" me with the "shooing." I locked the dogs in the house and got my shotgun. The sky was close to full dark. I did not want to shoot the bear, but I did want it to move on. My friend was scared, and so was I, by the noises the treed bear made—a cross between a low grunting sound and a half-throttle chain saw. I took about twenty paces from the house, held the gun to my shoulder and shot into the air.

The sounds were stunning. It was too dark to see the tree the bear was in, and when the bear came down, it sounded like the whole stand of trees was being ripped apart.

Mary was holding the only light, a large beam flashlight. I thought for a moment she had turned it off, but she had turned and run for the house. I followed, hot on her footsteps. As fate would have it, when I locked the dogs in the house, I also locked us out.

The noises of the bear continued and Mary opened the door—hinges and all! Adrenaline is a fine drug.

The third black bear learning came when I installed a dog door to the side porch, allowing the dogs access during the day. Friends were visiting from Seattle. They woke me one night with the news they believed there was a bear on the deck outside their bedroom. A cooler full of food sat on the side porch, along with some garbage in a black plastic garbage bag. The only entrance, other than the locked door, was the dog door. I looked out and, sure enough, there was a bear trying to get to the side porch goodies through the dog door. I banged loudly on the kitchen metal door and the bear jumped off the deck into the shadows. My friends kept an eye out while I got some plywood from the basement and securely nailed the dog door shut.

About two hours later, they woke me again with the same news. I told them it was OK, I had really nailed the dog door shut. They said the noise was worse.

When we looked out of the kitchen door window, we saw the bear sitting on his haunches, with both front paws busily working at the nailed plywood. When the paws got some purchase on the plywood, the bear flexed them, leaned back on his haunches and using his hind feet as leverage against the house, proceeded to tear off the nailed plywood along with a significant amount of siding on the house. He poked his head through the dog door and began to push his shoulders through with his hind feet.

It took me a while to register what I was seeing, and by the time my mind engaged and I started pounding on the kitchen door to scare him off the deck, he was firmly lodged in the dog door, not able to move forward or to retreat. I pounded a few more times before the house began to shake and the splintering sounds started.

I witnessed in the second bear episode what human adrenaline can do; I witnessed in this episode what bear adrenaline can do.

The dog door frame splintered; the two-by-fours around it were pulled out of the footing they were nailed to. As the bear backed up, most of the wall came with him.

The dogs went berserk, lunging at the glass kitchen door. I backed up; the bear looked in; the dogs continued to bark; and my friends left the room. The bear seemed in a momentary debate on whether to come through the glass door, or go for the garbage bag, located in plain view now the side of the house was removed. I reached for my hunting rifle and began to shake. The bear decided on the garbage. He dragged it off the deck, sat back on his haunches, threw it up in the air, and just before the bag hit the ground in front of him, he swiped with a black bear rendition of a round house punch. The plastic garbage bag exploded and the contents scattered halfway down the hillside toward the back of the house. The bear went through the garbage with the ease of a practiced yard sale enthusiast, picking out the exact items that were of the most value to him.

The next day I contacted Fish and Game. They informed me that there was a "problem" bear in the area where I lived. I informed them most likely their "problem" bear was in close proximity to my un-sided porch. When I returned the next day, the bear had been live-trapped in a large barrel trap used for such purposes and, in the words of Fish and Game, "relocated to a less populous area."

Aligning my internal rhythms to the seasonal provocation of the first fall and all the falls on the mountain, allowed me the practice of letting go. I let go of unfinished projects, of the warmth of summer, and practiced the ongoing letting go of the fear of living my life. With the letting go came the courage to embrace the contemplation of the winters.

Winter is a time of root and seed, a time of contemplation. The seeds of new beginnings lay dormant, waiting. The upward and offering energy of spring and summer, culminating in fall shedding, reverses to the downward, contractive forces of winter. The energy held in contemplation, in the roots. The cycle of life.

I learned to sing when I ski. I do not have a good singing voice, but the noise is sufficient to alert the deer to move. I learned the ski/sing combination one winter when a record snowfall and cold temperatures kept me from getting any closer to my house than a mile and a half from where the county maintained roads.

That same winter, the water to the house froze on Thanksgiving Day and did not thaw until St. Patrick's Day. I skied in and out with water and supplies during those months. One particularly cold, clear, full-moon night, I was skiing in with a toboggan full of five-gallon water containers. The toboggan had a five-foot lead rope which snapped to a belt at my waist, leaving my hands free for ski poles. I skied uphill toward home, pulling the toboggan. At the point where the slope crested and turned downward, I skied to the side of the road and allowed the toboggan to pass and begin to pull me.

This particular evening was the type of complete quiet experienced with a deep snowfall. This snow quiet was accompanied by millions of ice crystals reflecting the light of the full moon. It was like skiing through diamonds.

The rhythm of the skiing and the beauty of the night distracted me. I did not switch the toboggan to the pulling position until my downhill speed began to increase. In and of itself, the momentum was OK, but at the moment I skied aside to allow the water laden toboggan to pass, I skied into the deep snow and over the top of a deer bedded down for the night. The deer literally burst out from under my feet, knocking me over. I emitted my bladder through two layers of long johns and my ski pants. I regained my wits just as the toboggan full of water took the slack out of the towrope affixed to the belt around my waist. It jerked me into a butt first C-shape and then into a butt first V-shape. My skis came off and I careened down the steep slope, over the edge of the road, behind a toboggan full of water that was celebrating the ancient law of gravity.

I never found all of the plastic water containers. When the toboggan overturned and I wedged between two trees that were not separated enough to accommodate my V-shape, I could still hear the containers crashing through the woods below.

Henceforth, whenever I skied into my house, I sang loudly. I could hear the deer flushing ahead of me, which kept the water, both on the toboggan and in my bladder, exactly where it belonged. My favorite song to sing is a refrain from an old Mormon hymn, "Put Your Shoulder to the Wheel."

Don't ask me why.

I lived on the mountain for fifteen seasonal cycles. In my early work with Puppy I promised him and myself, that if he would learn to trust again, I would not move from the mountain until he died. He died during the fifteenth winter and I buried him overlooking his beloved mountain. There is so much I learned about myself from him—his healing and trust building were uncanny parallels to my own.

I learned you cannot teach trust without knowing it. Puppy never quite recovered enough trust to allow strangers to hug me or approach the house when I was not in view.

I learned when a trauma is sufficient, there are situations and/ or circumstances which override new wisdom, fueled with an instinctual, hard-wired survival fear. I saw that in Puppy when fear triggered his aggression; I see it in myself. There are always places I will "walk with a limp," with the fear of ancient memory embedded beyond recall. There is comfort in that knowing as I gather the wisdom of the mountain and move in the here and now of my life.

Reflections on the Present

*...I stand in the here and now in the light of the divine,
with a pair of white socks, cushioned by spring grass,
connecting me to the earth...*

To a great degree every job I have had has prepared me for
the present. I've loved every one—all forty of them. I know within
the diversity of my experience lies the essence of my wisdom,
which goes far beyond my formal education.

I worked in my Dad's shop, where I learned to fix, build, or
repair damn near anything. Dairy Queen gave me my first fast
food experience. Night crawlers were the focus of my first entre-
preneurial venture which prompted a keen observation of na-
ture that sustains me still.

At a mortuary, I answered the phone for the ambulance ser-
vice that provided emergency response for the small town I grew
up in. A job as a switchboard operator gave me a preview of what
would become the computer age. Working as a waitress was a
lesson in multi-tasking and public relations. As a swimming in-
structor, I learned the importance of knowing how to save your
own life in the water, of assisting the young and old to overcome
irrational fear, and of analyzing body movements that telecast
both physical and emotional imbalance. As a lifeguard, I learned
more about responding to emergencies and saving lives.

My job as a tennis program manager offered me the blending
of sports and small business. As a professional referee and coach,
I honed my observation skills and learned about working with
teams and honoring individual needs while creating a sense of
unity and belonging. I learned the skill of creating order through
cleaning motels and houses. Being a bartender and owner proved
to be the best school for observing and responding to human
response and behavior, and the power of addictions, as well as

mastering the checks and balances of running a small business. Through kitchen cabinet making, I developed skills in finish work, thus rounding out my building knowledge. The Navy gave me pride in my country and the gift of not having to decide what to wear.

Photography allowed me to make images of things in nature that touch others enough they're willing to pay for them. Through my private therapy practice, I've experienced owning a business in which I am the primary commodity. I assisted in founding a program for returning adult students that translates life and work experience into academic credit, participating with adults as they discover their wisdom. I have grown in my service as public school teacher, on-loan substitute principal, and adjunct faculty with five universities. I have grown in my role as a consultant to small business, Head Start programs, and Hospice. My present career in counseling and psychotherapy allows me on a daily, hourly basis to enter the rarefied air of trust, human distress, change and growth.

And last but not least, as a flute maker and player, I express the stories of my life through my playing in a way far exceeding my words.

Today, as I continue to reflect on the present, I look through the window of Ethyl. Ethyl is a 1972 motor home I bought from my secretary and her husband. She's a twenty-five-foot piece of fiberglass in shades of avocado and harvest gold. I use Ethyl annually to attend and support a Culture Camp in rural Montana. The camp is a learning place for Native American traditions. Tribal elders are selected for Culture Camp based on their skill and knowledge of Salish tribal traditions and language. They gather to camp all summer in a beautiful valley with a clear stream, cedar groves, and a large meadow.

The first week of camp is called "College Camp" where the young tribal members receive college credit for attending. The second week is "Basket Camp." The rest of the summer is open for young and old to come together to share and learn. The elders offer wisdom, the young ones offer hope for the future.

The camp is dedicated in memory of Agnes Vanderburg. Agnes was a Salish Indian woman who had a vision of not only providing a place and support for the young tribal members to learn the traditional language and skills from the elders, but to bring all people together in a celebration of sharing. It is the "all people" part of her vision, plus the friendship I have with an elder Kootenai Indian woman, Eva, that allows me the honor of offering support to the gathering.

As I drink in the experience, Eva, a basket weaver, sits by the fire, watching as the sun tops the Mission Mountains and spills light over the meadow full of tipis. Each tipi faces east, the direction of the sunrise, of new beginnings. The dew is heavy in this lush valley, and the droplets of water explode in prisms of light when the sun reaches the tips of each blade of grass. It is as if the sun ignites the meadow into a multi-colored fire. I breathe in the richness of the day and give thanks for my life. I ask to be of service this day to these people and listen with an open heart. I pray to remember the lost parts of myself which are mirrored in the prisms of light refracted by the sunrise and in the sharing of wisdom with the people.

Later in the day, a final gathering marks the end of college camp. The elders and teachers, as well as all the participants, share their experience of the week, a form of show and tell.

"I used to think it was not cool to be an Indian," one young women says, as she lifts a beaded pouch she made and shows it to the others. "I never came to camp until this year. My sister died last year. She came here all the time. She left me all her beads and beading things. I came here to learn what my sister knew. I am glad I am here."

My morning prayer is answered with the first speaker.

Others share what they learned and show their creations: buffalo hooves turned into bags for a stick game; yew wood bow soaking in the stream, the grain of the wood in the direction of the stream flow, and cured over the fire; a war stick, sally bags, root digging baskets, ya ya dolls, knapped arrow heads affixed to fire hardened shafts; ceremonial drums with rawhide stretched and drying over the frame; beaded medicine bags and pouches; gifts being exchanged. It is believed the first time you make or create an item is the time you learn the most, spend the greatest effort, and have the most pride in what you do. The tradition says the "first" is given away.

Eva offers a prayer and speaks of her knowing. She asks me to play my flute for this sharing. I did not know this was going to happen. I am embarrassed, scared. I feel very "white" and out of place. I draw strength from Agnes's vision. First I honor the flute maker, then Eva, and then I start to play. I am clumsy and the music isn't right. I take a deep breath, remember my prayer has already been answered. I am overwhelmed with gratitude for the privilege of being here. I forget about trying to make the music and the music begins to make itself. I quit playing and all the people are quietly staring at me. I sit down. Eva prays over the food and we eat.

Only three elders at this gathering stay the entire week. One of them is Eva. She is the elder recognized as the last of the split cedar root weavers. My friend. She teaches me and I am eager to learn. I learn not to plan my life so tightly that I forget to live it.

All the things I want to do and learn for the next few days are set aside when a young man kills a large white tale deer. At two hundred pounds, plus or minus, it is the biggest I have seen.

"A summer deer is only good for dry meat," Eva says. (Dry meat is like jerky.) Internally, I cringe slightly. Not only because am I not going to do what I planned, but because I have made dry meat with Eva before. It is a somewhat grueling process of rendering two hundred pounds of meat into hundreds of quarter-inch-thick strips suitable for the drying rack. Plans that do not meet the needs of now come to an end.

It's hot and the flies start to work early on the carcass. The hide soaks in the stream, preparing to be scraped, stretched, and soaked in a mixture made with the brain of the animal. The stretching and soaking are repeated again and again until the hide is pure white, with a soft velvety texture. Damp wood chips of cedar and larch, called "tamarack," are ignited. The smoke turns the white to a light tan as it enters the pores of the soft hide. At the tourist shop in the mission valley, one brain-tanned and smoked hide sells for about seven hundred dollars. Eva used hers this year to make 250 pairs of moccasins for the children of the tribe attending the Head Start program, so each step taken in their young experience is surrounded by the tradition of the people.

The fire is set under the drying rack—a mixture of apple and cottonwood. We cut meat until my hands cramp, and then we cut more. I give up after about five hours. Eva sits and cuts for the rest of the day and into the evening. Everyone participates in some way. Two young men keep the coyotes and bear away from the meat as they keep the fire going and dry meat all night. By morning the sacks of dry meat are full and suspended from the trees. My little city dog eats so many discarded scraps from the day's activity, her belly looks like she swallowed a basketball. She sleeps deeply and so do I.

The sinew is stripped for sewing and beading. There are hooves and long bones for decoration and a stick game. A male elder stops by: Agnes's son. He requests the tongue to eat, and accepts the offering with a toothless smile of thanks and a payment of story after story. Each story is delivered with the speech cadence, the hand and body gesturing that characterizes a unique tribal language that is mostly English with some Salish for emphasis.

The people give thanks and honor the animal's life by making use of every piece. There is a quiet reverence and friendly banter, a sense of belonging in the rhythm of cutting. I am shown again those things I have forgotten. I am reminded that neither tribal connection nor separatism exists when plans do not take on such importance they cannot be forgotten when there is a need to fill and all people come together.

The makers of dry meat share stories of loss, violence, kids neglected, fetal alcohol syndrome, crack babies, family situations, and other life events. They discuss the loss of a nation through the use of drugs and alcohol. They use this communal gathering as a forum for reflecting on the evolution of a people. They laugh and cry with the stories of tragedy, thankfulness and forgiveness. Then all discussion is set aside to honor one four-legged, to honor its life, to make dry meat.

I am thankful. I have a thriving private psychotherapy practice—A Center For Human Development located in a setting that utilizes the healing powers in nature with five acres of trees, ponds, waterfalls, and hiking trails. I celebrate the work my colleagues and I do there—work that focuses on honoring the innate wisdom that all have to find their pathways to healing and wholeness. I no longer wish to plan, so that when there is a need present, I can stop and, as I write in my fable, "stand in the here and now in the light of the divine, with a pair of white socks, cushioned by spring grass, connecting me to the earth."

In the honoring of a four-legged's life given, I've learned I can "make dry meat."

Reflections on the Future:

*...among the symbols on the shoe is the word CHOICE.
The letters circle above the shoe, pointing it in a direction
that somehow she knows is the future...*

As I enter my woodshop, the smell of aromatic cedar wood is strong. A fine coating of cedar dust clings to all the surfaces, including walls and ceiling. I wear a re-breathing dust mask, and as I glance at my reflection in the sliding glass door, I am reminded of faces in a *Star Wars* bar scene.

I pull out a chair, sit and begin to sand a flute I am making. The sound of sandpaper on cedar wood, back and forth, the rhythm, the smell, comfort me. Silence, except for the rhythmical sanding, is so complete it allows flute music to play in my mind, haunting and beautiful. I sense someone walking up behind me. I turn, no one is there. I smile. "Bob is here," I say out loud to myself. I feel his presence.

A feeling stirs inside me. I notice it in my stomach, it moves to my chest and throat. It is a pleasant sensation. I search for the word to describe the feeling. The word "joy" comes to my mind. I match it to my feeling; it fits.

This is my fourth attempt at writing about my future. I think that this should be the easiest writing; it is not. I attribute the difficulty in writing about my future to two things. First, one of the occupational hazards of being a counselor and therapist is with all the listening I do to other peoples' lives, few ask directly about mine. Second, so much of my energy throughout my life has gone into survival, I focus more on the "now" than on what may or may not be in the future. For many years, the question, "What do I need to do today to survive?" took priority over the question, "What is in my future?"

Approximately seven years ago I was gifted a Native American cedar flute by the wife of a flute maker, Bob Two Hawks. When I picked up the flute in an attempt to play, the music started easily. It has not stopped since. The flute opened the magic of music for me. It began a continuing journey of expressing my deepest feelings and beliefs using the infinite vocabulary of sound and music.

Four years after I played the first note on his flute, Bob died of complications of lung cancer. Bob was forty-three years old. The cause of the lung cancer was traced to the inhalation of cedar dust from all the years that he made flutes. The irony of his breath ending as a result of building the flute whose music was made beautiful with that very same breath, is stunning to me. His death is stunning to me. He had become the son of my heart.

Indirectly, the flute also began a journey of discovery about my relationship to money. I began to give away more money than I actually made, starting when I paid for part of Bob's alternative care for cancer. Up until the last ten or twelve years of my life, money was never in abundance. I remember times when I was hungry or had no place to stay. In the last ten years, I developed a pattern of donating or giving away money. While on the surface it seemed a noble act, I am aware my motivation for giving included an underlying guilt related to the belief I have too much. The phase continued from there. Now I can no longer afford to keep and/or maintain the tangible acquisitions of my life. I know on some level, this "atonement" of sorts is related to trying to "save the lost son," or the remorse of surviving when my family did not. The good news, however, is it's a timely occurrence in concert with my current and future theme of simplifying my life. I discover I am better at acquiring than I am at letting go.

I suspect I am done acquiring property, or manifesting tangible things in the world. I suspect I will get more practice at letting go, though I need to get more "user friendly" with that concept. I guess I've never really known what I will do after manifesting all the futures of my past.

As I write these reflections on my future, I decide to take a break and blow some bubbles. The bubble mix was left here by a friend. She blew bubbles for me the first time I thought I had finished my future writing. It made me smile. I know I want her in my life. The bubbles today are just as beautiful. They float in their multi-colored beauty, in the direction the wind carries them. Each of them is perfect. None of them are the same.

In my first attempt at writing about my future, I wrote a fable about a cactus and a castle, two symbols on my shoes. Those symbols represent to me the presence of Charlie and Charlotte, two members of my family of choice. I know I want them in my life, along with other members of my chosen family.

My second attempt focused on the difference between choices and reactions. Choice, according to Webster's, "implies the chance, right or power to choose by the free exercise of judgment." The word "react" as Webster's states, is "an opposing action to a force movement back to a former or less advanced condition." I discovered for me to make choices in this lifetime (rather than to simply react based upon survival instinct or out of old programming) required a number of years of life experience—a number I guess to be somewhere between thirty-five and fifty-five. I observe some enter the realm of choice earlier, some later, and some never enter. I was in my thirties before I could move out of the patterns that entered my blood and brain like some unsolicited vaccine or vitamin, hard-wiring my reactions. I know now I can short circuit the old wiring, so my primary energy is not spent in reaction to old survival tapes.

The third attempt contained the wisdom gathered from the choices I have made. This wisdom sustains my life today and in all my tomorrows:

❖ Speak my truth and let go of the response.

❖ Choose what I speak.

❖ Move toward those things I wish to occur in my life rather than moving away from those I wish to avoid.

❖ Remember binomial thinking (good/bad, right/wrong, black/white) is only useful in programming computers.

❖ Remember there are no comparisons, only the process of discovery of many right ways.

❖ Listen carefully to other right ways, rather than using all my energy to define or defend mine.

❖ Remember what I recognize outside of me (in nature or in the nature of other humans) is simply a mirror of what I already know, otherwise I would not be able to recognize it.

❖ Move out of judgment or the fear of being judged.

❖ Remember when judgment is present, it is because I have not lived in another's tears.

❖ Celebrate differences.

❖ Show those I love the truth about myself even when I am afraid I will not be loved in my truth.

❖ Remember setting a goal or accomplishing a task is not as important as living life on a daily basis.

❖ Simplify my life so I am not so tired managing the "things" in my life, that I have no energy for play and joy.

❖ Remember I am an elder.

❖ Recognize aging is more than cellulite, wrinkles, or waking up one morning to find my body has discovered gravity.

❖ Offer the wisdom of my experience to others.

❖ Celebrate my aging.

❖ Remember death defines life.

❖ Grieve well.

❖ Cry, laugh, and celebrate renewal and hope.

❖ Remember a sense of belonging has more to do with my relationship to myself than to another.

❖ Remember that to show and feel belonging, I must know the truth of my stories.

❖ Know that even though I am able to live solitarily, I heal in relationship.

❖ Celebrate moderation in all things.

❖ Surround myself with people who have the courage to act.

❖ Allow the breath of life to move in and out of me with the awareness of now.

❖ Remember resentment is useful only in identifying unmet need.

❖ Embrace conflict as an essential problem-solving tool.

❖ Enter conflict with an intention to learn why it is occurring, rather than to win or be right.

❖ Honor and live more closely to nature.

❖ Surround myself with the Light of the Divine.

❖ Play music every day.

❖ Drink daily from the pool of my imagination.

I see my dreams for the future revealed in all four of my writings. I embrace an awareness that reaches more deeply than gender, sex, language, sexual preference, money, ethnicity, religion, judgment, violence, all the action that follows thought, education, history, now or the "is" to come. I discover and touch the common connectedness that binds us all. It is in this oneness of commonality I choose to invite my future.

For three years, Bob's widow and I continued to build flutes in his memory. They became our flutes. Now, I am building his flutes again with the knowing I am simply a vehicle. The flutes belong to Bob and all the generations of traditional flute makers. When I step outside my woodshop, I breathe in the beauty of the forested hills, remove my dust mask, and play the flute I am making. The sounds of sorrow and joy mix to join the generations. I play all there is for me to feel—all the yesterdays, the sound of today, and the celebration of tomorrow.

My past is in the photo album on my right shoe. The album is full of images transferred through the lens of the camera of my experience. I gather those images in the here and now as I turn the pages of the album and step into my future.

Rashmi's Shoes

In Our Shoes

Fable

The Toy Train

The toy train chugged merrily through the emerald carpet of tea gardens, tooting its whistle at every treacherous hairpin bend. It hugged the side of the hill as it went along its twisted path like a caterpillar along a dusty track.

Outside, the fog had settled into the valley below, making it look like a magical white carpet to the heavens. In the distance, the purple of bougainvillea, the scarlet of poinsettia, and the exotic mauve of the orchid dotted the dense green of the mountains. The air was tea-scented, crisp and clean like newly washed laundry and the sun reflected off the magnificent snowcapped Himalayan peaks.

The cherubic faces of the mountain children smiled back at me, their cheeks a shiny polished red, like apples, their ragged clothes worn with use. They waved at the passengers on the train momentarily before going back to the game they were playing with sticks and stones.

I heard the strains of a familiar melody and turned to follow the sound. It came from a beaten-up transistor radio inside a little tea shack where local folk were taking a much-needed break from their day. Another, more ethereal sound drifted by, the tinkling of the prayer bells mingling celestially with the happy chaos around me.

All was well in this world—so why was I dying inside?

I closed my eyes and the bars of the train window became the bars of my cage. I wanted to break loose so desperately, to soar to the mountains ahead, but I couldn't shake the image of dogs hounding me as I stood immobilized with fear and despair.

I quickly opened my eyes and stared at the sparkling mountains, thirstily drinking in their awe-inspiring splendor.

"I will lift up mine eyes unto the hills, from whence cometh my help. My help cometh from the Lord, which made heaven and earth." The words of the ancient Psalmist truly came alive for me at this moment. I was returning to the mountains of my childhood, on a mission to heal from wounds I had ignored for much too long. I had become accustomed to the familiar naked pain in my heart and was hoping my journey back would be the elixir I was looking for.

I leaned back on my old wooden seat, its rigidity strangely comforting to me, and listened to the coordinated symphony of the Darjeeling Himalayan Railway. Chug-a-lug, Chug-a-lug, Chug-a-lug, Toot! Chug-a-lug, Chug-a-lug, Chug-a-lug, Toot!

I could hear my mother's voice from a long time ago encouraging me to sing along with this melody. It worked with any song, she said. I smiled at the memory and started to do exactly that. The children sitting opposite me joined in my refrain and soon we were chugging along the hillside singing "doe a deer a female deer" in such complete harmony, even Julie Andrews would have been proud of us!

Several hours later, the little train pulled wearily into Darjeeling, heaving a sigh of relief as it came to a standstill. People had already jumped off the train with their belongings before it had come to a complete halt.

I took one more look at the mountains and slowly stepped into the hustle and bustle of the memories of my childhood: street vendors hawking their wares, stray dogs scurrying along, beautiful Tibetan women selling their colorful trinkets proudly displayed on blankets on the ground, children weaving their way in and out through the bedlam.

A young man dressed in Levi's jeans and cowboy boots, obviously reminiscent of some American tourist, walked up and began taking my bags. Before I knew it I was hustled into a refurbished Land Rover, probably belonging to a Tea Planter in an earlier day, now relegated to a modest Darjeeling taxicab.

"Where to, Madam?" he asked.

"The Windermere," I replied.

As we approached the stately old hotel, nostalgic of the British Raj, a delicious feeling of anticipation overcame me.

I awoke the next morning in my beautiful four-poster bed and decided to explore the mountains that day—no schedule, no agenda, and definitely no tourist guide!

I took a taxi to a remote tea plantation and made arrangements with the driver to return at sundown to bring me back to the hotel. I had packed a little picnic basket for myself and, armed with my hiking boots and a sturdy windbreaker, I was ready to face whatever adventures awaited me.

My day unfolded perfectly as I trekked through the mountains, breathing in the crisp air, stopping occasionally to rest and savor my surroundings.

It was during a moment of rest I noticed an adorable little thatched cottage off to the right, and I wondered who could be living here in the wilderness. I stood up, stretched, and lifted my gaze to the sky, which had darkened suddenly, thickening with monsoon clouds. As if on cue, I saw a streak of lightning flash across the sky, followed by a clap of thunder, the magnificence of this display almost paralyzing me.

I quickly gathered up my belongings and walked toward the shelter of the cottage as the first monsoon raindrops pelted down, drenching me completely. I hurried onto the porch and turned to watch the rain washing the mountains. Behind me the door opened quietly. I turned around to see a man, his face covered with at least a thousand wrinkles, with a straw hat on his head and a smile so charming, I was immediately drawn to him.

"Beautiful isn't it?" he said. "I especially enjoy the smell of the earth, once the rain is over. Come on in, you're soaking wet. Let me give you something dry to put on and a hot cup of tea and we can watch the storm together."

I hesitated for a moment, my fear and lack of trust rearing their ugly heads, but the moment passed as quickly as it came, and I followed him in, introducing myself as I took the simple robe he handed me.

"Here's something for your feet," he said, handing me a pair of brilliant white socks and an old pair of shoes.

"You can change in here." He pointed to the door. "I'll put the kettle on. Join me on the porch when you're ready."

I walked into the tiny bathroom and turned on the light, marveling at his kindness and compassion, quite comfortable in my surroundings. I undressed, wrapped the robe around me, and bent down to take off my wet boots. In the light of the naked bulb, I noticed the shoes he had handed me. They were as colorful and unusual as my host—two old, black canvas shoes, each decorated quite differently from the other, yet obviously belonging together in a strange yet complimentary way.

White stripes ran vertically across the left shoe, like the bars of a prison cell, while two little birds' nests perched on the front. There were a few other bits and baubles behind: a lizard, a liquor bottle of some sort, a mask, and almost hidden from view, the letter "G" stuck to the tongue. The laces were tied securely. I felt the old familiar pain ripping through me as I lifted the shoe and took a closer look. The moment intensified as each wound from my past throbbed and bled copiously.

My catharsis had begun. I untied the laces deliberately, placed the shoe back on the floor, and picked up the right shoe. The first thing I noticed about this one was its free-flowing laces. Orange flames with purple tips encircled the base of the shoe, and brightly colored butterflies chased each other in sheer spontaneous abandonment around its mouth. On the front of the shoe, the word GOD proudly led the way. A couple of hearts, a hummingbird, a little dove, a pair of boots, and some money completed the ensemble.

I took a long deep breath and pulled on the new white socks my host had given me. I smiled through my tears at the utter bizarreness of the shoes as I slipped my feet easily into them. They felt wonderful, alive with discernment and possibility, luminous and free! And I knew right away that it took both shoes to make such a feeling possible.

I was going to be OK—in fact much better than OK—everything was in order in my world. My very essence was the result of all that I'd been through and all that I was yet to experience. Surrounded by the light, I stood there in that charming little cottage, a butterfly waiting to emerge. My heart overflowed with gratitude for this newfound feeling of love and peace. My healing had truly begun.

I literally floated out onto the porch where my new friend was pouring me a cup of tea. I sat with him in the silence, savoring the wonderfully fragrant, sweet aroma of Darjeeling Oolong tea, watching the raindrops dissipate and a magnificent rainbow emerge. A new day had dawned, bringing with it the guidance I'd been blindly searching for so long. I knew exactly what I needed to do. I had to release everything that didn't serve me anymore, to literally strip myself naked and start anew with complete trust, faith, and surrender. I was ready to return home.

Several hours later I heard the taxi horn in the distance, walked out to the front of the cottage, and waved to the driver to stop. I hurried back inside to change out of my robe and shoes, into my still damp clothes and boots. I thanked my friend, holding him tight as I took one last look at the mountains, intent on taking this newfound feeling back with me. My friend walked with me to my taxi and slipped a carrier bag into my hand as I was closing my door. We said "goodbye" and I knew without looking what was in the bag. I clutched my shoes and trembled with excitement and anticipation at the journey ahead.

I was finally free, my soul inseparable with everything that existed in this Universe and beyond.

⇒)⊂

Reflections on the Past

...All was well in this world - so why was I dying inside?
I closed my eyes and the bars of the train window
became the bars of my cage...

The cycle was finally broken.

The realization hit me as I stood by my husband's hospital bed. He was comatose, his eyes fixed in a doll-like gaze, tears gently streaming down his face. Years of alcoholism culminated in this quiet, eerie moment. I prayed for peace for him and recalled the many times I had fervently said the same prayer.

The nurse hurried in and busied herself with the breathing apparatus my husband was hooked up to. I leaned over, kissed him on the cheek, and began my way out of the hospital room. My life flashed before my eyes.

I saw a lonely little girl sitting cross-legged on the cool tiled floor of her bedroom, eyes as clear as crystal, entranced, almost in a hypnotic state as she gazed at her best friend's face and beseeched, "Then what happened?" I would sit for hours listening to Anjie tell her fantasy stories, escaping vicariously into them, her wonderful images pulling me away from the gray reality of my surroundings.

We traveled to distant places and spoke in different languages. In one of my fondest memories, the two of us are walking hand in hand in the park, talking to each other in gibberish, or as we preferred to call it, "our own special language." We would prattle on for hours, totally oblivious to the amused passersby. When we'd had enough of that, we would tumble down the grassy hills, laughing hysterically.

Our lives were enmeshed in fantasy; we would use our imaginations to become famous rock stars, brandishing our badminton rackets as makeshift guitars and forcing our parents to listen to our heartfelt renditions of "Yellow River." We vacillated between playing Elvis and Priscilla Presley one day, to the Swiss Family Robinson the next. I recall the absolutely beautiful shack we built in the back of my garden, using nothing more than a few twigs, branches, and leaves. Then there were the performances we staged for our loyal audience: my mother and father. "Rumpelstiltskin" was never rendered quite so passionately.

During precious sleepovers at Anjie's house, we would spend hours and hours in her tiny little attic uncovering hidden treasures in storage boxes. The sheer joy and laughter we shared was so precious, my little heart would ache when my father came to take me home. He would look at the disappointment on my face and say the same thing every time, "All good things must come to an end." A belief system he instilled in me, unconsciously perhaps, but one that has stayed with me almost all my life.

Anjie was stronger than I, but what sustained our friendship through the years was that she never perceived me as weaker. Growing up in India, I never had any revelations about what my life would be like. I had a mediocre childhood. I was comfortable and secure, but felt no strong attachment to either my mother or father. I do, however, have wonderful memories of my beloved maid, or surrogate grandmother as I prefer to think of her. She was the one who awakened me in the morning with kisses and tucked me into bed at night.

As I enfold my precious children in my arms today and tell them how beautiful they are, the little girl in me acknowledges she never had that from her parents. My parents loved me in the only way they knew. My mother never could demonstrate her affection, and my father would overcompensate for the lack of it when he was intoxicated.

Anjie became the light of my life, sustaining me through the weariness of my years.

I felt weary from the forced interaction with my family and from the shame of watching my father getting steadily drunk as the evening passed, knowing he would soon call upon us children to join in the festivities with him and cringing when he called my name.

I felt weary from seeing the quiet desperation in my mother's eyes as she resigned herself to yet another drunken evening, and from witnessing her final surrender to the situation by starting to drink herself, unable to fight it any longer.

The cold, dark, clammy grayness got steadily worse until the entire house was smudged by it. I had to run away and I did. I escaped to Boarding School in Darjeeling and then to University in Delhi, leaving my brother behind to deal with the slow disintegration of our family unit.

I blossomed during my time away in Boarding School in the mountains of Darjeeling. I felt at home. I embraced the mountains and knew I had been there many times before. I recall the first stirrings of young love when I met Ash. We explored each other's souls tenderly and those moments obliterated any loneliness my heart had ever felt growing up. He was beautiful, this boy love of mine. We went away to University together, but I walked away from him, bored with the steadiness of his devotion and hungry for whatever excitement I thought I needed.

Maybe my father was right. All good things must come to an end.

I let myself be engulfed by the craziness of university life and my days melted into long smoky sessions listening to Bob Dylan expounding on the meaning of life. Long, lazy, aimless days melted into one another as I perpetuated the "follies" of my young adulthood. I experimented with anything that would take away the pain and feeling of separation that became me. Legal or illegal, it didn't matter. It would all pass anyway!

And it did. By the time I graduated I wanted to get as far away as possible from dorm life and the bohemian existence I had submerged myself in for the last three years.

I finished college in London while living with Anjie, who had moved there with her mother a few years earlier. This was the high life—the classy restaurants, fancy food and wine. My search for love continued there, but this time it was all so elegant. I was eating escargot and frog legs and washing it down with Valpolicella and Soave. One year later I knew it was time to move on.

I had graduated from college there, and with another failed relationship under my belt, a heavy heart, and a degree in hand, I boarded the plane bound for India and another chapter in my life. I couldn't bear to return home to my parents. Things had only worsened during the five years I'd been away. I spent a month with them, listening to them reminisce as they got drunker and drunker every evening.

This time the loneliness I felt became almost suffocating. I returned to Delhi, got my first job there, and met my husband and father to my children. The only thing inappropriate about our coming together was he was a child himself, but I didn't see that until half a lifetime later. I loved him, or at least I thought I did, even when every cell in my body was screaming at me to stop and walk away from the dysfunction of the relationship.

Condoning his verbal and physical abuse, extreme possessive-ness, and maniacal jealousy, I followed him to the other side of the world, pursuing what I thought was my dream and praying fearfully without stopping for guidance. After all, he was my ticket to a new life in America. I would leave him once I got there, I kept telling myself. Anything was better than being alone or re-turning to live with my parents.

We were married in Chesapeake Bay. I remember gulping down the martini a friend handed me, and crying on my wedding night. Even then, I had no illusions about the sacredness of the union, but I was willing to settle because I had long ago lost sight of my truth and forgotten the brilliance of my being. As I wore my mask and did everything I was supposed to, that feeling of loneliness never left me.

I returned to India to spend two weeks with my father before he died of a sudden heart attack and alcohol-related complica-tions. "In my Father's house are many mansions." That was his favorite Biblical quote, and he was finally home.

I returned to America, to a new life in Los Angeles. I had everything I needed: a wonderful house, two shiny new cars parked in my two-car garage, a wonderful job, lots of friends and social acquaintances, and two precious children. This was my dream, so what was wrong with this picture?

Alcoholism had followed me from one side of the world to the other, and my cloak of fear became even more layered. This time there was no escape.

After my father's death, my brother embarked on his own journey of self-destruction, giving in to alcohol and drugs. When I learned he had gone through my father's estate in India, I brought him and my mother to Los Angeles to live with me. I will never forget the picture of those two broken spirits at L.A. Inter-national Airport, their clothes hanging on their gaunt frames, their eyes a lifeless shade of smoky beige. My brother fidgeted in the car all the way to my house, battling his heroin addiction, and my mother appeared as if in some distant land.

I prayed for strength and courage as I nurtured them back to health. I would rush home from work and cook them a meal every day, referring to myself as the mama bird.

I was in control again, or so I thought, and I would fix things for them.

The years passed and I busied myself, raising my children and pretending everything was all right, resigning myself to the futility of my situation, just as my mother had done before me.

My brother's descent started when he lost yet another job, becoming homeless one more time. He got onto a bus, rode downtown, and stayed there mingling with other kindred, homeless souls. He would call from time to time, or come to my door, and I would make sure he had a hot shower, clean clothes, and a meal. Then he would disappear into the night again. I remember him mentioning that he would like to see the mountains again. That thought stayed with me as I sprinkled his ashes in the mountains of Flagstaff.

He had come home to die. I remember the incredible feeling of sadness that overcame me that morning as I left for work after checking in on him. I covered him with a blanket as he lay on a hand-me-down mattress in my garage, his life slowly ebbing out of him. The phone rang later that afternoon; it was my mother informing me, very matter-of-factly, that he was in the hospital and things were not looking too good. The doctors convinced me that he had no quality of life left and it would be best to let him go. So we did.

Sweet baby brother, thank you for touching my life!

My mother never cried for him. Hers were the only dry eyes at his memorial. She was her usual stoic self. She held it together and cradled my children as the situations in my life began to crumble even further.

Years of deep hurt and feelings of long-standing resentment and futility had finally manifested in me. I recall the fear I felt sitting in the doctor's office, listening to his monotone as he informed me that my annual pap test had revealed pre-cancerous cells. He recommended I either monitor myself closely for the next few years or have a hysterectomy. I went with the latter recommendation.

Through all of this, my husband's drinking steadily increased until it crossed the fine line between recreational drinking to a continual state of intoxication. I reasoned, cajoled, and pleaded with him over and over again. When he stopped listening to me, I resorted to writing him letters, begging him to stop the madness and embrace the blessings we had. I later found my letters, all unopened, in the glove compartment of his car.

My mask was firmly in place by then, and I slowly retreated into my nest, closing the door to everyone on the outside. It was that same shame I felt growing up; however this time it was happening in my life, in my home, and I felt completely powerless to do anything about it.

I succumbed to the lure of alcohol myself as it melted my pain and promised a good night's sleep. I endured the insanity of my husband's abuse, ignoring the shame in my children's eyes as they watched this onslaught night after night. We drifted apart, existing in the same house as strangers, speaking not more than a few words to each other, turning to our children for comfort, neither one of us able to walk away.

Then something happened, something I like to refer to as my first spiritual revelation. I was sitting in the balcony of our hotel room with Anjie on a beautiful spring day, drinking in the beauty and splendor of the red rocks of Sedona, when I knew that something would happen to my husband. I didn't know what it would be, but I knew the children and I would be OK.

That started my spiritual initiation. I devoured every book I laid my hands on and went to every class I could. I discovered Louise Hay and the practice of New Thought, through which I learned that I could indeed change my life by changing my thoughts.

I got stronger every day until that February morning when I was able to stand tall in front of my husband, tell him I was releasing him and that I wanted a divorce. He pleaded with me for one more chance and promised he would go to the hospital and get cleaned out. I, in turn, promised him nothing but support in his recovery for himself, reiterating that the marriage was over and had been for a very long time. This time he listened, but it was too late. He had a cardiac arrest while in the hospital and was without oxygen for thirteen minutes, resulting in a condition called Anoxic Encephalopathy. Eighteen long months of rehabilitation followed where he had to relearn to eat, walk, talk, and think. He became my child and I nurtured him back to health. My release from him came when he walked onto the plane without looking back. He went to live with his brothers in Los Angeles, leaving the children, my mother, and me in Phoenix.

The children were my sanity through all this. I wrapped them in my arms, inhaling their love and laughter. I could breathe at last, and I slowly began emerging from my cage. Yes, there was life out there and it was OK for me to partake in it. Even better, there were people out there who genuinely cared and were willing to love me unconditionally. My broken spirit was on its way to being restored.

I started a new job at my church working with volunteers, making new friends and savoring all the love and affection my heart was so hungry for. Wrapped up in the euphoria of my newfound freedom, I failed to see, or should I say, refused to acknowledge, my mother's sudden lack of enthusiasm about everything. She was slowly fading away. She'd stopped eating and found no enjoyment in doing anything anymore. She would sit for hours staring out of her bedroom window, TV remote in hand, watching another episode of *Montel Williams*.

When I returned home one morning after dropping the children at school and found her still in bed, I knew it was time to admit her into the hospital. We drove in silence, both of us engrossed in our own thoughts, refusing to acknowledge our time was coming to an end. I spent the next day with her chatting about frivolous things, reading *People* magazine (one of her favorites) and cutting up her hospital Salisbury steak as she smiled at me affectionately and called me "a mother hen." She stopped talking a few days later. Her last words to me were "Enjoy yourself."

The doctors ran every test they could think of to determine what was wrong. Her spirit had simply left her and, for lack of a better term, the doctors referred to her condition as "Metabolic Encephalopathy," a complete shutdown of the system. I woke up that morning and knew exactly what I had to do. I had to let her go. I prepared the children in the best way I could. I remember them, valiant little souls sitting there across the table from me, their eyes welling up with tears as they prepared for yet another loss.

Another hospital bed in another hospital room. The smells were sickeningly familiar as I stood there and thanked my mother for all her love, courage, and support, and then let her go. And go she did, the very next day. Her soul was finally at peace, knowing I was starting my life all over again.

Summer came and with it came our healing. The children and I basked in the balmy summer sun, nurturing and loving each other, and rediscovering the simple pleasures of just being together again—being together without any more struggles or pain. I got my house in order, stripping the crumbling wallpaper, painting it a clean pure white, scrubbing the carpets, and replacing the blinds. I worked at a furious pace, determined to remove every trace of death. The energy was clean now and there was a sense of peace. My children would never feel the discomfort of being home the way I had while growing up.

The final release came a few months later. I was let go from my work after fifteen years. Another door closed, allowing me wonderfully crisp and refreshing breathing space to just be.

Suddenly everything was cleared away. A blank canvas beckoned me to start painting a new picture, but this time with thought, purpose, and intention. Yes, the cycle was finally broken, the yoke lifted and the chains snapped. I had made it through the dark night of my soul and could see the ray of light shining straight ahead. My mother had named me quite aptly. "Rashmi" means Ray of Light, and I guess I never quite lost sight of the light, even in the darkest of nights when there appeared to be none. I breathed in my life force, threw my arms open, and embraced my children as they came running to me.

Life was good. All good things needn't ever come to an end.

Reflections on the Present

…My heart overflowed with gratitude for this newfound feeling of love and peace. My healing had truly begun…

As I sit here in my study, formerly my mother's room, with the dancing flame of my candle in my peripheral vision, surrounded by all the little knickknacks I love so dearly, I am overwhelmed by the abundance of my blessings. I glance up to see my children smiling back at me from their photo frames, two incredible lights who have taught me so much about love and tenacity. Their persistent pursuit of joy and childhood pleasures has carried them and me through all our life experiences these last few years. The energy is wonderful in this room, buoyant and free as it is in the rest of the house. There is beauty everywhere, and the realization is crystal clear all is well in my life.

I reflect on the transformation that has occurred in me these last nine months, my gestation period, so to speak, and like the unborn fetus, I'm preparing for birth as I write this. Looking back, the summer of 2001 was a time when I closed the doors to all the ghosts of my past. Everyone I had loved had been removed from me: my father, my brother, my mother, and my husband. I had also been let go from my work of fifteen years. I had survived all the losses and was ready to start anew, to open my heart and love again.

It was a Saturday morning and I'd returned from Los Angeles, where I'd taken my children for a summer vacation to visit their dad. I'd finally made closure with my husband and returned to Phoenix with a sinking heart, grieving for all the love that had gone to waste. I went to church the next morning and walked into Richard. He looked like everything I'd ever imagined I wanted: tall with thick, dark hair, beautiful baby blue eyes, and a wonderfully open, honest face with laugh lines that crinkled so charmingly every time he smiled.

He brought so much joy into my life. I recall the words he said to me on our first date; "I don't know what you've been praying for, but this could be the answer." He certainly was the answer to my prayers as he moved into my life and surrounded me with so much beauty. He transformed my tired, dusty backyard into a Shangri-La. I now have lush, brilliant green grass, beautiful flowers, bird feeders, a birdbath—even a garden swing where I spend my leisurely afternoons delighting in the beauty around me. He went through the house, setting it in order; fixing everything he could find; putting up shelves; hanging pictures; replacing parts in appliances; and cleaning out the house and garage of junk accumulated through the years. He removed every hang-over from my past—stuff belonging to my husband and mother I didn't have the heart to throw out. He introduced me to plea-sures I'd long forgotten about—making love in the moonlight, music, jewelry, and cooking—and to some I'd never indulged in, such as gardening, hiking, bird-watching, and stargazing. I returned from a Christmas vacation to find the outside of my house painted a brilliant white, quite like the light that surrounds me now.

I fell blindly in love, literally devouring every part of him. I was so hungry and he was my world. He continually cautioned me to go slow, but as though in a whirlwind, I was carried away. I wanted it all and wanted it now. I had to make up for all the lost time, and like a spoiled child, I would kick and scream when I didn't get my way.

When I became excessively possessive and demanding, he began to pull away. What followed was heartache like I'd never known. I grieved for everyone and everything I had lost, and this time the grief was all mine. I could finally grieve for myself with-out concern for anyone else. After all, this was my pain and mine alone. The children were happy. I took care of them, and at the end of the each day when all my chores were done, I sat in my patio in the light of the October moon and cried for everyone and everything I had loved and lost.

It was a lonely Thanksgiving without Richard, but I pulled myself together and forged ahead. After all, I had gone through too much and come too far to give up now.

I began doing things for myself—quite a novel concept for me.

I joined a gym and even splurged on a few sessions with a personal trainer. I began walking every day and rediscovered the pleasure of having my feet touch the pavement in a smooth, steady rhythm. I attended a succession of wonderful classes, soaking up all the knowledge and wisdom I could. I unleashed the creativity in me as I wrote my story, decorated my altar, and painted my pictures. I spent time in daily meditation and prayer, embracing the God in me.

I got in touch with old friends and made new ones, even dating a succession of men—all in a valiant effort to stop loving Richard. My ego wallowed in their flattery, but I never stopped loving him. Through all this, I learned I was able to love again and this time began to see that it was possible to love someone without controlling and chaining his soul.

Richard came back into my life about Christmas, and it was so sweet to be able to learn to love him unconditionally. He continues to teach me there is no forever, to just embrace the mystery with him every day, taking one day at a time.

To live in the present and in the "wisdom of uncertainty" — that has been my greatest lesson. I glance over at the gift a friend gave me, a stone etched with the message, "Honor U." How appropriate. I was never able to do that. I always gave someone or something precedence over me. I have finally embarked on my journey of self-discovery, finding what brings me joy, how I like to be loved, and how to love myself. I am learning that trusting and surrendering to Spirit is the only way to attain peace and to achieve that wonderful sense of "knowing" I've had fortunate glimpses of.

Every time I'm tempted to fall back into my old familiar patterns and control issues, to start moving against the flow, crying to have my own way, the Universe gently reminds me to just let go and be. Being the good student I am, I obey...after a moment or two of whining. The Universe gives me ample opportunities to practice surrender, as in the incident with the cat.

Richard came home one day and found a cat in his bathroom, a beautiful Siamese cat, obviously lost and looking for a home. He took care of her for a few days. Then while I was at his house this last weekend, something came over me; I suggested we bring the cat over to my house for the weekend to cheer up my daughter who was recovering from a fever.

Now this may not sound unusual to you, but I've firmly affirmed over the years, much to the dismay of my children, that I do not want any pets. "I do not need anything else to take care of," is what I've said. However, the children fell in love with the cat and I'm now a pet owner!

So, here I am halfway through my life, learning to live each day for all it's worth.

I awake each morning glad to be alive. I give thanks for a second chance, a chance to do it right this time, a chance to love without leaning, a chance to do work that's meaningful, a chance to confront and relinquish my addictions and a chance to be able to count my blessings again.

Richard has shown me how to love again and has awakened the passion that lay hidden for so long within me. He's made me touch the depths of my sorrow and finally lay it to rest. He's made me dance with joy and live like there's no tomorrow. Now he's teaching me the final lesson—to enjoy my own company and to love myself in the moments when I'm alone and my children are at rest and my day is done.

These last few months have also been about my pursuit for my right and perfect work. As I sit here today I know whatever work I'm called to do will be the right and perfect work because I've finally learned to trust.

I have the possibility of two job offers, each one quite different from the other.

There is a wonderful sense of detachment, as I know I will be guided to make the right decision. This is the "wisdom of uncertainty" Dr. Deepak Chopra talks about, a concept I think I'm finally beginning to grasp. This is what frees us from the shackles of our past and opens us to all the wonderful possibilities of the future, possibilities we daren't even imagine!

So, as I sit here today, not knowing how long I'll have Richard in my life (yet willing to love him for every single moment that I have), and not knowing where my perfect work lies (yet willing to step into whatever is provided), I revel in the Now and in the grace of the woman I have become. As Emily Dickinson puts it so aptly:

'If I can stop one Heart from breaking,
I shall not live in vain:
If I can ease one Life the Aching,
Or cool one Pain,
Or help one fainting Robin
Unto his Nest again,
I shall not live in Vain.'

It has been an incredible journey, and it gets better every day.

Reflections on the Future

...I was finally free, my soul inseparable with everything that existed in this Universe and beyond. I was home at last...

Her long black hair flowed freely in the wind as she twirled her body sensuously to the music of the October moon. She was dressed in long flowing white chiffon which molded itself gracefully around the curves of her body, like a meandering stream pouring itself over a mountain. Her eyes were closed and there was a gentle and serene smile on her beautiful face. She was free.

She deliberately performed her Moondance, paying homage to all the heavenly beings that had cradled her so many times before.

The music built itself up to a gradual crescendo, and as she completed her final spin, she knew exactly what her future held—sheer, simple and profound joy in the moment.

Her dancing was an expression of joy and that's really all that mattered, all she had control over—to simply go for the joy in whatever was before her to do, to be and to love.

This knowing manifests itself in me completely as I write my future reflections today. I am that Moon Dancer and my quest is for Joy. I see myself as the perfect creation Spirit intended me to be, emerging whole and free through all my life experiences. All the births and deaths, the tears, the fears, and serendipitous moments of my existence have created the person I am today.

I see myself comfortable in the quiet moments when my day is done, and I can hear the gentle breathing of my children sound asleep. I can be still in the midst of all the chaos that might surround me, sitting in faith, patience, and love. I see myself climbing the tallest mountain and shouting joyously from its peak, accepting every invitation that comes my way—not holding back in fear, but trusting life will take care of me. I stand back when I need to and move forward at other times, always living to the fullest with a passion that's ceaseless and insatiable.

I see myself doing work I am meant to do—reaching out, touching and changing lives with gentle compassion. I heal men, women, and children through my words and silence.

My home reflects the peace and beauty that is within me, and I tend to it with love and care. I plant my own garden with grace and open my doors to welcome friends and loved ones.

I raise my children well and let them go when they need to, surrounding them with love and blessings to create their own life tapestries. I do not tell them how to live their lives but am there to laugh and cry with them in those special moments.

I see myself walking this Earth's journey with my beloved. I have known him many times before and will continue to encounter him in all my lifetimes. His body is strong, his mind is gentle, and his eyes hold all the memories we've shared together. We sit in the silence and know the thoughts the other is thinking. We dance with unabashed joy to the music that plays only for us. We are connected, yet free to pursue our individual dreams and goals.

I am finally one with Spirit, my intention and will aligned with my Father/Mother God, my every thought a prayer.

The drums beat faster and faster, and I move almost in a hypnotic trance. My skirt swishes around me in celebration of every single nuance of my existence. It is indeed a marvelous night for a Moondance, and I immerse myself totally in the beauty of the music, the fragrance of the night, and the heady romance of the moonlight.

If this is not the stuff that dreams or futures are made of— then what is?

> *Well, it's a marvelous night for a Moondance*
> *With the stars up above in your eyes*
> *A fantabulous night to make romance*
> *'Neath the cover of October skies*
>   —*Van Morrison*

Wind Dance

Our stories are released
Like long-held breath
Upon a silent land
Each woman exhales
And is set free
By the howling
Of the raucous wind
The cacophony
Of voices rising up
Twisting into a tornado
Then inside me
All is still

—Courtney Dyer

In Our Shoes

Guidelines for Creating Your Own "Shoe Group"

We the authors of this book have come to think of this experience of forming a 21st century quilting, though instead of telling our life stories over squares of hand-stitched fabric, we tell them on sheets of paper, then watch as our laughter and tears of recognition bind them together into one exquisite image of our humanity. To gather together a group of shoe women, is to seize an opportunity to discover, honor, and share the wisdom inside each and every one of us.

Before forming your own group of "shoe women," it is important to be clear about your purpose in coming together. A *shoe group* is not designed to be a traditional "writers' group" in which people come together for the sole purpose of honing their writing skills, although shoe women support each other in expressing themselves with clarity and passion.

A shoe group also is not intended to be a therapy or support group—although participants are likely to experience a great deal of growth and support through the process of sharing their stories—nor should it ever be a forum for debating the morality or ethics of any individual's life choices or beliefs.

The sole mission of a shoe group is *to provide a space for women to come together and share their memories, experiences, reflections, dreams—the stories of their lives—free of judgment or criticism. A foundation of mutual respect is absolutely essential.*

To assist you, we've outlined some suggestions that either worked for us in creating a positive and productive experience, or that we *wished* we had considered before we started. Hindsight—it's a beautiful thing.

I. Select your members.

Every woman has a story, so from that standpoint, every woman makes a perfect prospective member. You needn't know anything about her story to know that she'll have a wealth of experience and wisdom to offer. You needn't know her experience or credentials as a writer. To be a "shoe woman," she simply must be willing to commit to the group's mission and ground rules.

In choosing women to invite, simply allow your intuition to guide you. The only question posed to the women in our group was, "Would you be interested in participating?" Although one of the women had never done any formal writing before, we knew she, like each one of us, was there by Divine appointment.

How many members is up to you, but an optimum number for a group of this kind is from six to eight members. Too few and it's difficult to create a synergy among the members—too many and time may run short for all members to have the opportunity to share.

II. Choose a facilitator.

Designating someone to facilitate will help your meetings to run smoothly and efficiently. The role of the facilitator is to keep the group focused on its mission and ground rules, and to keep an eye on the clock to ensure that each person gets the opportunity to share. You may choose one facilitator for all the meetings, or rotate the duty of facilitating among all the members.

II. Set the "ground rules."

Any group is made up of individuals, each with her own personality, beliefs and opinions. Even if all the personalities blend perfectly, following an agreed upon set of ground rules will help to create an environment where each individual feels safe to express, not only the experiences of her life, but her thoughts and feelings about those experiences. Should individual personalities occasionally bump up against each other—which is not an uncommon occurrence in group interactions—the ground rules become even more important in maintaining the safety and well-being of each member. Reviewing them at the beginning of each meeting—at least for the first several meetings—will help keep the group on track.

Here are some basic ground rules (you can add more of your own) we strongly recommend:

1. **Mission.** All members must adopt the spirit and scope of the group's stated mission: *to share the stories of their lives without judgment or criticism.* Each member acknowledges and respects that the stories shared by the other members represent the truth for *them*, even if she does not share their perspectives.

2. **Attendance.** Each member must commit to attending every meeting, to the best of her ability.

3. **Confidentiality.** Every story told within the context of the group must be kept confidential. Only the writer/teller of each story has the power to decide if and when to share it with anyone outside of the group.

4. **Honesty.** This is the rule that demands the most courage of any shoe woman: to be willing to risk being open, honest, and authentic in reflecting on, writing, and sharing her life stories. This does not mean that a member must agree to open every aspect of her private life to the group. She need only be willing to gently extend the boundaries of feelings and experiences she has risked sharing in the past, and to tell any story she chooses to tell honestly, without pretense. Wisdom can only be exchanged through an open door.

5. **Professional intervention.** Each member must agree that if the process of writing and sharing personal stories raises memories or issues she finds troubling or distressful, she

will call upon a professional therapist, member of the clergy, or trusted friend for assistance and support.

6. **Critiques.** In critiquing any story or set of reflections, comments or judgments about any member's personal life or feelings are ***strictly forbidden***. The idea is not to critique the content of another person's life, but the clarity of her expression. Therefore, members must agree to restrict their critiques to matters related to a story's *pacing* and *clarity*, such as

❖ Passages that seem unclear or confusing.

❖ Passages which move too slowly, containing extraneous details.

❖ Passages which move too quickly, leaving the listener/reader wanting to know more.

7. **Communication.** Should an issue arise between members of the group, each must agree to address it directly with each other, or within the safety of the entire group—not with other members apart from the group setting.

III. Set the Stage.

A gathering of shoe women is a celebration—a celebration of our lives and spirits. And what would any celebration of women be without candles, flavored coffee, and chocolate? The idea of "setting the stage" for your gathering is simply to make every member feel honored and at home. Members may each contribute toward the purchase of snacks and beverages, or each may bring something to share with the others at each meeting.

While our group elected to meet at the same house every week, you can choose to have members take turns hosting the meetings. Either way, we believe that for women to be greeted by the light of candles burning, the aroma of coffee brewing, and the majesty of a plate of chocolate-dipped biscotti (or whatever the snack of choice) sets the proper tone for the story sharing to follow.

IV. Agree on a time frame.

You can, of course, get together as often as you want, for as long as you want. However, we suggest meeting weekly for a period of sixteen weeks, divided into four, four week segments:

❖ Segment 1: Members decorate their shoes and write/share their fables.

❖ Segment 2: Members write/share their reflections on the past.

❖ Segment 3: Members write/share their reflections on the present.

❖ Segment 4: Members write/share their reflections on the future.

V. Design Your Shoes and Socks

1. The process of story sharing begins by each woman deco-rating a pair of shoes and socks to represent her life—past, present, and future. We strongly recommend that you do this activity as a group, rather than individually, allowing at least an hour to complete. A glue gun and glue sticks work best for affixing items onto shoe surfaces from canvas to patent leather. Additional decorating supplies might include:

   ❖ acrylic paint
   ❖ magic markers
   ❖ yarn
   ❖ pom poms
   ❖ pipe cleaners
   ❖ play money
   ❖ beads

❖ bells
❖ sequins
❖ glitter
❖ shells
❖ stones
❖ specialty buttons (craft stores have a wide variety)
❖ doll house miniatures

2. Choose a pair of shoes from your closet you no longer plan to wear. It is important the pair you decorate be *your* shoes—shoes you have walked in, lived in.

3. Select one shoe—either the right or the left—to represent the journey of your life from birth until today. The other shoe will represent your vision of your life from today forward

4. Decorate your "past shoe" with symbols that represent the people, places, events, interests, beliefs, dreams, pets, jobs, etc., that have shaped your life up to today. Choose the symbol—color, shape, object, word, letter, number—that most closely illustrates the feeling or image evoked by each one.

5. Decorate your "future shoe" with symbols that represent the kind of people, places, events, dreams, beliefs, etc., that you envision creating in your life from today forward.

6. Decorate a pair of socks to represent your life as it is in the present.

7. When everyone is finished decorating, share your shoes and socks with each other, describing the meaning and context of each symbol.

VI. Write Your Fable

The purpose of this exercise is not to produce a polished piece of literature, but to reveal your feelings about the mirror of your life you have just created with your shoes and socks. As soon as each member finishes decorating—OK, after a short break for coffee and biscotti—she should choose a comfortable place to sit and begin writing. This is not as intimidating a prospect as it may sound to those who don't do much writing, or who prefer to avoid it altogether. We're going to provide the one thing needed to write a fable that will surprise and delight you—a place to begin. Once your pen is moving across the page, you can trust your spirit to do the rest. Simply begin your story by following this format:

Imagine you have come across this particular pair of shoes and socks in some way—such as while digging through a closet, walking on a beach or hiking in a forest. Begin your fable by writing about how and where you found them. Follow this with a brief description of the shoes, noting the style of shoes, for example, along with some of the objects or symbols that adorn them. Then describe how it feels to place the shoes and socks on your feet. Now that your pen is in motion, finish your story by answering this question: *Where do these shoes take me from here?* This activity should take no more than 45 minutes. Don't think, don't edit yourself as you go, just write. Write whatever comes to your mind, without judgment or censure.

Then read your stories aloud to each other, although this will probably have to wait until the next meeting. At this point, you may choose to spend a week or two revising your fables—to play with the words and images—or to move on to writing your reflections.

VII. Write your reflections—past, present, and future.

There is no right or wrong way to do this. The style and content of these reflections will be as unique as each woman who writes them. As Karolyne would say, "You can't flunk reflections." The whole idea is to spend some time reflecting upon your life and to write down whatever memories, thoughts and feelings that come rising to the surface.

As a group, you can decide whether you want to write and share these reflections at each meeting, or whether you want to do the writing in the time between meetings, and use the group time to share what you have written. Because every story will likely trigger so many memories among all the members of the group, we suggest you write on your own time so that you can devote your time together reading and talking.

VIII. "At-distance" members.

You can, of course, design your "shoe group" any way you want. You may choose to use the shoe group idea to connect friends, or family members, all of whom live in different locations. (Keep in mind that whether family, friends, or strangers, the ground rules still apply.) You may have several small groups of two or three members each in two or three locations, all connected via telephone, e-mail and regular or "snail" mail.

You may decide to form a single core group, as we did, and invite one or two "at-distance members," those who live far enough away as to preclude them from participating in person. Whatever arrangement you choose, here are a few guidelines that will help ensure a meaningful experience for everyone:

❖ Arrange for each at-distance member to fax, e-mail, or snail mail her writings in advance of each meeting, so another member can read them aloud to the rest of the group. Have the other members send their writings to the at-distance participant.

❖ Set a chair for each at-distance member at every core group meeting as an acknowledgement of her presence in spirit and her value to the group as a whole. Display a photograph of her at each meeting, and send her a group photo of the other members.

❖ As budget and time zones allow, call the at-distance member(s) during the meeting to touch base and offer any comments on the writings submitted that week. Otherwise have all the members e-mail, fax, or snail mail their comments to each other. The idea is simply to foster an ongoing atmosphere of camaraderie, whether a member is sitting right there in the room or hundreds of miles away.

❖ If at all possible—again if budgets and personal schedules allow—at least once during the series of meetings, arrange for all of you to be in the same place at the same time. While our stories alone connect us as women, as human beings, there is no substitute for seeing into another's eyes, for holding another's hands. Any time a group of "shoe women" can share their stories face to face is cause for great celebration.

Our hope is, in gathering together your own group of shoe women, you will find all the wisdom of heart, mind, and soul—all the magic of being—we discovered in ourselves and each other. Whoever and wherever you are, our love and admiration go with you.

Charlotte, Courtney, Jami, Ramona,
Jane, Karolyne, and Rashmi
The (original) Shoe Women

The "shoe women" are available to assist you in starting your own "shoe group" through Wonder Weavers, Inc. For information on seminars, workshops, and presentations, please visit our website at www.wonder-weavers.com

Top row, L to R: Ramona, Karolyne, Jane
Front row, L to R: Rashmi, Jami, Charlotte, Courtney

About the Authors

Charlotte Rogers Brown earned a degree in journalism from Gonzaga University, and has won numerous awards from the Associated Press and the Society of Professional Journalists for her work as a news reporter and feature writer. She is a co-author of the book, *A Weaving of Wonder: Fables to Summon Inner Wisdom,* published in 1995 by LuraMedia (now Innisfree Press) and co-authored by therapist Karolyne Rogers, Ph.D. Their book earned endorsements from, among others, actress/author Patty Duke and Louise Wisechild, author of *The Obsidian Mirror* and *The Mother I Carry.* She currently facilitates classes and work-shops through her business, *Wonder Weavers, Inc.*

Courtney Dyer grew up in Jamaica, West Indies. Although an artist from the day she was born, she wandered onto a different path, becoming a registered nurse in a Post Anesthesia Care Unit. Upon regaining her artistic senses, she left nursing in 1998 and eventually started her business, EtchArtStudio.com, where she creates sandblast etchings on stone. She also expresses her artis-tic vision through painting, and writing. A U.S. Army veteran, Courtney now lives in Phoenix, Arizona, with her cats, Sage and Rose.

Jami McFerren currently serves as Communications Direc-tor for an Arizona state agency. The former award-winning jour-nalist worked in radio and television news and still does on-air fundraising for the local PBS affiliate. Jami also serves as guest speaker, moderator, and mistress of ceremonies for a variety of civic and social service organizations. Her volunteer work includes service as a chaplain and trustee of her church.

Jane Norde has lived in Phoenix, Arizona, since 1959. She was trained by the Center for Educational Development in San Antonio, Texas, to assist high schools in drug and alcohol pre-vention in the All Star Program. She self-published her first book of poetry, *Feather*, in the fall of 2001. She continues to write and volunteers her time as a chaplain at her church.

Ramona Sallee earned her MBA in Finance from Xavier University in Cincinnati, Ohio. She has spent thirty years in this career field. After serving as Vice President of Finance for an international company based in Phoenix, Arizona, she decided to downsize her career and concentrate on her interests in creative writing and oil painting. She has studied creative writing in Boston and Phoenix and is currently writing a novel.

Karolyne Smith Rogers, earned her Ph.D. in adult learning theory from the University of Idaho. She is co-founder of A Center for Human Development in Coeur d'Alene, Idaho, where she maintains a private counseling practice. Her life-long belief in the celebration of differences is reflected in her professional history as a public school teacher; regional and national consultant for Head Start and Hospice; and adjunct faculty for several colleges and universities. She also was awarded the Idaho Governor's Award for Creative Excellence for her writing and implementation of substance abuse prevention programs.

Rashmi Goria grew up in India. After earning her degrees in Commerce and Fashion Merchandising from Delhi University and from the College for the Distributive Trades in London, England, she began her career in fashion design and the garment industry. She immigrated to the United States twenty years ago and went on to work in both the garment and travel industries.

Printed in the United States
1114400002BA